# Environmental Politics in Latin America

Since colonial times the position of the social, political and economic elites in Latin America has been intimately connected to their control over natural resources. Consequently, struggles to protect the environment from exploitation and contamination have been related to marginalized groups' struggles against local, national and transnational elites. The recent rise of progressive, left-leaning governments—often supported by groups struggling for environmental justice—has challenged the established elites and raised expectations about new regimes for natural resource management.

Based on case studies in eight Latin American countries (Argentina, Brazil, Chile, Ecuador, Colombia, Bolivia, El Salvador and Guatemala), this book investigates the extent to which there have been elite shifts, how new governments have related to old elites, and how that has impacted on environmental governance and the management of natural resources. It examines the rise of new cadres of technocrats and the old economic and political elites' struggle to remain influential. The book also discusses the challenges faced in trying to overcome structural inequalities to ensure a more sustainable and equitable governance of natural resources.

This timely book will be of great interest to researchers and masters students in development studies, environmental management and governance, geography, political science and Latin American area studies.

**Benedicte Bull** is a Professor at the Centre for Development and the Environment, University of Oslo, Norway.

**Mariel Aguilar-Støen** is Associate Professor at the Centre for Development and the Environment, University of Oslo, Norway.

# Routledge Studies in Sustainable Development

This series uniquely brings together original and cutting-edge research on sustainable development. The books in this series tackle difficult and important issues in sustainable development including: values and ethics; sustainability in higher education; climate compatible development; resilience; capitalism and de-growth; sustainable urban development; gender and participation; and well-being.

Drawing on a wide range of disciplines, the series promotes interdisciplinary research for an international readership. The series was recommended in *The Guardian*'s suggested reads on development and the environment.

**Institutional and Social Innovation for Sustainable Urban Development**
*Edited by Harald A. Mieg and Klaus Töpfer*

**The Sustainable University**
Progress and prospects
*Edited by Stephen Sterling, Larch Maxey and Heather Luna*

**Sustainable Development in Amazonia**
Paradise in the making
*Kei Otsuki*

**Measuring and Evaluating Sustainability**
Ethics in sustainability indexes
*Sarah E. Fredericks*

**Values in Sustainable Development**
*Edited by Jack Appleton*

**Climate-Resilient Development**
Participatory solutions from developing countries
*Edited by Astrid Carrapatoso and Edith Kürzinger*

**Theatre for Women's Participation in Sustainable Development**
*Beth Osnes*

"The importance of elite politics to environmental governance is undeniable and yet the actual operations of this politics and the shifting constitution of elites have received far too little attention in studies of environmental governance in Latin America and beyond. This book provides a trove of valuable insights into the ways in which elites affect Latin American environments and the political possibilities for more equitable and sustainable relationships between society and natural resources. A super contribution."

*Anthony Bebbington, Clark University, USA*

"With the arrival of new left-wing governments to Latin America, and as elites shift in the region, this book offers an original look at their performance. Featuring several case studies, the chapters in this book simultaneously assess different economic sectors and countries governed by different versions of the Latin American left, both in terms of political power over society and over nature."

*Eduardo Gudynas, Latin American Centre for Social Ecology, Uruguay*

# Environmental Politics in Latin America

Elite dynamics, the left tide
and sustainable development

**Edited by Benedicte Bull
and Mariel Aguilar-Støen**

Routledge
Taylor & Francis Group
LONDON AND NEW YORK

from Routledge

First published 2015
by Routledge

2 Park Square, Milton Park, Abingdon, Oxon OX14 4RN
711 Third Avenue, New York, NY 10017, USA

*Routledge is an imprint of the Taylor & Francis Group, an informa business*

First issued in paperback 2016

*British Library Cataloguing-in-Publication Data*
A catalogue record for this book is available from the British Library

*Library of Congress Cataloging-in-Publication Data*
Environmental politics in Latin America : elite dynamics, the left tide and sustainable development / edited by Benedicte Bull and Mariel Aguilar-Støen.
pages cm. -- (Routledge studies in sustainable development)
1. Environmental policy--Latin America--Case studies. 2. Natural resources--Government policy--Latin America--Case studies. 3. Sustainable development--Latin America--Case studies. 4. Elite (Social sciences)--Latin America--Case studies. I. Bull, Benedicte, 1969- editor of compilation. II. Aguilar-Støen, Mariel, editor of compilation.
GE190.L29E68 2014
333.7098--dc23
2014020184


ISBN: 978-1-138-79026-1 (hbk)
ISBN: 978-1-138-21245-9 (pbk)


Typeset in Goudy
by GreenGate Publishing Services, Tonbridge, Kent

# Contents

## PART 1
## Agriculture and biotechnology

## PART 2
## Mining

## PART 3
## Forestry

# Figures

# Tables

# Contributors

**Mariel Aguilar-Støen** is Associate Professor at the Centre for Development and the Environment (SUM), University of Oslo, Norway. Her research interests focus on environmental governance in the Latin America region, particularly as related to monetized approaches for forest conservation, mining conflicts and land tenure.

**Pablo Andrade** is a Professor at Universidad Andina Simon Bolivar, Ecuador. His work focuses on development studies and political economy, with emphasis on the political economy of state formation and on the governance of natural resources in the Andean Region.

**Benedicte Bull** is a Professor at the Centre for Development and the Environment (SUM), University of Oslo, Norway, and Director of the Norwegian Network for Latin America Research (NorLARNet). Her main research areas are Latin American politics, political economy and development, with a particular focus on Central America and issues of elites and inequality.

**Nelson Cuéllar** is a Senior Researcher and Deputy Director of PRISMA, El Salvador. His work includes such issues as territorial dynamics, climate change, REDD+, territorial rights and governance and compensation for ecosystem services.

**Eivind Hanche-Olsen** was a Research Affiliate at the Centre for Development and the Environment (SUM), University of Oslo, during the time of this research. He is now a school teacher at Eidebakken Skole.

**Cecilie Hirsch** is a PhD fellow at the Centre for Development and the Environment (SUM), University of Oslo, and a PhD candidate at the Norwegian University of Life Sciences (NMBU), Norway. Her research interests include environmental governance, climate change and forest policies and social movements in Latin America, particularly Bolivia.

**Barbara Hogenboom** is an Associate Professor in Political Science at the Centre for Latin American Research and Documentation (CEDLA), the Netherlands. Her main fields of interest are contemporary politics and the governance of development and the environment, studied from the angle of international political economy.

**Marte Høiby** was a Research Affiliate at the Centre for Development and the Environment (SUM), University of Oslo, Norway, during the time of this research. She is now a research assistant at Oslo University College. Her research interests include media and climate change, and globalization and the security of journalists working in conflict zones.

**Susan Kandel** is the Executive Director of PRISMA, El Salvador. Her research interests include territorial dynamics and governance, climate change, migration and rural livelihoods, compensation for ecosystem services and institutions for natural resource management.

**Cristián Parker G.** is Director of the Master's program in Social Sciences and Civil Society at the Universidad de Santiago de Chile. His research interests focus on development sociology and religious and cultural sociology.

**Héctor Sejenovich** is a Senior Researcher at the Gino Germani Research Institute, Buenos Aires, Argentina. Since 1968 he has worked in teaching and counseling, and research about environmental governance and related issues in almost all Latin American countries and in several prestigious international organizations.

**Bruno Taitson Bueno** is a PhD candidate in Sustainable Development at the University of Brasilia, Brazil. His interests include environmental policies, sustainable development, international relations and international journalism.

**Fabiano Toni** is a Professor and Graduate Coordinator at the Center for Sustainable Development, University of Brasília, Brazil, where he teaches environmental governance. His research interests include decentralization of forest policies and the impacts of climate policies on land use, with a focus on the Brazilian Amazonia and Cerrado.

**Larissa C. L. Villarroel** works at the Brazilian Ministry of Environment. Her interests include environmental policies, climate change and sustainable development.

**Joaquín Zenteno Hopp** is a Junior Researcher at the Centre for Development and the Environment (SUM), University of Oslo, Norway. His research interests include environmental governance and the use of modern biotechnology.

# Acknowledgements

This book is the result of the four-year collaborative research project Environmental Governance in Latin America and the Caribbean (ENGOV), led by the Centre for Latin America Research and Documentation (CEDLA) in Amsterdam, The Netherlands and funded by the Framework Program 7 of the European Union. One of this book's editors, Benedicte Bull, was the leader of the "work package" on "Elites, institutions and environmental governance" and this book presents the results of the work conducted for that part of the project.

Being a part of a large research project such as ENGOV, which included collaboration between six Latin American universities and four European universities, has been challenging as well as rewarding. The researchers involved came to the project with different perspectives, backgrounds, political inclinations as well as views on what research and science is and what it can achieve in society. That has led to long discussions conducted in meetings across the region: from Chile and Argentina, to Ecuador, Brazil and Mexico. It has been especially challenging to reach a common understanding of what elites are and why to study elites in a region where a long-standing commitment to the poor and marginalized in social sciences (that we share) has led many to ignore the need to study the attitudes and actions of elites. We would like to thank every one of those who have contributed to those discussions and thus to make this volume what it is. In addition to those who are contributing to this book, we would like to thank: David Barkin, Mina Kleiche, Mariana Walters, Joan Martínez-Allier, Carlos Larrea, Gloria Baigorrotegui, Fernando Estensorro and Thomas Ludewigs. We would furthermore like to thank in particular the CEDLA team of Fabio de Castro, Michiel Baud and Leontine Cremers, who not only have contributed to the discussions, but also logistically managed to coordinate so many different scholars with even more different backgrounds and experiences. Barbara Hogenboom, who has also contributed to this book, deserves a very special mention for her endless patience with the groups' inquiries. We would also like to thank the ENGOV-project's reference group, a remarkable group of experts that have contributed very constructively to our discussions: Eduardo Silva, Anthony Bebbington, Barbara Goebbels and Leticia Merino.

We would also like to express our gratitude to the European Union's Framework Program 7, for its generous support, without which this project would never have been undertaken.

Further, we would like to thank our home institution, the Centre for Development and the Environment (SUM) and the University of Oslo, in particular Marie Thörnfeld, who, with an impressive persistence, has managed to fit the bureaucratic requirements of the University of Oslo with those of the European Union. Line Sundt Næsse also played an important role in that regard at the beginning of the project, and Joaquín Zenteno has in addition to contributing strongly to three of the book's chapters made an indispensable contribution to the filling in of all the required forms from the EU. Finally, our director Kristi-Anne Stølen and our Head of Office Gitte Egenberg showed, as they have always done in the past, a remarkable commitment to support our work and ideas. Thank you all!

In the final stage of the process, Armando de la Madrid deserves special thanks for translating parts of the book from Spanish and for editing English as well as our multiple species of Spanglish into a publishable product.

Benedicte would like to thank Osvaldo for taking care of the whole family while she spent her days doing research and discussing finding with ENGOV colleagues in distant parts of the world.

Finally, we would like to thank all the informants—whether elites or those struggling for respect for their cultures, natural resources and lands—for their patience with our queries. We hope we have conveyed your viewpoints, whether we share them or not, with respect.

# Abbreviations

| | |
|---|---|
| AADEAA | Environmental Lawyers Association of Argentina |
| AAPRESID | *Asociación Argentina de Productores en Siembra Directa/* Argentinean No-Till Farm Association |
| ADS | Agency for Sustainable Development |
| ALBA | *Alianza Bolivariana para los Pueblos de Nuestra América/* Bolivarian Alliance for the Peoples of Our America |
| ANAPO | *Asociación de Productores de Oleaginosas y Trigo/*Oilseed and Wheat Producers Association |
| ANEP | *Asociación Nacional de la Empresa Privada/*National Association of Private Enterprises |
| ARENA | *Aliança Republicana Nacionalista/*Nationalist Republican Alliance |
| ASA | *Asociación Semilleros Argentinos/*Argentine Seed Association |
| BINGO | big international non-governmental organization |
| CACIF | *Comité Coordinador de Asociaciones Agrícolas, Comerciales, Industriales y Financieras/*Coordinating Committee of Agriculture, Commercial, Industrial and Financial Associations |
| CAFTA-DR | Central America and Dominican Republic Free Trade Agreement |
| CCBA | Climate Community and Biodiversity Alliance |
| CD | *Cambio Democrático/*Democratic Change |
| CDB | China Development Bank |
| CELAC | *Comunidad de Estados Latinoamericanos y Caribeños/* Community of Latin American and Caribbean States |
| CES | *Consejo Económico y Social/*Economic and Social Council |
| CGN | *Compañía Guatemalteca de Níquel/*Guatemalan Nickel Company |
| CI | Conservation International |
| CIFOR | Center for International Forestry Research |
| COCODE | local development community councils |
| CODIDENA | Diocese Commission for the Defence of Nature |
| COENA | *Consejo Ejecutivo Nacional/*National Executive Council |
| COICA | *Coordinadora de las Organizaciones Indígenas de la Cuenca Amazónica/*Coordinator of Indigenous Organizations of the Amazon River Basin |

| CONABIA | *Comisión Nacional Asesora de Biotecnología Agropecuaria/* National Advisory Commission on Agricultural Biotechnology |
| CONICET | *Consejo Nacional de Investigaciones Científicas y Técnicas/* National Scientific and Technical Research Council, Argentina |
| CONINAGRO | *Confederación Intercooperativa Agropecuaria/*Inter-Cooperative Agrarian Confederation |
| CONTAG | *Confederação Nacional dos Trabalhadores na Agricultura/* National Confederation of Rural Workers |
| COP 15 | 15th Conference of the Parties of the United Nations Framework Convention on Climate Change |
| CRA | *Confederaciones Rurales Argentinas/*Argentinean Rural Confederations |
| CSR | Corporate Social Responsibility |
| ECLAC | Economic Comission of Lation America and the Caribbean |
| EMAPA | *Empresa de Apoyo a la Producción de Alimentos/*Enterprise for the Support of Food Production |
| ENGOV | Environmental Governance in Latin America and the Caribbean |
| ESIA | Environmental and Social Impact Assessments |
| EU | European Union |
| FAA | *Federación Agraria Argentina/*Agrarian Federation of Argentina |
| FAB | *Foro Argentino de Biotecnología/*Argentine Forum for Biotechnology |
| FAS | *Fundação Amazônia Sustentável/*Sustainable Amazon Foundation |
| FCPF | Forestry Carbon Partnership Facility |
| FLACSO | *Facultad Latinoamericana de Ciencias Sociales/*Latin American Faculty of Social Sciences |
| FMLN | *Frente Farabundi Martí para la Liberación Nacional/*Farabundo Martí National Liberation Front |
| FPIC | Free, Prior and Informed Consultation |
| FUSADES | *Fundación Salvadoreña para el Desarrollo Económico y Social/*Salvadoran Foundation for Economic and Social Development |
| GANA | *Gran Alianza por la Unidad Nacional/*Grand Alliance for National Unity |
| GCFT | Governors' Climate and Forest Taskforce |
| GDP | Gross Domestic Product |
| GEF | Global Environment Facility |
| GenØk | *Senter for biosikkerhet/*Centre for Biosafety |
| GHG | greenhouse gas |
| GIZ | *Deutsche Gesellschaft für Internationale Zusammenarbeit/*German International Cooperation Agency (formerly GTZ) |
| GM | genetically modified |

| GMO | genetically modified organism |
|---|---|
| GRIF | Guyana REDD Investment Fund |
| IBAMA | *Instituto Brasileiro do Meio Ambiente e dos Recursos Naturais Renováveis*/Brazilian Institute of Environment and Renewable Natural Resources |
| IBCE | *Instituto Boliviano de Comercio Exterior*/Bolivian Institute for Commercial Exports |
| IDB | Inter American Development Bank |
| ILO | International Labor Organization |
| IMAC | *Instituto de Meio Ambiente do Acre*/Acre Environmental Institute |
| IMF | International Monetary Fund |
| INE | National Bureau of Statistics |
| INTA | *Instituto Nacional de Tecnología Agropecuaria*/National Institute for Agricultural Tecnology |
| ITEAM | Amazonas Land Tenure Institute |
| IUCN | International Union for Conservation of Nature |
| LCDS | Low Carbon Development Strategy |
| MAM | *Movimiento Amigos de Mauricio*/Friends of Mauricio (Funes) Movement |
| MARN | *Ministerio de Ambiente y Recursos Naturales*/Ministry of the Environment and Natural Resources |
| MAS | *Movimiento al Socialismo*/Movement towards Socialism |
| MDB | *Movimento Democrático Brasileiro*/Brazilian Democratic Movement |
| MEM | *Ministerio de Energía y Minas*/Ministry of Energy and Mines |
| MERCOSUR | *Mercado Común del Sur*/Southern Common Market |
| MINAGRI | *Ministerio de Agricultura, Ganadería y Pesca*/Ministry of Agriculture, Livestock and Fishery |
| MNC | multinational company |
| MoU | memorandum of understanding |
| NGO | non-governmental organization |
| PA | protected area |
| PAF | Plan for Family Agriculture |
| PAIS | *Patria Ativa I Soberana*/Proud and Sovereign Homeland |
| PAPXIGUA | *Parlamento del Pueblo Xinka de Guatemala*/Parliament of the Xinka People of Guatemala |
| PDS | *Partido Democrático Social*/Social Democratic Party |
| PDVSA | *Petróleos de Venezuela S.A.*/Venezuelan Petroleum Inc |
| PFG | Partnership for Growth |
| PMDB | *Partido do Movimento Democrático Brasileiro*/Brazilian Democratic Movement Party |
| PNBV | *Plan Nacional para el Buen Vivir*/National Plan for the Good Life |
| PP-G7 | *O Programa Piloto para a Proteção das Florestas Tropicais do Brasil*/Brazilian Pilot Program to Conserve the Rainforest |

| | |
|---|---|
| PREP | *Programa Nacional de Restauración de Ecosistemas y Paisajes*/National Program for the Restoration of Ecosystems and Rural Landscapes |
| PSDB | *Partido da Social Democracia Brasileira*/Brazilian Social Democratic Party |
| PT | *Partido dos Trabalhadores*/Workers' Party |
| RDS | *Reserva de Desenvolvimento Sustentável*/Sustainable Development Reserve |
| REDD | Reducing Emissions from Deforestation and forest Degradation |
| REDU | *Red Ecuatoriana de Universidades y Escuelas Politécnicas para Investigación y Posgrados*/Ecuadorian Network of Universities and Polytechnic Schools for Research and Graduate Studies |
| RFS | Rainforest Standard |
| SENESCYT | *Secretaria Nacional de Educación Superior, Ciencia, Tecnología e Innovación*/National Secretariat of Higher Education, Science, Technology and Innovation |
| SENPLADES | *Secretaría Nacional de Planificación y Desarrollo*/National Secretariat of Planning and Development |
| SNUC | *Sistema Nacional de Unidades de Conservação*/National System of Protected Areas |
| SRA | *Sociedad Rural Argentina*/Rural Society of Argentina |
| TNC | transnational company |
| UDP | *Unidad Democrática y Popular*/Democratic and Popular Unity |
| UFM | *Universidad Francisco Marroquín*/Francisco Marroquín University |
| UNASUR | *Unión de Naciones Suramericanas*/Union of South American Nations |
| UNDP | United Nations Development Programme |
| UNFCCC | United Nations Framework Convention on Climate Change |
| VCS | Verified Carbon Standards |
| WB | World Bank |
| WCS | Wildlife Conservation Society |
| WCSD | World Council for Sustainable Development |
| ZEE | *Zoneamento Ecológico-Econômico*/Ecological–Economic Zoning |
| ZFV | *Zona Franca Verde*/Green Free Trade Zone |

# 1 Environmental governance and sustainable development in Latin America

*Benedicte Bull and Mariel Aguilar-Støen*

## Elites and natural resources in Latin America: the main arguments

Since colonial times, the differentiation of the social, political and economic elites from the rest of the population in Latin America has been built, in part, on the control over natural resources that the elite has secured through history. Securing control over land, minerals, water, oil, gas and forests has been equally as important as their control over labor in order to be able to dominate societies and state apparatus, as for example shown by Coronil (1997) accounting for the role of oil in the evolution of the Venezuelan state. A further historical characteristic of Latin America is that this elite control has been intimately linked to the insertion of Latin America into the global economy as exporters of raw materials, and to the elite's cultural, ethnic and economic ties to foreign countries, companies and organizations, as well as to the racialized patterns of social domination prevalent in most Latin American countries (Quijano, 2000).

Consequently, socio-environmental conflicts in Latin America often involve disputes over the distribution of economic resources and goods, access to and control over natural resources, as well as representation and subjective meanings (Escobar, 2011). They are often traversed by political, social, ethnic and economic claims; they have involved struggles against local, national and transnational elites by indigenous peoples, small farmers and other marginalized groups as well as middle-class actors sympathizing with their cause (Carruthers, 2008).

There also exists an elitist environmental movement in Latin America, and it has exerted considerable influence on environmental policy making and in the framing of environmental problems in the region. This elitist environmental movement has often had an urban base and has been inspired by global conservationist movements and ideas. This is reflected for instance in the early instauration of natural parks and other forms of "fortress conservation" in the region, the development of market-based incentives for water and forest conservation and the institutionalization of environmental management. The ideas and initiatives have been brought to the national agenda by non-governmental organizations (NGOs), academic and official research institutes, or policy makers often linked to international organizations and more attuned to international intellectual currents than to the needs of the local populations (see e.g. Mumme *et al.*, 1988; Nugent, 2002). Consequently, this form of conservation has been criticized for failing to understand environmental issues in the context of the creation of livelihoods for marginalized groups (Holmes, 2010). In fact, this type of conservation has often been opposed by local populations dependent on the use of biological reserves for small-scale agriculture and grasslands.

Recently, Latin America has seen new groups rise to political power and old economic elites being challenged by multifaceted economic and political processes. Many of the left-leaning governments that came to power in this period were supported by indigenous organizations, peasants associations and other movements pursuing environmental justice and a more equitable and sustainable use of natural resources. Thus, there were great expectations regarding their willingness and ability to shift development strategies towards more sustainable and equitable policies that pay more attention to the concerns of local populations and indigenous peoples than to the exigencies of global capital and domestic elites.

However, apparent contradictions in policies related to environmental governance soon appeared in many countries: in Bolivia the government of the Movement Towards Socialism (MAS) led by indigenous labor unionist, Evo Morales, launched plans to construct highways through indigenous territories and protected areas (PAs) while pursuing the good life in harmony with "Pachamama" in official discourse; in Brazil the expansion of hydroelectric dams threatened biodiversity and indigenous livelihoods at the same time as the government made major efforts to reduce deforestation; and in Ecuador mining concessions expanded while efforts were made to restrict oil extraction. Thus, doubts arose about the sustainability of the development strategies pursued during Latin America's "pink tide" (Gudynas, 2010).

The purpose of this book is to better understand the dynamics of environmental politics of the so-called pink-tide governments in Latin America. The starting point is a view of the government as a body that controls a certain set of resources, including economic and political resources. However, it is not omnipotent. In most of Latin America governments have relatively weak state apparatuses at hand to implement their will, and much of societies' economic, political, coercive, knowledge and organizational resources are controlled by elites—national and international—that do not necessarily share the government's agenda. Thus, we approach the question of how to understand the dynamics of environmental politics from an elite perspective. We ask: To what extent has the "pink tide" involved a shift of elites? To what extent has that contributed to more sustainable policies and to what extent has it led to the opposite? How do the new governmental elites relate to old elites? Do they accommodate their interests? Do they pursue alliances with them? Do they try to undermine them? Do they compete with them? To what extent have new economic, knowledge or political elites emerged as a result of the rise of the center-left governments? Do they share the same visions of development and the environment or do they diverge? And how do they relate to non-elites or subaltern groups?

This book is the result of a four-year joint research project on environmental governance in Latin America and the Caribbean funded by the European

Union's FP7. Our strategy for researching the contradictions and dynamics of environmental governance in this project has been to study the governance of economic sectors of major importance in a number of different countries. As a result, in this book we deliver case studies of the soy sector in Bolivia and Argentina, agriculture in El Salvador, mining in Chile, Argentina, Colombia, Ecuador and Guatemala, biotechnology in Ecuador, and forestry in Brazil. In addition, the book includes two chapters that cover several cases and countries: one on the new elites arising in connection with the global "Reducing Emissions from Deforestation and forest Degradation" (REDD) program and one on shifting elites in the mining sector in several Andean countries. Although we explore different countries and sectors, across the cases, the focus is on how the incorporation of environment issues in the governance of economic activity depends on which groups that have come to power, how they relate to elites outside their own political projects and how they relate to subalterns.

The main argument of this book is that the new, leftist governments overall were faced with many constraints as they in fact controlled limited resources resulting from weak state institutions and strong societal elites. In that situation they had the choice of attempting to strengthen the states (depending on state revenues), grooming new elites, allying with outside elites (economic elites, international elites, knowledge elites, etc.) or confronting competing elites. All of these strategies had environmental implications. Moreover, the degree to which environmental considerations and governance mechanisms were incorporated in their development strategies depended not only on their own development priorities but also on their success in enrolling or competing with alternative elites. In what remains of this chapter, we will first give an introduction to the so-called "pink tide" in Latin America. Thereafter we will discuss the concepts of environmental governance and sustainable development as a basis for what follows in the subsequent chapters, before we detail our main argument and provide an overview of the book.

## The "pink tide" in Latin America

Over the last ten years a number of governments that define themselves as belonging to the center-left entered power in Latin America. Out of 49 presidential elections in Latin America in the 2003–13 period, 22 were won by center-left candidates, and with the exception of Mexico and Colombia, all the large economies in Latin America were governed by center-left governments in most of this period.

However, there were significant differences among the center-left governments in Latin America. Early attempts to classify them in distinct categories of moderate and radical or contestatory[1] regimes (see e.g. Castañeda, 2006; Weyland, 2010) have been widely rejected (Beasley-Murray et al., 2010; Cameron and Hershberg, 2010; Lievesley and Ludlam, 2009; Levitsky and Roberts, 2011), because it became evident that there were significant differences in policy style and content among these governments. Yet a main distinction may be drawn between those who sought gradual socio-structural change (i.e. greater equality) within the framework of a liberal democracy, existing institutions and the market economy, and those who have sought alternatives for political economic inclusion that go beyond liberal democracy and a market economy, requiring constitutional and institutional changes.

In attempting to explain such differences, most authors have focused on the type of social movements or political parties from which they emerge. For example, Roberts and Levitsky distinguish between leftist regimes based on their concentration of power and degree to which they are based on an established party or a new political movement (Levitsky and Roberts, 2011). Beyond that, the center-left governments were based on highly diverse coalitions, with groups ranging from indigenous movements (as in Ecuador and Bolivia), and labor unions (as in Brazil, Argentina and Bolivia), to peasant and landless movements (as in Brazil and the Lugo government in Paraguay), and broad democracy movements (as in Chile and Brazil). Environmental issues played very different roles in the different cases. It was an integral part of the discourse of change in the cases of Bolivia and Ecuador, and a major issue for important actors in the government coalition in El Salvador and Brazil. In other cases, it has entered the stage at later points (such as in the case of Chile, where particularly socialist Michelle in her second presidential period (2014–18) will have to pay major attention to environmental issues).

It is difficult to characterize the diversity of development strategies that have resulted from the center-left governments in simple phrases. However, they may be considered as varieties of a regional developmental nationalism. This is characterized by an increasing direct state engagement in developmental policies, and increasing economic nationalism, but embedded in regional integration and open to trade and investments from abroad (Bull, 2015). While this has been pursued with the aim of filling state coffers to enable distribution and poverty reduction (among other aims), in many cases it has happened at the expense of relations with local populations and environmental considerations, as we will discuss in the chapters that follow.

However, whereas many authors have emphasized the support coalitions of different governments to explain their policies, much less attention has been paid to the obstacles that the regimes have met in power, and thus many studies have erroneously conflated a political phenomenon with the policy output (Luna, 2010, p. 29). The dilemmas and challenges that leftist governments encounter faced with opposition from socio-economic elites that control the means of production have provoked splits within the left for more than a century in Latin America as well as Europe. As will be further elaborated in Chapter 2, historically resource limitations and the opposition from socio-economic and political elites have presented particular obstacles to Latin American governments aiming for structural change (Weyland, 2010, p. 6). As shown by Buxton in the case of Venezuela, the choice of a certain strategy may not only be a result of ideologies and a pleasing support coalition, but equally of the elites' opening or blocking the possibility for dialogue and reaching agreements (Buxton, 2009). Indeed, although the composition, ideology and strategy of the political movement in power is important for understanding the direction of the policy-making process and the policies proposed, the outcome cannot be understood without taking into account the interaction with the former elites and the institutional framework that they have left in place.

## Environmental governance

Environmental governance is a concept that has gained much currency among scholars from a range of disciplines including geographers, sociologists, environmental managers and development scholars to analyze how decisions about the environment and nature are made (Bridge and Perreault, 2009). It involves a focus on systems of governing, means for the allocation of resources and the exercise of control and coordination in which state and non-state actors play various roles (Bulkeley, 2005).

The concept environmental governance emerged in the neoliberal era (Baud *et al.*, 2011) and signaled an analytical focus that moved beyond the state. The perceived obsolescence of state-oriented analyses of environmental policies as a governmental affair had both empirical and ideological reasons. Thus, Lemos and Agrawal (2006) argue that environmental governance is used to analyze the globalization of environmental policy-making; the decentralization of environmental management; the role of market- and agent-focused incentives as regulatory mechanisms; and the challenges involved in the cross-scalar nature of environmental problems (Lemos and Agrawal, 2006).

As it has become associated with neoliberalism and a focus on management issues rather than power and inequalities, environmental governance has been criticized for engendering analyses "that flatten uneven relations of power, and which mask competing claims to, and about the environment" (Bridge and Perreault, 2009, p. 492).

We understand environmental governance in a broader sense, as the set of mechanisms, formal and informal institutions and practices by way of which social order is produced through controlling that which is related to the environment and natural resources. In other words, we are not only interested in the "management of nature" but in how, through governing nature and natural resources, the conditions of what is possible for actors in a given context, are established.

As such, environmental governance stands in no contrast to an approach based on political ecology for which inequalities and power are key concepts. In our use of the term, studying environmental governance deals with analyzing the re-scaling of environmental decision making; commodity chain coordination; the role of institutions in environmental policy making; the role of different non-state actors and their participation in socio-environmental conflicts; as well as the role of the state in environmental regulation within the context of capitalist accumulation and the commodification of nature and to explore the production of socio-environmental order (Bridge and Perreault, 2009).

While political ecology tends to "privilege the rights and concerns (often livelihood-based) of the poor over those of powerful political and economic elites" (Bryant and Jarosz, 2004, p. 808) and thus tends to blackbox[2] elites, environmental governance studies have also largely failed to study elites in any detail. A focus on the role of elites in environmental governance is found almost exclusively in studies dealing with international trade regimes or international environmental treaties (Cashore, 2002; Levy and Newell, 2002, 2005; McCarthy, 2004), and these studies are limited to the business elites although, more recently the role of other actors, that we define as elites, has also been included in analysis of environmental governance (see Bock, 2014). Our contribution in this book is that through various case studies we set out to analyze the role of different and various types of elites (see Chapter 2) in national or regional contexts on the production of social order through the environment and natural resources.

Our understanding of environmental governance allows us to weave together the economic and the political in environmental decision making. We also focus on the relationship between institutions and social action. This means that we highlight the role of, and interactions between, state and non-state actors (NGOs, social movements, private corporations), and between elite and non-elite actors in allocating and regulating the environment and resources. In doing so, we shift the understanding of power in environmental decision making away from a state-centric perspective. Rather, we see power as social boundaries that define the fields of action for all actors, and define what is possible for the self and for others (Hayward, 1998). The mechanisms of power consist in laws, rules, norms, customs, social identities and standards that constrain and enable inter- and intra-subjective actions; we focus on "whether the social boundaries defining key practices and institutions produce entrenched differences in the field of what is possible for different actors" (Hayward, 1998). Institutional arrangements, organizations and the relationships involved in environmental governance embody political and economic power, acting through the control of the environment. In our analysis we seek to shed light on power dynamics involved in environmental decision making and to trace back the origins of such dynamics and their implications for sustainable development. By analyzing different cases, we hope to demonstrate that the relationships involved in environmental governance also have historical and structural determinants.

In this sense, we find it problematic to assume a definition of elite that is blind to the complex, dynamic and at times conflictive relationship between different groups of actors controlling key resources (see Chapter 2). Given the current situation in Latin America, in which groups that have been on the barricades to oppose the elites in power, find themselves in power, we cannot assume that elites will always essentially be mainly a part of the cause of inequality and environmental degradation. Moreover, the fate of agendas for environmental protection and more sustainable production patterns of other actors, such as social movements, depends not only on their own ability to mobilize and articulate their demands, but crucially also on the elite's reaction to them. This situation urges a closer scrutiny of the dynamics of interaction of elite and non-elite actors in environmental decision-making.

Decisions about the environment are affected by actors and processes at various and multiple scales. This is especially important when considering the important role played by Latin American countries in the export of agricultural products and the growing importance of international standards for the regulation of food production, the contribution that Latin America might do to solve global environmental problems such as climate change or biodiversity conservation, as imagined by policy-makers and development agencies, the transboundary nature of certain resources such as water or the increasing focus on the extractive industries in the region. Governance is thus useful as an analytical framework to explore complex and multi-scalar institutional arrangements, social practices and actors engaged in environmental decision-making.

## Sustainable development

The literature on environmental governance ironically often leaves out a discussion of development. Indeed, "development" has for long been discredited due to its association with foreign development cooperation, capitalism and megaprojects with little sensitivity to the needs and livelihoods of local populations and vulnerable environments (Escobar, 2011). Also the term "sustainable development" has been misused to the degree that it has lost its ability to capture a desirable path of societal change.

Sustainable development can be considered a "boundary term"; a term where science meets politics and politics meets science (Gieryn, 1999)—in that sense, the concept of sustainable development has depended on epistemic communities (Forsyth, 2003) that share an understanding of and common commitment to linking environmental and economic development concerns (Scoones, 2010). Thus, sustainable development as a concept has had an important political role in processes of policy making on development around the world and at different scales (Mansfield, 2009).

The term was launched in 1987 by the UN-commissioned report *Our Common Future* (popularly known as the "Brundtland report"; WCED, 1987) defining sustainable development as "development that meets the needs of the present without compromising the ability of future generations to meet their own needs." Sustainable development signified a change by way of which issues of environment and economic growth are going to be considered together. To a significant extent, and because of the ambiguity of its definition, sustainable development allowed different concerns and interests to meet. On the one hand, environmental activists from the North concerned with "the limits to [economic and population] growth" sought to incorporate environmental thinking in development planning as, to them, development projects and population growth caused the loss of biodiversity and natural habitats. On the other hand, governments and activists of the global South had argued for decades that environmental concerns could not be de-linked from concerns about economic growth and equity (Mansfield, 2009).

For many activists and academics in the South, particularly in Latin America, the causes of environmental degradation are the same as those of poverty (see for example Faber, 1992; Leff, 1994). Furthermore, attempts to get countries of the South to renounce development in the name of conservation were seen largely as neocolonial efforts to control resources in the South (Mansfield, 2009). During the UN Conference on Environment and Development in Rio de Janeiro in 1992 (also known as the Earth Summit), the idea that economic growth can be reconciled with environmental conservation gained wide support from countries in the North and in the South (Adams, 2008). One of the reasons is perhaps that both the Brundtland report and policy-makers at the Earth Summit argued that while overpopulation was a problem (as environmentalists in the North suggested), it was the result of poverty, and because poverty was the problem (as activists in the South suggested) economic development would become the solution to both socio-economic problems and environmental degradation. Economic growth in the South will decrease poverty, control population growth, relieve direct pressure on resources and provide economic resources for conservation (Mansfield, 2009). In other words, as Mansfield (2009, p. 39) argues, "no longer seen as an environmental threat or cause of global inequality, development became the route to sustainability"; in this way, by taking up the idea of sustainable development, governments around the world could circumvent discussions of politically challenging issues necessary to reduce poverty, increase equity and create more environmentally friendly ways of living. The idea that sustainable development should be linked to capitalist development and neoliberal globalization was not challenged at the global level during the subsequent World Summits on Sustainable Development in 2002 (Mansfield, 2008) or in 2012.

However, the last decade in Latin America offers interesting points to reflect about the term sustainable development and the politics around it. On the one hand, ideas of the good life and the value of mother earth, as well as granting constitutional rights to nature (as in the cases of Bolivia and Ecuador) represent radical innovations in the ways in which (sustainable) development can be thought. At the same time, governments in Latin America have placed much weight on generating economic growth by way of state interventions, with the aim of not only preparing the ground for market actors, but as a means of improving the lives and livelihoods of the majority of the population. We do not consider that this can be reduced to serving the interests of elites, global capital or international aid agencies; rather it is a necessary means to bring millions out of poverty.

The range of meanings attached to sustainable development reflects the contested question of what development itself means (Forsyth, 2005). For the purposes of this book, we will not offer yet a new way of defining sustainable development. Rather, the approach we take is that we examine the ways in which governments and elites are creating "new" socio-ecological relations in a range of cases and sectors in Latin America. By this we mean relations that promote the reduction of inequality in access to and control of resources, the bearing of environmental costs and in access to environmental and economic benefits.

Thus, our analysis focuses on the politics of creating new socio-ecological relations addressing the relations of power that shape what people can do in a given
context and how, who should have access to what resources, on what basis and
for what purposes is defined through different political processes.

## Changing elites and sustainable development: the contribution of this book

The following chapters will address these issues in a range of different ways. In
Chapter 2, Benedicte Bull addresses from a theoretical standpoint, the question
of when and how we may expect elites to pursue sustainable development policies and an equitable form of environmental governance. She discusses not only
different elite concepts and how they perceive the possibilities for democracy and
sustainable development, but she also discusses another concept that has perhaps
been even more salient in Latin American social sciences, namely classes. She
also identifies factors that may lead to a change in elites' compositions or attitudes that may allow for new environmental politics to emerge.

The subsequent chapters are organized by sectors. In Part 1 we research the
agricultural sector. In Chapter 3, Bull, Cuéllar and Kandel discuss the experience
of the government of Mauricio Funes in El Salvador (2009–14) in attempting to
transform the country's development model, particularly in the agricultural sector. Funes was the first president in El Salvador to be supported by the left-wing
former guerilla party *Frente Farabundi Martí para la Liberación Nacional* (FMLN),
and he thus ended 17 years of right-wing rule. He took over a country in a triple
crisis: with dismal growth performance, deep social problems and major environmental challenges, not least due to vulnerability to climate change. However,
the government faced major obstacles posed by old elites in their pursuit of a new
development agenda, as well as differences between groups within the government coalition favoring different development models, and limitations due to the
close integration of El Salvador into the US economy.

Chapter 4 takes us to Bolivia. In 2006, the former coca-grower and labor union
leader Evo Morales took power in Bolivia as leader of the MAS (*Movimiento al
Socialismo*) party. One of the main issues that MAS promoted in the election
campaign as well as in the first governmental program, was a more sustainable agriculture focusing on the needs of small farmers and rejecting the use of
genetically modified crops. In the new constitution that was adopted in 2009,
genetically modified organisms (GMOs) were banned while the "good life"
(*buen vivir*) in harmony with Mother Earth (Pachamama) was set as a national
development goal. However, in the aftermath, genetically modified (GM) soy
production has increased significantly. In this chapter Marte Høiby and Joaquín
Zenteno Hopp discuss the relations between old/traditional soy elites and new
soy elites associated with the MAS party.

The theme of GMO continues in Chapter 5, on Argentina. Over the past
years, Argentina has become the world's number one producer of GM soy, while
a national discussion of environmental implications of soy production has been

largely absent. Hanche-Olsen, Zenteno Hopp and Sejenovich try to understand this through focusing on the relationship between the governments of Néstor Kirchner and Cristina Fernández de Kirchner, on the one hand and on the other hand, old rural elites and emerging agribusiness elites. New techniques and ownership structure (including by transnational companies (TNCs)) have led to land concentration, but also increased the role of urban-based businessmen in the management of the production process. Thus, the old rural elite is considerably weakened and new agribusiness elites with different subgroups emerge. At the same time, the experience of a hostile attitude towards agricultural production by the Kirchner governments, with increased tax burdens and lack of technical support and incentives, made many farmers choose the most secure way of making money quickly, namely to move into GM soy. In the very narrow room for dialogue between the different agricultural elites and the government, environmental issues arising from the no-till practice, the use of glyphosate and the expansion of the agricultural frontier, have been weak or absent.

Chapter 6, on Ecuador, also discusses the issue of GM soy but from a different perspective. Pablo Andrade and Joaquín Zenteno Hopp find that in the case of Rafael Correa's government there has been a significant change in position from the first rejection of GMOs to embracing the general use of modern biotechnology in agriculture. While this is partly accounted for by the president's focus on growth and development and the marginalization of the environmentalist faction in the governing coalition, Andrade and Zenteno find that another part of the story is the rise of a group of young technocrats in different governmental offices with largely similar backgrounds and education that strongly favor biotechnological solutions. This group increasingly dominates the agenda on agricultural development, and it is in the process of developing as a technocratic elite.

Part 2, on mining, starts with a broad overview of the changes in mining, oil and gas politics in South America, with a particular focus on the Andean region. Barbara Hogenboom (Chapter 7) discusses the policies towards resource extraction of the "center-left" governments in Venezuela, Bolivia, Ecuador and Brazil, and looks at how they interact with new international elites with major roles in the extractive sectors, including Chinese companies and new financial actors. She argues that the new "center-left" elites have placed equal emphasis on the so called "strategic resources" as their neoliberal predecessors, and that in spite of employing a new discourse and new means (including more state involvement) in the extractive sectors, their policies have equal potential for generating conflicts and have major shortcomings in terms of environmental governance and sustainable development.

Mariel Aguilar-Støen enters into detail on such mining conflicts in the case of Guatemala in Chapter 8. Guatemala is not strictly a country that has been a part of the "pink tide." Between 2008 and 2012 it was governed by Alvaro Colom of the self-declared center-left party *Unidad Nacional de la Esperanza.* However, Guatemala is characterized by the entrenchment of old elites in the economy as well as the political system that has continued to pursue mega-projects, not least in the mining sector that has seen a steep increase in concessions. This chapter studies the conflict regarding the silver mine project "El Escobal" in south-eastern Guatemala between various local groups on the one hand, and on the other hand, the Canadian company "Tahoe Resources Inc"[3] managing the mine, and its associates among the national elite. The argument of the chapter is that mining conflicts are located within the politics of place. Ongoing mining conflicts in rural Guatemala are connected to broader political struggles in the country, but manifest in the way in which different actors try to build and contest the identity of particular places and of the people connected to such places. Place meanings are connected to conflicting ideas about property to land, environmental governance, participation and development. The elites' ideas and values in this respect are often opposed to local movements' ideas and values.

In the final chapter on mining, Cristián Parker (Chapter 9) studies the attitudes towards sustainable consumption and production among elites with key positions in mining and energy industries in Colombia, Ecuador, Argentina and Chile. The chapter focuses on the view, social representations and practices of elites as a means to shed light on whether these actors are beginning to assume (or not) a real shift towards real sustainable consumption of water and energy in production patterns in the context of structural (global, local and strategic) constraints and dynamics. The chapter identifies four different discourses among the elite groups interviewed: (1) responsible mining/energy production but without reduction in consumption; (2) efficiency and good management of water and energy; (3) a focus on sustainable use within the context of a holistic governmental policy, and (4) a more critical stance that suggest finding alternative models.

Part 3 discusses forestry. In Chapter 10, Mariel Aguilar-Støen and Cecilie Hirsch discuss the international REDD initiative launched at the Conference of the Parties of the United Nations Framework Convention on Climate Change (UNFCCC) in 2005. Currently there are REDD projects that aim to reduce deforestation in several Latin American countries. Aguilar-Støen and Hirsch discuss how the REDD process has led to the emergence of a new science-policy elite that control specific knowledge resources. The requirement of having acquired this specific, technical knowledge, may also exclude other marginal groups from meaningful participation in environmental governance of the resources upon which they depend.

Chapter 11, on forest governance in Brazil, by Toni, Villarroel and Bueno, starts by observing the contradictions of the environmental policies of the last Brazilian governments (those of Luiz Inácio Lula da Silva and Dilma Rousseff). While praised internationally for the reduction of deforestation in the Amazon, under the recent governments the use of GMOs has been approved, land-use restrictions have been lifted, mega-dams have been licensed and the creation of PAs and indigenous lands has slowed down. Parts of the many contradictions are due to the size of the country and its federal structure that allows for much environmental policy to be carved out at the state level. Thus Toni *et al.* analyze the dynamics of environmental governance in two Amazonian states, Acre and Amazonas, that have reached impressive results in terms of forest protection due to a set of innovative environmental policies pursued by the local administration.

They find that in both states the new policies depended on an elite shift: in the case of Acre, change meant a new elite coming to power, whereas in Amazonas, elections brought a change within the ruling elite.

## Notes

1 In Weyland's definition a contestatory strategy includes "enacting reforms step by step in a determined, cumulative strategy ... privileging prudence, gradualism and realism" (Weyland, 2010, p. 7).
2 We use the term "blackboxing" as a parallel to its use in international relations. In international relations theory states are often assumed to be unitary, rational, self-interested actors, and the actual decision-making processes of the state are disregarded as being largely irrelevant and thus not subject of research. Thus, Graham Allison (Allison, 1971) argued that the state was considered a "black box" leaving important fields of knowledge unexplored. In a related meaning but referring to the hard sciences, Bruno Latour has used the term as a verb "blackboxing" (Latour, 1987). We use it here to argue that political ecology by considering elites as self-interested, rational actors without considering internal differences and decision-making processes, in effect has "blackboxed" them.
3 The El Escobal project has the potential to become one of the largest silver producers of the world. Tahoe Resources Inc. plans to invest a total of US$406 million in this mine. See www.industrialinfo.com/news/abstract.jsp?newsitemID=220200; see also www.tahoeresourcesinc.com.

## References

Adams, B. (2008) *Green Development: Environment and Sustainability in a Developing World.* Routledge, London.

Allison, G. (1971) *Essence of Decision Making: The Cuban Missile Crisis.* Little Brown and Company, Boston, MA.

Baud, M., Castro, F. D. and Hogenboom, B. (2011) Environmental governance in Latin America: Towards an integrative research agenda. *Revista Europea de Estudios Latinoamericanos y del Caribe/European Review of Latin American and Caribbean Studies,* 90, 79–88.

Beasley-Murray, J., Maxwell, A. C. and Hershberg, E. (2010) Latin America's left turns: A tour d'horizon, in A. C. Maxwell and E. Hershberg (eds), *Latin Americas Left Turns: Politics, Policies and Trajectories of Change.* Lynne Rienners Publishers, Boulder, CO, pp. 1–23.

Bock, S. (2014) Politicized expertise: An analysis of the political dimensions of consultants' policy recommendations to developing countries with a case study of McKinsey's advice on REDD+ policies. *Innovation: The European Journal of Social Science Research,* 1–19.

Bridge, G. and Perreault, T. (2009) Environmental governance, in N. Castree, D. Demeritt, D. Liverman and B. Rhoads (eds), *A Companion to Environmental Geography.* Wiley-Blackwell, Oxford, pp. 475–497.

Bryant, R. L. and Jarosz, L. (2004) Ethics in political ecology: A special issue of *Political Geography.* Introduction: Thinking about ethics in political ecology, *Political Geography* 23, 807–812.

Bulkeley, H. (2005) Reconfiguring environmental governance: Towards a politics of scales and networks. *Political Geography,* 24 (8), 875–902.

Bull, B. (2015) Latin America's decade of growth: Progress and challenges for a sustainable development, in A. Hansen and U. Wethal (eds), *Emerging Economies and Challenges to Sustainability*. Routledge, London, pp. 19–33.

Buxton, J. (2009) Venezuela: The political evolution of Bolivarianism, in G. Lievesley and S. Ludlam (eds), *Experiments in Radical Social Democracy* Zed Books, London and New York, pp. 57–74.

Cameron, M. and Hershberg, E. (2010) *Latin Americas Left Turns: Politics, Policies and Trajectories of Change*. Lynne Rienners Publishers, Boulder, CO.

Carruthers, D. V. (2008) *Environmental Justice in Latin America: Problems, Promise and Practice*. The MIT Press, Cambridge, MA.

Cashore, B. (2002) Legitimacy and the privatization of environmental governance: How non-state market-driven (NSMD) governance systems gain rule-making authority. *Governance*, 15, 503–529.

Castañeda, J. G. (2006) Latin America's left turn. *Foreign Affairs*, 85, 28–43.

Coronil, F. (1997) *The Magical State: Nature, Money and Modernity in Venezuela*. University of Chicago Press, Chicago, IL.

Escobar, A. (2011) *Encountering Development: The Making and Unmaking of the Third World*. Princeton University Press, Princeton, NJ.

Faber, D. (1992) The ecological crisis of Latin America: A theoretical introduction. *Latin American Perspectives*, 19(1), 3–16.

Forsyth, T. (2003) *Critical Political Ecology. The Politics of Environmental Science*. Routledge, New York.

Forsyth, T. (2005) *Encyclopedia of International Development*. Routledge, London.

Gieryn, T. (1999) *Cultural Boundaries of Science: Credibility on the Line*. Chicago University Press, Chicago, IL.

Gudynas, E. (2010) Si eres tan progresista ¿Por qué destruyes la naturaleza? Neoextractivismo, izquierda y alternativas, *Ecuador Debate*, 79, 61–81.

Hayward, C. R. (1998) De-facing power. *Polity*, 31, 1–22.

Holmes, G. (2010) The rich, the powerful and the endangered: Conservation elites, networks and the Dominican Republic. *Antipode*, 42, 624–646.

Latour, B. (1987) *Science in Action: How to Follow Scientists and Engineers Through Society*. Harvard University Press, Cambridge, MA.

Leff, E. (1994) *Ecología y capital: racionalidad ambiental, democracia participativa y desarrollo sustentable*. Siglo XXI Editores, México D.F., Mexico.

Lemos, M. C. and Agrawal, A. (2006) Environmental governance. *Annual Review of Environment and Resources*, 31, 297–325.

Levitsky, S. and Roberts, K. (2011) Latin America's "Left turn": A framework for analysis, in S. Levitsky and K. Roberts (eds), *The Resurgence of Latin America's Left*. Johns Hopkins University Press, Maryland, MD.

Levy, D. L. and Newell, P. J. (2002) Business strategy and international environmental governance: Toward a neo-Gramscian synthesis. *Global Environmental Politics*, 2, 84–101.

Levy, D. L. and Newell, P. J. (2005) *The Business of Global Environmental Governance*. MIT Press, Cambridge, MA.

Lievesley, G. and Ludlam, S. (2009) *Latin America: Experiments in Radical Social Democracy*. Zed Books, London and New York.

Luna, J. P. (2010) The left turns: Why they happened and how they compare, in M. A. Cameron and E. Hershberg (eds), *Latin America's Left Turns: Politics, Policies and Trajectories of Change*. Lynne Rienner Publishers, Boulder, CO and London, pp. 61–80.

Mansfield, B. (2008) Global environmental politics, in K. Cox, M. Low and J. D. Robinson (eds), *Handbook of Political Geography*. Sage, London, pp. 235–246.

Mansfield, B. (2009) Sustainability, in N. Castree, D. Demeritt, D. Liverman and B. Rhoads (eds), *A Companion to Environmental Geography*. Blackwell Publishing, Oxford, pp. 37–49.

McCarthy, J. (2004) Privatizing conditions of production: Trade agreements as neoliberal environmental governance. *Geoforum*, 35, 327–341.

Mumme, S. P., Bath, C. R. and Assetto, V. J. (1988) Political development and environmental policy in Mexico. *Latin American Research Review*, 23, 7–34.

Nugent, S. (2002) Gente Boa: Elites in and of Amazonia, in C. Shore and S. Nugent (eds), *Elite Cultures: Anthropological Perspectives*. Routledge, London, pp. 61–73.

Quijano, A. (2000) Colonialiadad del poder y clasificación social. *Journal of World-Systems Research*, 2, 342–386.

Scoones, I. (2010) Sustainability, in A. Cornwall and D. Eade (eds), *Deconstructing Development Discourse: Buzzwords and Fuzzwords*. Oxfam, pp. 153–162.

WCED (1987) *Our Common Future*. Oxford University Press, Oxford.

Weyland, K. (2010) The performance of leftist governments in Latin America: Conceptual and theoretical issues, in K. Weyland, L. Madrid and W. Hunter (eds), *Leftist Governments in Latin America: Successes and Shortcomings* Cambridge University Press, Cambridge, pp. 1–28.

# 2 Elites, classes and environmental governance
## Conceptual and theoretical challenges

*Benedicte Bull*

## Introduction

The main question that has motivated this book is: why, given the political shifts experienced in Latin America over the last decades, has there not been a more profound policy shift towards a sustainable development model? The hypothesis that we launched in the introduction was that the degree of change depends on the dynamic interplay between elites and non-elite groups, how the former have changed and how those changes impact on the elite–non-elite dynamics.

However, discussing this requires a clarification of several concepts and questions: What is an elite? When and why do elites pursue policies and practices leading to sustainable development and when do they not? To what extent can democracy overcome the impediments to greater equality as well as improved environmental governance of an elitist state and society?

The purpose of this chapter is to provide an analytical approach to those questions. It starts by defining elites. In doing so, the concept of elite is compared to another concept that is much used in Latin American social sciences to define the upper strata of society, namely classes. In a region in which the Marxist claim that "political power is an offshoot of economic power" has often rung true, there has been a certain distrust in attempts to distinguish elites from classes (Rovira 2011). Both concepts reflect dimensions of social inequality, but while the distinction of an upper class refers to its command of economic means, elites are defined by way of their influence in society and exertion of power over political outcomes (Etzioni-Halevy 1997, p. xxv).

After defining elites, the chapter discusses the role of elites in development. This is a topic that has been a subject of increasing scholarly attention in recent years (see e.g. Amsden *et al.* 2012; Acemoglu and Robinson 2012). However, the recent literature has mostly taken a very traditional concept of development as a starting point. Development has been understood—implicitly or explicitly—as economic growth, based on technological progress and industrial upgrading. Attempting to understand the role of elites in sustainable development (i.e. development that encompasses equitable environmental governance and a sustainable use of natural resources) poses additional challenges. Given that we assume that some kinds of elites will always appear, we do not only have to grapple with the question of how and under what conditions elite's self-interests can become compatible with fostering general development processes. We also have to consider under what conditions they will pursue policies and practices compatible with a more sustainable development.

Another problem with the recent literature on elites and development is that it has been based on a concept of elites that is uncoupled from that of class. For that reason, it also lacks an understanding of the role of elites in the capitalist economy. Marxists would argue that precisely due to the fact that elites (understood as the capital holding class) can never disassociate themselves from a global capitalism that is by definition incompatible with sustainable development as defined above, an elite dominated economy can never be sustainable. Yet, if we define elites in line with the "Italian school" discussed in the next section, we would rather consider the challenge to be the emergence of elites whose view on long-term economic development interest includes a consideration for a sustainable and equitable use of natural resources and avoidance of environmental degradation. The contradictions between these two views on the relationship between elites and sustainable development will be discussed in Part three.

The final part of the chapter focuses on the prospect of change towards more inclusive and sustainable development oriented institutions. It identifies three factors that can contribute to change, but argues that they do so mainly when they act together. The first is democratic change: new elites may emerge as a result of the rise of new non-elite groups to power as occurred in many Latin American countries during the 2000s. The second is changes in the global economy that may contribute to a "breaking of elites" (J.A. Robinson 2012, p. 43). The third is a "reorientation of elites": when elites adopt new perspectives, ideas or even ideologies that lead them to change practices and policies pursued.

## What is an elite?

A surprising number of studies that claim to speak about elites fail to define the concept (Woods 1998; Smith 2006). Among those that do address the concept explicitly, one may identify three main approaches. The first is a structural political economy (sometimes Marxist) approach that defines elites based on their relationship to capital and means of production. This has been dominant in elite studies in the highly unequal and class divided societies in Latin America.[1] The term elite is indeed sometimes used interchangeably with "the upper middle and upper classes," as opposed to the "popular classes." In other cases, the "elite" is used as including business, landholding and political elites, considered to operate in close alliances, and often allied with global political–economic elites. This is the case, for example, in the historical sociological literature on the role of the land-holding elites, and their relations to industrial capital (Torres-Rivas 1989; Paige 1997). Also, newer contributions that study elite constellations associated with regional and global configurations of ownership to capital regard elites as being a function of their role in the capitalist economy, and the interests and attitudes of the elites are essentially derived from their relationship to capital (W.I. Robinson 2003; Segovia 2005). Their influence in politics and society in general is assumed as a result of their relationship to capital.

The second approach is found in the classical elite studies (often called the "Italian school") and takes what in many respects is an opposite view: Elites are identified based on their influence in politics and society. Their control over different resources is assumed. While having its roots in the writings of Mosca, Michels and Pareto (Mosca 1939; Michels 1962; Pareto [1935] 1997), it is still dominant in elite studies that define elites as a distinct group within a society that enjoys privileged status and exercises decisive control over the organization of society (Wolf 2012, p. 120).

A further difference to the class-based definition of elites is that while class-based approaches link elite dominance mainly to the control over economic resources (capital), the classical elite studies consider elites to potentially emerge from their control of various and possibly overlapping resources (thus we will here call it a "resource-based approach"). These may include organizational resources (control over organizations), political resources (public support), symbolic resources (knowledge and ability to manipulate symbols and discourses) and personal resources (such as charisma, time, motivation and energy) (Etzioni-Halevy 1997, p. xxv). Such a multi-resource approach leads to the focus on a number of different elites, based on the control over different resources. For example, Solimano and Avanzini include three different elites: the "knowledge elite," the "entrepreneurial elite" and the "political elite" in their study of transnational elite circulation, although admitting that they might be overlapping (Solimano and Avanzini 2012).

A third approach, that could be called an institutional approach, would, following Mills, define elites as the groups populating the "upper skeletons" of important social and political institutions. As argued by Mills: "The power elite is composed of men whose positions enable them to transcend the ordinary environments of ordinary men and women; they are in positions to make decisions having major consequences" (Mills 1956, pp. 2–3). Although broadening the definition of institutions from that of Mills and focusing rather on social structures, the first major study of Latin American elites was based on this approach. Lipset and Solari's study from 1967 defines elites as the "people holding positions in society which are at the summits of key social structures, i.e. the higher positions in the economy, government, military, politics, religion, mass organizations, education, and the profession" (Lipset and Solari 1967, p. vii). Based on this, they studied the values, skills and capabilities of political, economic, military and labor elites. Their justification for focusing on elites was their assumed superior impact on decision-making in developing countries such as those found in Latin America in the absence of the constraints of large-scale bureaucracies and mass political pressure such as those to be found in "modern" societies.

Currently, it is common to take an institutional approach in studies of bureaucratic (including technocratic) elites (Ai Camp 2002; Montecinos 1996; Joignant and Güell 2011) and parliamentary elites (Alcántara Sáez 1995, 2008) in Latin

America. However, in general, elite studies tend to move beyond studies of institutional elites and include also other groups that stand in a privileged position to influence society.

What I will call a resource-based approach has the advantage in a study of environmental governance and sustainable development of focusing more directly on the groups that influence decisions and practices. Moreover, compared to an institutional approach, a resource-based approach gives us a more complete picture since it is clear that not only the holders of specific positions are able to influence environmental risk, costs and benefits. It leads to the influence not only of capital owners but equally of increasingly influential groups that control knowledge or organizations, or exert influence based on their personal resources and networks. A further advantage is that it allows us to distinguish between different elites and thus make visible struggles between different elite groups as well as alliances between them.

Thus, for the purpose of this book, we define elites as:

> Groups of individuals that, due to their control over natural, economic, political, social, organizational or symbolic (expertise/knowledge) resources, stand in a privileged position to influence in a formal or informal way decisions and practices with key environmental implications.

Using such a definition means that we in theory may include a wide number of different groups. It obviously includes business elites that control economic resources including capital and often major institutions regulating its use. They may also control natural resources (including land, hydrocarbons, water, etc.), but their control over such often crucially depends on additional political and organizational resources. It includes groups at the height of important societal institutions including the different powers of the state (executive, legislative and judicial), and media elites controlling the stream of information and knowledge. However, it may also include intellectual or scientific elites and elites that base their influence on the control over organizations, such as non-governmental organizations (NGOs).

Such a broad elite concept is not without its disadvantages. By including such diverse groups in the term "elite," we run the risk of detaching it from important underlying dynamics of the capitalist economy that undoubtedly have a strong impact on the possibilities for a sustainable use of resources. Moreover, such a concept does not specify the implications of elite dominance for environmental governance, as elites according to the plural "resource-based" definition may both be in opposition to each other and have different interests and goals related to environmental governance. We may, for example, talk about an "environmental elite" whose key interests relate to environmental goals. These may run into conflict with the variety of political elites that may pursue a multitude of goals, both personal and general, all with important environmental implications, as well as a business elite with essentially capitalist goals.

In the following, therefore, we will outline such a resource-based approach to elites, but keep embedding our understanding of elites in an understanding of their broader dynamics of the sphere in which they are dominating, including the capitalist economy.

## Elites, institutions and sustainable development

The recent renewed interest in elites and development is closely connected to an increasing consensus that the main explanation for differences in economic performance is variation in institutions (J.A. Robinson 2012). Economic and political institutions are decisive for the channeling of resources in society and the making of rules that regulate their use. Acemoglu and Robinson argue that economically prosperous countries are characterized by inclusive political institutions, meaning that they are both centralized (i.e. that institutions have ensured sufficient control over a geographical area) and pluralized (i.e. that there exists an agreed division of power). In contrast, extractive political institutions concentrate power in the hands of a narrow elite and place few constraints on the exercise of this power (Acemoglu and Robinson 2012, p. 81). Extractive political institutions enable the elites controlling political power to choose economic institutions with few constraints or opposing forces, and that mainly enrich the same elites. Inclusive institutions in contrast create checks and balances and enable the entire society to take part in a process of economic growth, thereby creating long-term sustainable growth.

This focus on institutions is in no way new in development theory. Institutions as a foundation for development has been a central element in Weberian development theory, from Gunnar Myrdal to the literature on the "developmental state" (Myrdal 1968; Woo-Cumings 1999). This focused on the conditions for—and evolution of—a state with monopoly on legitimate violence, and an institutional bureaucracy capable of implementing policies and controlling the masses. In spite of the fact that many geographical areas have experienced more violence related to the process in which state elites' have gained control of competing groups offering functional equivalents to the state, than benefits emerging from an institutionalized state, the weberian image of a centralized, autonomous state has remained an ideal in development studies (e.g. Migdal *et al.* 1994; Evans 1995). Such a state, in which a given set of institutions' right to tax and demand loyalty in return for protection and the extension of benefit are no longer questioned, is for example considered a precondition for the high-growth policies and business–state relationship of the east Asian developmental states (Amsden 2001; Wade 1990) as well as the more historical examples of development such as the European (Tilly 1992).

The role of elites related to institutions is also no new concern. Elites have long been in focus due to their direct influence on the allocation of resources in society, and their indirect influence through controlling political institutions. In the development literature elites have just as frequently been considered a part of the problem as the solution to development challenges. As argued by Myrdal "In fact, [elites] are best defined as people who are in a position to hinder reforms or to manipulate them, and, in the end, to obstruct their implementation"

(Myrdal [1979] 2010, p. 335). Elites may choose to redistribute resources, or act as rent-seekers and direct resources towards favored and inefficient social groups (Amsden *et al.* 2012, p. 5). Although their decisions about this are often depicted as "choices" (Acemoglu and Robinson 2012), in concrete situations, their decisions are based on a combination of ideas and ideologies and their desire to survive and get stronger—as elites, as governing elites or as human beings. Their "choices" depend on the institutions in which they are embedded, but in turn, they contribute to upholding these institutions or weakening them. One of their possible goals may be to contribute to centralizing the state in order to acquire a greater degree of institutional control as a means to pursue a number of other objectives. However, they may also seek to do the opposite if that serves their interests as individuals or groups better.

One of the main questions posed in the literature on elites and development is: when and under what conditions are the elites' goals compatible with the centralization and pluralization of power and the creation of development oriented institutions? In fact, there are numerous linkages, and virtuous as well as vicious cycles between development, the strengthening of some elites and institutional strengthening. For example, economic growth may create bases for taxation that can be used for institutional strengthening, that in turn may spur further growth through investments as well as including larger parts of the population in economic processes. However, taxation depends on relatively strong institutions, and economic growth can perfectly well also be pocketed by rent-seeking elites, contributing to hollowing out institutions.

The concept of development underlying these accounts of the relationship between elites and institutions is almost exclusively focused on economic growth and industrial upgrading. Furthermore, the term "institutions" is largely equated with "state institutions" and "development" is understood as national development. The literature on elites and development has to a very limited degree problematized the environmental sustainability of development, and its distributional implications are only considered to the extent that it has long-term national growth and development consequences. That means that it is considered a problem if growth is so narrowly focused that it misses out large amounts of human resources, but apart from that, distribution among social groups and geographical areas is generally ignored.

As a result, this view on development is largely rejected by the literature on *political ecology*. This takes inequalities of economic resources and power-relations as a point of departure and engages in how development in contexts of structural inequality at multiple levels produces environmental degradation. Political ecology:

> accept[s] the idea that costs and benefits associated with environmental change are for the most part distributed among actors unequally ... which reinforces or reduces existing social and economic inequalities ... which holds political implications in terms of the altered power of actors in relation to other actors.
>
> (Bryant and Bailey 1997, pp. 28–9)

The many contributions to political ecology from Latin America draw heavily on their origins in neo-Marxism (Durand Smith *et al.* 2011), and often critically take "Capitalism and its historical transformations [as] a starting point for any account of the destruction of nature" (Peet *et al.* 2010, p. 23). What was characterized above as "development" is in this literature characterized as the privileging of certain exploitative productive systems over others, which is one reason for current intertwined distributive and ecological conflicts and the degradation of the environment making long-term improvements of peoples' living conditions less likely (Alimonda 2011).

Elites appear in the political ecology literature largely as the perpetrators: they are the capital owners, the business and knowledge elites and the groups controlling the state. However, they are rarely the object of direct scrutiny. Elites are mostly blackboxed[2] and treated implicitly as synonymous with the capitalist class or their "executive committee" (the state) or "organic intellectuals" (scientists, etc.). Their interests are considered to depend on their location in structural relations of domination, and their privileges to derive from their positions in the structures that configure Latin America as a subaltern region open to exploitation according to the needs of a globally integrated capitalism. The double exploitation of people and nature also forms the basis of the construction of the modern states, dominated by national elites.

Thus, the emergence of a "national development project" that simultaneously ensures centralization of and inclusive political and economic institutions is considered a contradiction in terms. National development projects would be considered instruments of domination, creating conflicts not only between more or less economically privileged groups, but also between groups with unequal exposure to environmental degradation and access to resources. It is also a matter of the relationship between sub-national communities/localities and national institutions. The potential conflict between national and sub-national interests is perhaps most strongly present related to natural resource extraction where the natural resources are based in a specific locality that may experience most of the negative impacts of their extraction, while the positive impacts will benefit rather the national or transnational elites (Bebbington 2013). However, short of a prior settlement between national and sub-national elites, any national development project may provoke such conflicts. Moreover, even if the environmental implications are so diffuse that they do not provoke immediate social conflicts, development projects and policies may have serious long-term distributional as well as environmental implications.

The question to be posed will thus not only be under what conditions can we expect elite objectives to be aligned with national development goals, but how to make those goals aligned with sub-national and long-term goals for the entire population. A common answer to that has been to emphasize pluralism and democracy. In other words, to provide good mechanisms of representation, participation and accountability that can lead to the establishment of institutions of environmental governance with the potential of less elitist and more sustainable development outcomes. This has been what many hoped would occur in Latin

America during the last decade. However, elite theory has never been convinced of the merits of pluralist democracies to make societies more egalitarian.

## Elites, the state and democracy

Both class and elite theory originally had a quite dismal view on the potential of democracy for transforming society, a matter that is rooted partly in their view of the state. The interpretation of Marx's view of the state as being "the executive committee of the capitalist class" has been criticized for being reductionist and overly instrumentalist (see e.g. Jessop 1990). However, Marxist analysis is generally skeptical of changes in the state without underlying changes in the mode of production upholding it. Elite theory does not necessarily disagree with the bleak outlook for democracy to change the state; it is rather on how and why the state may change that the two approaches differ.

Class theory originally considered the possibility of two potential processes of change to the capitalist state. The first was the rise of the working class that would liberate the state from the capitalist economy, and move towards a non-elitist proletarian democracy belonging to the whole nation. Short of such a revolution, the rise of leftist parties was considered to make little difference. Although there could be a functional separation between the capitalist classes and state elites, the latter would serve the formers' interests since those who manage the state apparatus are dependent on the maintenance of some reasonable level of economic activity, and that in a capitalist economy the level of activity is largely determined by private investment. Groups in power cannot ignore capitalists since the capacity of the state to finance itself depends on the state of the economy, and that public support for a regime will decline sharply if it presides over a serious drop in the level of economic activity with a parallel rise in unemployment and shortages of key goods (Block 1977). The result is that without acquiring control over capital, or acquiring support from abroad, the concern for "generating business confidence" will always be in focus for even a reformist government. Therefore, the state cannot really be democratized within a capitalist economy in spite of the establishment of pluralist institutions.

This quite pessimistic view on the possibility of democratizing the capitalist state has led social movements across Latin America to reject the route of formal politics. As argued by the Peruvian sociologist Aníbal Quijano: democratic socialism can be little more than "the pact in which the subaltern classes give up revolution in exchange for negotiating the conditions of their own exploitation" (Quijano, cited in Borón 2007, p. 2). In practice, different social movements have chosen different paths, ranging from the Zapatist's rejection of all engagement with the formal political system, to the formation of political parties based on social movements in, for example, Bolivia (Bull 2012). However, there is a general recognition of the need to maintain a degree of autonomy from political parties as well as the state, and that priority should be given to "the transformation of political society" (Costilla 2009, p. 2). One of those transformations would be towards a development model emphasizing living in harmony with nature and community values (Zibechi 2003).

However, not only class theory, but also elite theory was skeptical of the virtues of pluralist democracies. Gaetano Mosca regarded universal suffrage and parliamentarianism as unable to dissolve the principle that an "organized minority" is able to "impose its will on a disorganized majority" (Mosca 1939, p. 154), while Vilfredo Pareto famously divided society into three groups: the non-elite and the elite, subdivided into the governing elite and the rest. However, the fact that an elite was always governing, did not mean that there were necessarily the same people always ruling. Rather, the governing elites were exchanged by slowly ascending families and groups from lower classes, and would thus be replaced in a slow process of elite circulation (Pareto [1935] 1997). A conclusion to be drawn related to the question above, about possible changes resulting from democracy, was thus that although the political institutions would remain elitist, they could nevertheless change as new people would acquire positions. Indeed, it is this elite circulation, not the construction of political subjects among the dispossessed classes that would lead to change (Pareto, cited in Hartmann 2007). Thus, if we want to understand social change, we should study elites.

The second process of change envisioned by Marxists emerges from the space opened for the "relative autonomy of the state" in situations of weak or split class forces (Jessop 1990). One argument related to the need for the state to free itself from specific capitalist forces in order to implement policies serving the fundamental interest of the ruling classes. One major task that the capitalist classes themselves are not able to perform is to establish a "political hegemony" ensuring the dominance of the lower classes. In order to do this, the state assumes a relative autonomy with regard to the bourgeoisie (Poulantzas 1978). This would lead to the emergence of a state elite that is set functionally apart from the capitalist class, and may give rise to a separate class of bureaucrats and state functionaries, although it may serve the ultimate interest of the capitalists.

The issue of state autonomy is also essential to the followers of Weber's view on elites. The state bureaucracy is, according to Weber, not only a by-product of capitalism, but the most effective form of legitimate power and the source of the emergence of an entire new class (Weber 1978). Understanding the structure and power of the bureaucracy is much more important than the electoral institutions since the demos itself is "a shapeless mass [that] never "governs" larger associations, but rather is governed" (Weber 1978, pp. 984–985). This assertion and its theoretical foundation have given rise to a literature on the structure and resources of bureaucracies, their *esprit de corps* and management of knowledge. This literature has inspired the study of technocratic elites in Latin America and elsewhere (see e.g. Montecinos 1996; Ai Camp 2002; Joignant and Güell 2011). Although never autonomous from state power, they are considered to be a superior power instrument with a high degree of autonomous dynamic that is superior to any form of collective action. The dilemma presented to new political forces gaining formal power over a state apparatus is that while the bureaucracy may hinder a shift in policies and practices, they are institutions that may take decades to construct, and irrespective of how much popular support a ruler may enjoy, without the instrument of a modern bureaucracy, his or her ability to enact, implement and enforce his/her will is severely limited.

In sum, both elite theory and class theory have reservations with regards to the ability of democracy to reform and transform institutions and development models. For class theory, the main limiting dynamic lies within the capitalist system. The logic of capitalism is the drive towards increased profit and deeper exploitation—by definition incompatible with a sustainable development model. The class-based nature of the state also makes transformation through state-democratization difficult if not impossible, due to the imperative of generating business confidence for ensuring investments, employment and further political support. New capitalist elites may appear, but they will never make a real difference as their main interests are the same. For some, the "hope" is not a shift in elites, but rather a transformation coming from new kinds of organization of subaltern groups, transcending the old "working class" and labor movements and transforming political society (Sousa Santos 2001). For others, to take political power is considered to be inevitable, and what is required is a state transformation "from above," making it a tool to serve the oppressed classes rather than capitalist forces (García Linera 2004; Borón 2007).

For elite theory, the doubt about democracy's ability to transform the state and give impetus to more sustainable development models relates to two different dynamics: first, it relates to the idea of elite circulation that refutes the possibilities of egalitarian political institutions. However, this may still be a source of change regarding environmental governance. As mentioned above, elites may potentially have different interests and preferences regarding development and the environment. Therefore, the entering of new elites into important positions could also potentially mean a substantial shift in development policies and environmental governance. Second, it relates to the imperative to construct a state and ensure its legitimate presence in the entire territory. The construction of a weberian state with territorial control and a bureaucratic elite whose ascent is based on merit, requires not only political support but also resources. Since most resources are concentrated in the hands of economic elites, those resources can only be accessed by taxing or taking control over resources directly. Both are complicated processes requiring significant political "capital." It appears as highly unlikely that any new governing elites succeeding in taking control over such resources, should, once they had taken control over these resources, place limitations on their use in terms of environmental precautions if that would lead to reduced income in the short term, even if it could increase the profitability in the long term.

Which one of these dynamics will predominate remains an empirical question: the capitalist elite dynamics, elite circulation or the state–elite dynamics. In the following we will flesh out some hypotheses based on recent experiences in Latin America, while we will leave it to the following chapters to discuss actual cases of these different dynamics.

## Elite dynamics and three paths to change in Latin America

In spite of all the obstacles discussed above, elite shifts do occur. In explaining how and why, some have focused on "critical junctures" in history. These are major watersheds in political life that establish certain directions of change and foreclose others in a way that shapes politics for years to come (Collier and Collier 1991, p. 27).[3] Rather than being caused by one specific change, during critical junctures, "a major event or confluence of factors disrupts the existing balance of political and economic power in a nation" (Acemoglu and Robinson 2012, p. 106).

The question is: to what extent can we see such disruptions occurring in Latin America? And will they contribute to better environmental governance and a more sustainable development? One may identify three factors that jointly have the potential of causing disruptions although the direction of it is unclear and it varies across countries. The first is the already mentioned political disruption related to the entering of power of center-left governments, many of whom represented groups that had not previously held political power. These political shifts have so far mainly been studied as processes emerging "from below" (Silva 2009). Indeed, the turn to the left is frequently interpreted as the result of social uprisings against the neoliberal economic model implemented across the continent from the 1980s, and against elitist democracies that continued mainly to represent the groups that had exploited the peoples and the nature of Latin America for centuries. However, these processes have also contributed to the creation of new elites, and many governments that have previously enjoyed support from grass-roots movements have later disqualified them or consciously attempted to co-opt them (Zibechi 2010; Bowen 2011).

These new political elites differ significantly from each other and have followed very different development policies as well as developed different relationships to institutions. Some of them have introduced piecemeal reforms within the framework of the existing constitution and institutions, while others have embarked on a more radical path of social reform arriving at new forms of governance and distribution. A lot of effort has been put into trying to understand why they evolved so differently (Lievesley and Ludlam 2009; Cameron and Hershberg 2010; Weyland 2010; Levitsky and Roberts 2011). One conclusion from this is that although there has been a certain disruption from the past in each country, there has also been a high degree of continuity. The parties and social movements that brought the center-left governments to power are rooted in distinct historical trajectories (Levitsky and Roberts 2011), and the type of disruption they have created depends on the resource limitations and the opposition encountered from old socio-economic and political elites (Weyland 2010, p. 6).

Thus, it seems that for change to occur there has to be additional factors present. One of those is a shift in the global economy. Two major interrelated trends have occurred in the global economy parallel to the Latin American political shifts: a rise in demand and prices of commodities, and the rise of China as a major economic power (see Chapter 7 in this volume and Durán Lima and Pellandra

2013). This not only had the effect of increasing "policy space" for the Latin American countries by making them less dependent on markets and sources of capital that tend to place conditionalities on their lending or market access (such as the World Bank, International Monetary Fund and the United States). It has also contributed to the increasing activity in terms of establishment of new integration mechanisms and organizations, including the Union of South American Nations (UNASUR) and the Bolivarian Alliance for the Peoples of Our America (ALBA) with an aim of being alternatives to the integration mechanisms of the old elites.[4] In turn it has contributed to the emergence of new economic elites in several countries. This has occurred perhaps most markedly in Venezuela (Al Jazeera 2010), but also in smaller countries such as El Salvador and Nicaragua (Carrión Fonseca 2012; Lemus 2014).

A second main factor is what could be called "elite reorientation," i.e. that the dominating ideas of an elite shift. Historically, we have two major examples of such elite conversion in Latin America: one is the neoliberal transformation during which groups that previously had promoted state-led development policies became firm believers in market-driven, export-oriented models. In some cases, this was a result of the ascent of new groups of "technocrats" (such as the (in-)famous Chicago boys in Chile (Silva 1996), while elsewhere it was the combined result of intellectual influences and economic reorientations (such as in the conversion of the Central American business elite; see Bird and Oglesby 2014).

A quite different process of elite reorientation is the gradual conversion of large groups of Latin American elites from support for dictatorships towards a commitment and belief in democracy, creating a new "value consensus" (Di Palma 1973). In neither case did this "elite conversion" happen out of the blue. Rather the new ideas achieved influence due to a crisis or the exhaustion of prior models, and a gradual shift of interests. Currently, one could imagine that the seriousness of the environmental—and climate—crisis could open the space for new ideas brought about by new elite groups, the conversion of old groups or a new dynamic interplay between different elite groups.

A third process is what Burton *et al.* call an "elite settlement" (Burton *et al.* 1992). This is a process of negotiation between competing elite groups that may have fundamental and lasting consequences in a common elite acceptance of a new code of political conduct. Thus, although the most important effect of such elite settlements is the transformation of institutions, it also, in this process, may transform not only who the elites are, but also the views and behaviors of those elites.

## Conclusion

The problem of elites in democracy and development has been a concern in the social science literature for many decades. Much of the literature discussed here looks at the tendency of societies, institutions and organizations to sustain elites as a hinder for the emergence of more democratic forms of governance and more egalitarian distribution of resources. However, some have formulated arguments in favor of the possibility of a renewal of elites and its potential for driving positive changes in democracy and development. Yet, sustainable development and environmental governance have not been considered specifically, and much of the specialized literature on that consider "elites" primarily as a part of the problem.

In the chapters that follow, we will explore the extent to which elite shifts have occurred in these three ways. Rather than sticking to one specific perspective, we will start from the definition of elites provided above and seek to understand what it means for environmental governance and sustainable development that new elites have emerged where they have, whether we see an "elite conversion" and whether there are tendencies to "elite settlements." Furthermore, we will explore how new and old elites relate to non-elites or "subalterns" and the impact of that on sustainable development and environmental governance. With that we aim to contribute not only to an understanding of the possibility for more equitable, just and sustainable development models, but also to the knowledge on how elites form, change, relate to each other and to subaltern groups.

## Notes

1  See for example Hershberg and Pérez Saínz (2014) and Meza *et al.* (2009).
2  For more information on blackboxing, see page 12 this volume, note 2.
3  The concept "critical juncture" is originally from Lipset and Rokkan 1967: 33ff.
4  UNASUR was created in 2008 with the aim of bridging the two existing integration initiatives in South America: the Andean Community (CAN) and the Southern Common Market (MERCOSUR). In parallel, ALBA was created by Venezuela and Cuba in 2004, incorporating Bolivia, Ecuador and Nicaragua in addition to Cuba and four small Caribbean states.

## Bibliography

Acemoglu, D. and Robinson, J. A. (2012) *Why Nations Fail: The Origins of Power, Prosperity and Poverty*. Profile Books, London.

Ai Camp, R. (2002) *Mexico's Mandarins: Crafting a power elite for the twenty-first century*. University of California Press, Berkeley and Los Angeles, CA.

Alcántara Sáez, M. (1995) El estudio de las elites parlamentarias en América Latina. *Inguruak Revista Vasca de Sociología y Ciencia Política*, 13, 25–37.

Alcántara Sáez, M. (ed.) (2008) *Politicians and Politics in Latin America*. Lynne Rienner Publishers, Boulder, CO and London.

Alimonda, H. (2011) La colonialidad de la naturaleza: Una aproximación a la ecología política latinoamericana, in H. Alimonda (ed.), *La naturaleza Colonizada Ecología política y minería en América Latina*. CLACSO, Buenos Aires, pp. 21–58.

Al Jazeera (2010) Venezuelan boligarchs doing well. May 22, 2010, available at: www. aljazeera com/news/americas/2010/05/201052242911266217.html (accessed 30 July 2014).

Amsden, A. (2001) *The Rise of "The Rest": Challenges to the West from Late-Industrializing Economies*. Oxford University Press, Oxford.

Amsden, A., Di Caprio, H. A. and Robinson, J. A. (2012) *The Role of Elites in Economic Development*. UNI-Wider Studies in Development Economics. Oxford University Press, Oxford.

Bebbington, A. (2013) Natural resource extraction and the possibilities of inclusive development politics across space and time. Effective States and Inclusive Development Working Paper No 21, available at: www.effective-states.org (accessed 30 July 2014).

Bird, A. and Oglesby, L. (2014) Las crisis de gobierno: Las geografías insurreccionales y los impactos de la guerra en las elites Centroamericanas en la década de los 80, in E. Hersberg and J. P. Pérez Saínz (eds), *Elites y la configuración de poder en Centroamérica: El siglo XX y su desmorono*. FLACSO, San José Costa Rica, forthcoming.

Block, F. (1977) The ruling class does not rule: Notes on the Marxist theory of the state. *Socialist Review*, 33, 6–27.

Borón, A. (2007) Crisis de las democracias y movimientos sociales en América Latina: Notas para una discusión. *Cronicón Observatorio Latinoamericano*, Bogotá Fundación Taller de Comunicaciones No. 13 Versión, online, available at: www.cronicon.net/paginas/edicanter/Ediciones13/17.htm (accessed 30 July 2014).

Bowen, J. D. (2011) Multicultural market democracy elites and indigenous movements in contemporary Ecuador. *Journal of Latin American Studies*, 43, 451–483.

Bryant, R. L. and Bailey, S. (1997) *Third World Political Ecology*. Routledge, New York and London.

Bull, B. (2012) Social movements and the "pink tide" governments in Latin America: Transformation, inclusion and rejection, in K. Stokke and O. Törnquist (eds), *Democratization in the Global South: The Importance of Transformative Politics*. Palgrave Macmillan, London, 75–99.

Burton, M., Gunther, R. and Highley, J. (1992) Introduction: Elite transformations and democratic regimes, in J. Highley and R. Gunther (eds), *Elites and Democratic Consolidation in Latin America and Southern Europe*. Cambridge University Press, Cambridge, pp. 1–37.

Cameron, M. and Hershberg, E. H. (2010) *Latin America's Left Turns: Politics, Policies and Trajectories of Change*. Lynne Rienners Publishers, Boulder, CO.

Carrión Fonseca, G. M. (2012) New clothes for the emperor or is ALBA naked in Nicaragua? *Revista Envío*, 375, October, available at: www.envio.org.ni/articulo/4607.

Collier, R. B. and Collier, D. (1991) *Shaping the Political Arena: Critical Junctures, the Labor Movement and Regimes Dynamics in Latin America*. University of Notre Dame Press, Notre Dame, IN.

Costilla, O. (2009) *Programa Latinoamericano de Revista Electrónica de Psicología Política*, Año7 No 20, Julio/Agosto, 94, Educación a Distancia en Ciencias Sociales, Centro Cultural de la Cooperación Floreal Gorini, Buenos Aires.

Di Palma, G. (1973) *The Study of Conflict in Western Societies: A Critique of the End of Ideology*. General Learning Press, Morristown, NJ.

Durán Lima, J. and Pellandra, A. (2013) El efecto de la emergencia de China sobre la producción y el comercio en América Latina y el Caribe, in Enrique Dussel Peters (ed.), *América Latina y El Caribe: China Economía Comercio e Inversiones*. Unión de Universidades de América Latina y el Caribe, México DF, pp. 105–127.

Durand Smith, L., Figueroa Díaz, F. and Guzmán Chávez, M. G. (2011) La ecología política en México: ¿Dónde estamos y para dónde vamos? *Estudios sociales*, 19(37), June, 283–307.

Etzioni-Halevy, E. (1997) Introduction, in E. Etzioni-Halevy (ed.), *Classes and Elites in Democracy and Democratization*. Garland Publishing, New York and London, pp. xxiii–xxxv.

Evans, P. (1995) *Embedded Autonomy: States and Industrial Transformation*. Princeton University Press, Princeton, NJ.

García Linera, Á. (2004) Democracia: Liberal versus democracia comunitaria. *El Jugete Rabiosa*, 2(96), 20 January, available at: www.cronicon.net/paginas/edicanter/Ediciones13/17.htm (accessed 30 July 2014).

Hartmann, M. (2007) *The Sociology of Elites*. Routledge, London.

Hershberg, E. and Pérez Saínz, J. P. (eds) (2014) *Elites y la configuración de poder en Centroamérica: El siglo XX y su desmorono*. FLACSO, San José, Costa Rica.

Jessop, B. (1990) *State Theory: Putting Capitalist States in their Place*. Penn State University Press, University Park, PA.

Joignant, A. and Güell, P. (eds) (2011) *Notables tecnócratas y mandarines: Elementos de sociología de las élites en Chile 1990–2010*. Ediciones Universidad Diego Portales, Santiago de Chile.

Lemus, E. (2014) La millonaria revolución de Alba. *El Faro*, available at: www.elfaro.net/es/201401/noticias/14423/ (accessed January 19, 2014).

Levitsky, S. and Roberts, K. (2011) Latin America's left turn: A framework for analysis, in S. Levitsky and K. Roberts (eds), *The Resurgence of Latin Americas*. Johns Hopkins University Press, Baltimore MA, pp. 1–29.

Lievesley, G. and Ludlam, S. (2009) *Latin America: Experiments in Radical Social Democracy*. Zed Books, London and New York.

Lipset, S. M. and Rokkan, S. (1967) *Party Systems and Voter Alignments: Cross-National Perspectives*. Free Press, New York.

Lipset, S. M. and Solari, A. (1967) *Elites in Latin America*. Oxford University Press, Oxford.

Meza, V., Salomón, L., Romero, R., Torres Calderón, M. and Illescas Oliva, J. (2009) *Honduras Poderes Fácticos y Sistema Político*. Centro de Documentación de Honduras, Tegucigalpa.

Michels, R. (1962) *Political Parties*. Free Press, New York.

Migdal, J. S., Kohli, A. and Shue, V. (1994) *State Power and Social Forces: Domination and Transformation in the Third World*. Cambridge Studies in Comparative Politics. Cambridge University Press, Cambridge.

Mills, C. W. (1956) *The Power Elite*. Oxford University Press, Oxford.

Montecinos, V. (1996) Economists in political and policy elites in Latin America. *History of Political Economy*, 28, 3–425.

Mosca, G. (1939) *The Ruling Class*. McGraw-Hill, New York.

Myrdal, G. (1968) *Asian Drama: An Inquiry into the Poverty of Nations*. Pantheon, New York.

Myrdal, G. ([1979] 2010) Underdevelopment and the evolutionary imperative. *Third World Quarterly*, 1(2). Reprinted in Benedicte Bull and Morten Bøås (2010), *International Development*, Vol. II, Sage Library of International Development. Sage, London.

Paige, J. M. (1997) *Coffee and Power Revolution and the Rise of Democracy in Central America*. Harvard University Press, Cambridge, MA.

Pareto, V. ([1935] (1997) The governing elite in present-day democracy, in E. Etzioni-Halevy (ed.), *Classes and Elites in Democracy and Democratization*. Garland Publishing, New York and London, pp. 147–152.

Peet, R., Robbins, P. and Watts, M. (eds) (2010) *Global Political Ecology*. Routledge, London.

Poulantzas, N. (1978) *State Power Socialism*. Verso, New York.

Robinson, J. A. (2012) Elites and institutional persistence, in A. Amsden *et al.* (eds), *The Role of Elites in Economic Development*. UNI-Wider Studies in Development Economics. Oxford University Press, Oxford, pp. 29–52.

Robinson, W. I. (2003) *Transnational Conflicts: Central America, Social Change and Globalization*. Verso, New York.

Rovira, C. (2011) Hacia una sociología histórica sobre las elites en América Latina: Un diálogo crítico con la teoría de Pierre Bourdieu, in A. Joignant and P. Güell (eds), *Notables*. Ediciones Universidad Diego Portales, Santiago de Chile, pp. 271–291.

Segovia, A. (2005) *Integración real y grupos de poder económico en América Central*. Friedrich Ebert Stiftung, San José Costa Rica.

Silva, E. (1996) *The State and Capital in Chile: Business Elites, Technocrats and Market Economics*. Westview Press, Boulder, CO.

Silva, E. (2009) *Challenging Neoliberalism in Latin America*. Cambridge University Press, Cambridge.

Smith, K. E. (2006) Problematising power relations in elite interviews. *Geoforum*, 37, 643–653.

Solimano, A. and Avanzini, D. (2012) The international circulation of elites: Knowledge, entrepreneurial and political, in A. H. Amsden, A. DiCaprio and J. A. Robinson (eds), *The Role of Elites in Economic Development: Wider Studies in Development Economics*, Oxford: Oxford University Press, pp. 53–86.

Sousa Santos, B. (2001) Los nuevos movimientos sociales. *OSAL Debates*, September 2001.

Tilly, C. (1992) *Coercion, Capital and European States AD 990–1992*. Wiley-Blackwell, Oxford.

Torres-Rivas, E. (1989) *Repression and Resistance The Struggle for Democracy in Central America*. Westview Press, Boulder, CO.

Wade, R. (1990) *Governing the Market: Economic Theory and the Role of Government in East Asian Industrialization*. Princeton University Press, Princeton, NJ.

Weber, M. (1978) *Economy and Society*. Berkeley University Press, Berkeley, CA.

Weyland, K. (2010) The performance of leftist governments in Latin America: Conceptual and theoretical issues, in K. Weyland, R. L. Madrid and W. Hunter (eds), *Leftist Governments in Latin America: Successes and Shortcomings*. Cambridge University Press, Cambridge, pp. 1–27.

Wolf, A. (2012) Two for the price of one? The contribution to development of the new female elites, in A. Amsden *et al.* (eds) *The Role of Elites in Economic Development*. UNI-Wider Studies in Development Economics. Oxford University Press, Oxford, pp. 120–139.

Woo-Cumings, M. (1999) *The Developmental State*. Cornell University Press, Ithaca, NY.

Woods, M. (1998) Rethinking elites: Networks, space and local politics. *Environment and Planning*, 30, 2010–2119.

Zibechi, R. (2003) Los movimientos sociales latinoamericanos tendencias y desafíos. Observatoario Social de América Latina (OSAL), January, available at: www.pensamientocritico.Org/rauzib1003.htm (accessed 30 July 2014).

Zibechi, R. (2010) América Latina: Nuevos conflictos, viejos actores. *America Latina en Movimientos*, 7(8), available at: http://old.kaosenlared.net/noticia/america-latina-nuevos-conflictos-viejos-actores (accessed 30 July 2014).

# Part 1

# Agriculture and biotechnology

# 3 El Salvador

## The challenge to entrenched elites and the difficult road to a sustainable development model

*Benedicte Bull, Nelson Cuéllar and Susan Kandel*

### Introduction

The election of Mauricio Funes as president in El Salvador in 2009 marked a watershed in the history of the country, as it was the first time that a president backed by a left-wing party was elected. The Funes government was supported by the rather diverse coalition of the former left-wing guerrilla party *Frente Farabundi Martí para la Liberación Nacional* (FMLN), the small center-left party *Cambio Democrático* (CD) and a diverse group of supporters of Mauricio Funes who joined in the *Movimiento Amigos de Mauricio* (MAM). They took power in the midst of a deep economic, environmental and social crisis after 20 years of government by the *Alianza Republicana Nacionalista* (ARENA), a party established and run by the country's economic elite, in close association with the top business association *Asociación Nacional de la Empresa Privada* (ANEP). During those 20 years, El Salvador had been transformed from an agro-export economy to a transnationally integrated service based economy, heavily dependent on remittances from Salvadoran (often undocumented) immigrants in the United States. In parallel, the national economic elites transformed from an agro-export based national elite into transnationally integrated business groups. Their investments focused on reaping the benefits of the inflow of remittances by investing in commerce and services, but with a propensity to move into whatever sector where opportunities for quick profits would appear (Bull 2013).

In this context, the Funes government set out to conduct a structural reform aimed at modifying the manner in which the government exercised power, introduce new forms of governance, and set the basis for a new and sustainable economic and social model. Yet this was to occur within the frames of the existing constitution, as the government emphasized that what had occurred was a democratic electoral victory, not the beginning of a revolution (Gobierno de El Salvador 2012).

The new economic and social model was intended to reduce poverty and inequality but also incorporated a concern for reducing the country's vulnerability to the impact of climate change, given the catastrophic effects of repeated climatic events. A number of governmental policies and programs were launched intending to reinvigorate small-scale production and regulate the use of natural resources and environmentally harmful practices. This was combined with a governance model based on participation and dialogue with stakeholders at the local as well as national levels.

Yet, in the critical economic situation in which El Salvador found itself in 2009, the governmental endeavor had to be combined with policies aimed to generate employment and economic growth. That required investments that the state under no circumstances could undertake alone. Thus, it strongly felt the limitations of a leftist party in power, as discussed in Chapter 2. The new government had to turn to local economic elites, as well as international cooperation agencies, to attempt to reach common ground regarding development policies and encourage investments. However, the dialogue with the national economic elite soon soured, and threatened to halt many of the initiatives proposed by the government.

In this chapter we ask: why has it been so difficult to pursue a new model of environmental governance in El Salvador? The conventional wisdom is that such forms of governance run counter to the interests of capital holders since environmental regulation may introduce new costs. While this is part of the truth, it does not fully explain the extremely hostile reactions by the Salvadoran economic elite to new governance initiatives. We argue that this can only be understood by taking three other factors into account: (1) the amalgamation of the economic and political elite, leading the economic elite to pursue political as well as economic interests, (2) the structural impediments to change due to the weakness of the state and the transnational integration of the Salvadoran economy, and (3) the lack of a basic consensus about the desired development path. These elements must in turn be understood by incorporating simultaneously an international, national and local perspective. The case of El Salvador also shows that short of state power to back multi-stakeholder dialogue and provide strong incentives for the variety of sectors to participate, such processes may be weak devices for altering destructive practices.

The chapter proceeds as follows: first, we discuss the recent transformation of the Salvadoran economy and implications for elite power and environmental governance. Second, we discuss environmental governance under the ARENA administrations. Third, we analyze policies pursued by the Funes government to establish a new development model with improved environmental governance. Fourth, the evolution of the relationship between the government and the economic elites during the implementation of these policies are discussed. The final section draws conclusions regarding the viability of consensus-based forms of environmental governance in hyper-politicized contexts of deep structural inequality.

## The economic transition in El Salvador: implications for elite-composition and the environment

El Salvador is often presented as the "quintessence" of the Latin-American oligarchic state, dominated by a small agro-export elite with investments in several sectors and crops. The origins of the fortunes of the Salvadoran elite can be traced back to the production of indigo and cattle ranching during colonial times. From around 1860, coffee gradually replaced indigo as the main export crop. The coffee elite invested in sugar plantations beginning in the late nineteenth century. Sugar production expanded with the US embargo of Cuban sugar (Bulmer-Thomas 1987, pp. 158–159), and between the late 1950s and 1975, cotton production was introduced (Williams 1994). Sugar and cotton required larger investments and members of the main cotton and sugar growing families were frequently also owners of banks (Williams 1986, p. 44–48; Wilson 1978).

In terms of environmental impact, indigo production required clearing large areas of forests that along with cattle-ranching caused major deforestation. The shade-grown coffee that replaced indigo production provided new forest cover, and was thus less destructive from a hydrological point of view. However, it did cause large-scale elimination of tropical forests, and the coffee mills became an important source of contamination of surface waters. Moreover, the introduction of coffee caused large-scale displacement of peasants and changes to land tenure (Barry and Rosa 1995). The environmental impact of the sugar cane production was much more severe, resulting from the spraying of the crop with pesticides, and the burning of the cane before being cut, causing major impacts on nearby crops and communities. The cotton production applied higher concentrations of pesticides per hectares than in any other part of the world, poisoning the soil, water sources and aquatic ecosystems (Barry and Rosa 1995). Furthermore, the cotton production took place in the low lands along the pacific coast and both the cultivated areas and the construction of necessary infrastructure contributed to the destruction of the remaining forests, including the mangrove forest of high importance for marine biodiversity.

The combined effect of these activities was that, by the end of the 1970s, less than 6 per cent of El Salvador's natural forest was considered undisturbed by agro-export or other activities (Utting 1991). Its rapid deforestation was accompanied by loss of biodiversity, rapid soil degradation, particularly in the areas of cotton and sugar cultivation, sedimentation of rivers, lakes and reservoirs, and unchecked contamination of surface water (Acevedo *et al.* 1995).

From the late 1950s to the early 1970s a number of industrial enterprises were established based on the surplus from the agro-export that circulated through national banks owned by the same agro-export elite. However, economic diversification did not create more heterogeneous elites since it was mostly the old coffee growers and exporters that moved into new sectors (Baloyra 1989; Colindres 1977).

The dominance of the agro-export groups started to wither in the 1980s due to a combination of the reforms adopted by the civil-military junta that took over El Salvador after the 1979 coup, falling world prices of the major export crops, and the 1980–92 civil war. The reforms included nationalization of banks, financial institutions and coffee exports, and a partial land reform that changed the patterns of landownership and increased the land controlled by cooperatives. However, due to the combined effect of the war, declining commodity prices, outward migration and the incompleteness of the reform, it had little positive effect on rural livelihoods. The weight of traditional agriculture (coffee, sugar and cotton) in the Salvadoran gross domestic product (GDP) decreased from an average of 20.6 percent in the 1975–79 period to 2.4 percent in 1999. As a percentage of exports it was reduced from 64 percent to 11.7 percent in the same period (Segovia 2002).

These changes resulted in the weakening of the agricultural–financial nexus that had dominated El Salvador for decades. What ended up making up for the loss of agro-export income were remittances from Salvadoran migrants in the United States. Remittances grew from virtually nothing in 1980 to 3.5 billion dollars annually in 2006, representing 55 percent of the generation of income from abroad (Gammage 2006; Rosa 2008). In the period after the signing of the Chapultepec peace accords in 1992 the old agro-export elite reoriented its investments. After the re-privatization of the banks in 1992, the financial institutions became the focal point for dense investment networks extending into all sectors of the economy (Paniagua 2002). Most of these evolved into regional financial conglomerates, and between 2005 and 2007 they were all sold to foreign banks, as were most of El Salvador's industrial enterprises. The former agro-export elites focused rather on reaping the benefits from the remittances by focusing on commerce, services, construction and real-estate depending largely on their alliances with transnational companies (TNCs) for access to technology (Bull 2013).

The economic transformation occurred in the context of a reduction of cultivated land for some crops, while cotton production experienced what Barry and Rosa called an "environmental collapse" (Barry and Rosa 1995). The abandoning of former cotton farms in turn led to the recuperation of the highly polluted areas used for cotton production (Hecht *et al.* 2006).

However, another effect of the war was the displacement of small farmers that started to cultivate in marginal areas including steep slopes, causing heavy increases in soil erosion (Acevedo *et al.* 1995). Furthermore, after an initial decline, the areas of coffee cultivation increased. Moreover, sugar returned as a key sector of interest to the elite: between 1978 and 2006, the areas of cultivated land set aside for sugar cane production tripled (Rosa 2008), and increased further towards 2010 (MARN 2012c). Sugar continued to be controlled by the five owners of the six sugar mills in the country, of which one family (Regalado Dueñas) owns two mills that cover 50 percent of the production. The increase in areas used for sugar cane caused pressure on the surrounding subsistence agriculture, and due to the low degree of mechanization and widespread burning of the canes before cutting, contributed to soil erosion.

## Elite practices and environmental governance of the ARENA-led El Salvador

Between 1989 and 2009, the right-wing ARENA party won four consecutive presidential elections (1989, 1994, 1999 and 2004) with a relative ample margin (except for in the 1999 elections), and controlled in the same period between 206 (1994) and 111 (2004) municipalities (Fundaungo 2011). ARENA remained a party controlled by the country's economic elite. Within the highest socio-economic class, the percentage of people that supports ARENA is about twice as high as among the rest of the population (Artiga Gonzales 2004). Its leadership has incorporated a strata of mid-level businessmen, but the executive committee, the National Executive Council (COENA) of ARENA is dominated by members of the business elite.

The success of ARENA must be understood as a result of the control of at least four resources. First, ARENA has mobilized more economic resources than any other political party in El Salvador for campaign financing. Mejía (2009) shows that in the 2009 campaign ARENA spent more than three times as much on media advertisement as did the FMLN, and has in addition depended on the personal fortunes of candidates for campaigns (Koivumaeki 2010, p. 94). Second, ARENA has mobilized technical expertise. Shortly before he joined ARENA, later president Alfredo Cristiani had established the think tank, the Salvadoran Foundation for Economic and Social Development (FUSADES), generously supported by the USAID, and counting among its founding members the majority of the Salvadoran economic elite (Paige 1997, p. 37). ARENA also established two institutes that conduct technical research: ARENA Estrategia, founded in 2003, and Centro de Estudios Políticos Dr. José Antonio Rodríguez Porth (CEP) (Koivumaeki 2010). Third, the elite controlled the media. Historically, two families—the Altamirano and Dutriz families—have dominated the printed news in El Salvador (Rockwell and Janus 2005). Television is dominated by the Telecorporación Salvadoreña owned by Boris Eserski that controls three of the most popular channels, a number of radio stations, advertising agencies and the main TV guide.[1] Radio follows along the same line, as it is dominated by five business groups, of which former President Elías Antonio Saca (ARENA) (2004–09) owns the largest one. A final component of the elite control has been the control over the judicial system, particularly the Supreme court which has historically been loyal to the elite, often echoing the most conservative forces within them (Freedman 2012).[2]

The ARENA governments pursued one of the clearest examples of neoliberal economic policies in Central America. Among the most significant elements in this was the privatization of banks and public services in the 1990s, the 2001 dollarization, and the signing of the free trade agreement between Central America, the United States and the Dominican Republic (CAFTA-DR) that entered into effect on January 1, 2006. These changes strengthened groups related to the financial and service sector in relation to the agro-industrial sector (Towers and Borzutzsky 2004). However, while privatization ensured a short-term upsurge of investments (as did the massive sale of the re-privatized banks in 2007), the policies failed to ensure sustained investments and growth (see Table 3.1). Rather, while the domestic elite invested their proceeds from the sale of enterprises abroad, depending on remittances to fuel domestic demand for their services, the government was left with very little room to maneuver in terms of development policy.

The forms of environmental governance established under ARENA rule were characterized by: (i) gradual increase of governmental regulative capacity, (ii) lack of public participation, and (iii) a focus on conservation of protected areas (PAs) whereas the productive sectors of interest to the elite were left untouched.

The war had wiped out the little El Salvador could count on in terms of environmental management and control. It was not until 1997 that the Ministry of the Environment and Natural Resources (MARN) was established, based on the US funded Executive Secretary for the Environment (SEMA) attached to the Milplan (the Ministry for Planning and Coordination of Economic Development). Initially, ARENA opposed fiercely an Environmental Law that would require environmental assessment of private development projects. However, the law was passed, albeit in a watered down version in 1998 (Moreno 1998). Since elite interests were increasingly focused in urban areas where the population was concentrated, these urban environmental problems gained importance (MARN 2012c). Simultaneously to the urban focus of governmental development efforts, in rural areas multiple development projects with innovative governance mechanisms were established. Many were inspired by liberation theology and the late Salvadoran economist Aquiles Montoya's theories of a solidarity economy.[3] While these initiatives often were in conflict with the central state, and received little support, many were supported by international cooperation.

One example was the development projects occurring in the area of Bajo Lempa.[4] Bajo Lempa, in the coastal plains at the mouth of the Lempa river, is characterized by its highly fertile soil and rich biodiversity. It was of little importance in the indigo and coffee production and therefore became both an ecological reserve and an escape for the population that did not fit into the agro-export economy and could live off fisheries and subsistence agriculture. In the 1960s, Bajo Lempa was colonized by a handful of rich families and transformed into one of the main cotton producing areas, and one that was quickly deforested and severely polluted, with grave consequences in the fragile coastal areas. However, as a combined effect of the collapse of world prices, the aforementioned ecological collapse, the land reform, the civil war and an unsuccessful take-over of the haciendas, cotton-production dropped steeply between the late 1970s and early 1980s. The war led to an exodus of people from the Bajo Lempa area and a partial ecological recovery. With the peace agreement of 1992, a process of repatriation with the Land Transfer Program and new productive projects emerged, many of which were supported by foreign aid. Many of the families that had been repatriated were supporters of the left-wing insurgencies and they believed in collective and sustainable agriculture. With support from various foreign non-governmental organizations, multiple new projects were established, and so were new local governance mechanisms aimed at jointly managing natural resources. These increased particularly after Hurricane Mitch devastated the region and exposed once again the extreme environmental vulnerability of the region. As a result, bodies such as the Committee for Local Development of Bajo Lempa and the Committee for the Management of the Biosphere Reserve of Xirihualtique-Jiquilisco were established. However, as these forums for dialogue and governance mechanisms often were in opposition to the governmental policies of intensive export agriculture, dialogue with the national government was deficient. The conflicts increased as sugar-cane production started to increase again, often threatening local agriculture.

## The Funes government's quest for a new development path

Thus, when the Funes took over the government it was in a polarized context with a central government that supported a market-based transnationally integrated service oriented economy, but with an expanding sugar sector, and multiple local initiatives for an alternative model of development and environmental governance.

The government also confronted a triple crisis: an economic, an environmental and a social crisis. After economic growth had been low for several years, it was negative in 2009 due to the international financial crisis (see Table 3.1). Moreover, poverty levels that showed few signs of being reduced in the 2000s (see Table 3.2) rose by ten percentage points between 2008 and 2009 according to the Multipurpose Household Survey.[5] Furthermore, the long term environmental crisis had become by this point evident and critical. Deforestation that was reversed during the war increased again, including deforestation of the mangroves which are of high value to marine biodiversity as well as an important defense against flooding caused by extreme weather. Furthermore, the country's water supply and quality was at critical levels, and the vulnerability to climatic changes was devastating to both crops and livelihoods. In 2009, El Salvador was hit by tropical storm Ida that caused 198 deaths, and a number of other phenomena such as landslides and rising sea levels threatening both lives and livelihoods. Moreover, the agricultural crisis that had endured since the 1980s had new consequences in the context of the 2008 financial crisis. By 2010, El Salvador was no longer able

*Table 3.1* Export/import, investment flows and GDP growth 2000–10

|  | 2000–05 | 2006 | 2007 | 2008 | 2009 | 2010 |
|---|---|---|---|---|---|---|
| Inward FDI flow (million US$) | 325* | 241 | 1551 | 903 | 366 | 117 |
| Export of goods (million US$) | 3267.8* | 3758.6 | 4029.1 | 4610.7 | 3860.9 | 4478.6 |
| Remittances (million US$) | 2,362* | 3,316 | 3,695 | 3,742 | 3,387 | 3,431 |
| GDP growth % | 2.4* | 3.9 | 3.8 | 1.3 | –3.1 | 1.4 |

Source: Authors' elaboration based on CEPAL (2010, 2011); Solimano and Allendes (2007).
* Average 2000–05.

Table 3.2 Poverty levels (percentage of people living on less than US$2 a day)

| Year | Total | Urban | Rural |
|------|-------|-------|-------|
| 1995 | 54.2 | 45.8 | 64.4 |
| 1999 | 49.8 | 38.7 | 65.1 |
| 2004 | 47.5 | 47.5 | 56.8 |
| 2009 | 47.9 | 42.3 | 57.6 |
| 2010 | 46.6 | 41.1 | 55.8 |

Source: Authors' elaboration based on CEPAL (2010, 2012).

to ensure supplies of basic grains and had to import beans from China. On top of that, Funes was faced with a crisis of the right wing, one that could have worked to his favor, but that in the end did not.

Funes's team had a different profile than those of the former governments. It was a negotiated blend of representatives of the ranks and file of FMLN and CD with a diverse political experience, and people selected by MAM. Many were recruited from international organizations and think tanks.[6] Whereas these groups can hardly be called an "elite" in the same manner as the country's economic elite, they did control significant resources in terms of technical expertise and many had very different views on environmental issues than the old elites.

Funes came to power promising change, and his government entered into a hectic transition period in which a number of plans were elaborated in order to guide the process of change. The first plan for such change was the Programa de Gobierno 2009–14: Nace la Esperanza, Viene el Cambio,[7] which was the programmatic platform promoted by Funes as a presidential candidate and his vice-presidential candidate Salvador Sánchez Cerén, of the FMLN. Subsequently, the Global Anti-Crisis Plan was launched, with an estimated investment of US$ 587.5 million to be executed over the course of 18 months. While envisioning major social reforms to combat poverty and improve public services, it also included measures of austerity. That was partly a requirement of the Stand-By agreement worth US$ 800 million that the government signed with the International Monetary Fund (IMF) that allowed it to overcome the immediate financial crisis in which it found itself. The Stand-By agreement was designed to increase social spending and provide economic stimulus to help El Salvador out of the crisis, but also included requirements for control on current expenditures and a 17 percent increase of fiscal income by 2014.[8]

In order to ensure implementation and impact of the plans, the government considered it necessary to establish a new type of relationship with the business sector that would not imply a subordination of the Government to private interests, and, on the other hand, generate a climate with the minimal requirements of confidence both for national and international investment.

(Gobierno de El Salvador 2012, p. 19)

One of the means to do so was to establish links to the more moderate and progressive groups among the business elites, including the Salume and the Cáceres families. Another measure was to ensure funding elsewhere as a means to encourage the creation of an alternative elite. Some parts of the FMLN also advocated stronger ties with the Venezuelan-led Bolivarian Alliance for the Peoples of Our America (*Alianza Bolivariana para el Pueblo de Nuestra América*—ALBA) and related organizations in order to get access to alternative sources of finance. This happened to a certain extent with the entry of ALBA Petróleos and ALBA Alimentos. ALBA Alimentos's (ALBA food) made a US$90 million investment to reactivate 100,000 *manzanas* of farmland, generate jobs and increase food production, and ALBA Petróleos. By 2014, a new economic group was emerging with ALBA Petróleos at its core but with investments in a number of companies, and leaders closely linked to FMLN (Lemus 2014).

The government also placed strong emphasis on establishing new forums for dialogue and governance mechanisms with the traditional elite. In 2009 it created the Economic and Social Council (*Consejo Económico y Social*—CES) with representatives of organized business, social organizations, labor organizations, academics and the government. Although some business chambers, parts of the most radical left wing and the radical right boycotted CES, initially it had broad representation. Its first task was to agree on a five-year development plan (2010–14) to be implemented after the initial anti-crisis measures. CES came to an agreement about such a plan that gave priority to (i) the reactivation of the productive economy and reduction of poverty; (ii) structural reform of the state and public administration; (iii) prevention of violence and the creation of a new model of integrated development; and (iv) efficient management of environmental risks (Gobierno de El Salvador 2010a, pp. 52–53). A main innovation in the plan was to develop a model of territorial management that would ensure citizens' participation in governance, as a means to achieve the goals of universal social protection and environmental management.

Parallel to this, the government initiated the National Strategy for Productive Development aimed to restructure the economy to stimulate innovation and improve the conditions for small and medium sized enterprises (Gobierno de El Salvador, 2010b, p. 92). It proposed to convert El Salvador into (a) a producer of its own food, (b) a specialized industrial center, (c) an international logistics center by modernizing the system of harbors and network of roads, given its strategic position in the region and (d) an international center for tourism. This meant that it opened for megaprojects to be developed jointly between the public and the private sector.

However, it also focused on aiding small farmers, a group that had been largely neglected in the former governments. The main means to do so was the Plan for

Family Agriculture (PAF) that re-established the institutional mechanisms of support that had provided small family farms with credit, technical assistance, access to land and other important inputs, but that had been removed as a part of the structural adjustment process of the last decades (MAG 2011, p. 10). It included a Program for National Supplies for Food and Nutritional Security (PAN), a program to support family agriculture, and one to strengthen their links with commerce and industry. Among the concrete goals were to increase by 70,000 hectares (100,000 *manzanas*) the cultivated areas for basic grains in 2014, a means assumed to reduce rural poverty by 12 percent (MAG 2011).

However, although several plans dedicated space to environmental issues, it was clear to the community of environmentalists that this was actually not given high priority on the agenda. Groups of environmentalists went to lengths to attract the attention of the transition team to the urgent environmental issues that the country faced, but with little success.

When the two tropical storms Alex and Matthew hit in 2010 and the tropical depression 12-E hit in 2011, they caused major damage on rural infrastructure and agricultural crops, and incurred major human costs. This led not only to a reorientation of governmental funds to reconstruction but also to placing the issue of climate change, risk management and vulnerability reduction higher on the national agenda. The tropical depression 12-E also revealed the limits of PAF, that was based on non-ecological production process and failed to consider the enormous vulnerabilities and the situation of climate risk that the small Salvadoran farmers were faced with. As a response, PAF was adjusted with the Environmental Strategy for Adaptation and Mitigation to Climate Change in the Agricultural, Forestry, Poultry and Fishery sectors coordinated by MARN.

After the storms, the government also initiated the National Program for the Restoration of Ecosystems and Rural Landscapes (PREP) aimed at promoting the restoration of ecosystems and landscapes as a way to reduce the risk and increase the capacity for mitigation and adaptation to climate change of the agricultural sector and infrastructure. In contrast to PAF (whose main area of work is the individual farm), PREP sought to promote organic and sustainable agriculture eliminating the use of agrochemicals; make the practices by the large producers (of sugar, coffee and cattle) more sustainable; and introduce "natural infrastructure," including vegetation jointly with physical construction in order to reduce risk (MARN 2012a). Moreover, it intended to do so in dialogue with the communities (Grupo Dialogo Rural 2012).

The government also initiated dialogue with particular sectors of the international elite on many of these policies, but with different degrees of success. For example, it initiated conversations with the sugar industry to end the use of the most polluting pesticides and reduce the areas of burning cane by 12,500 hectares. This caused fierce clashes with the sugar mill owners who argued that the government had no intention of ensuring necessary dialogue:

> The topic of the environment is different. There the government is imposing things. I will give you an example: MARN and some congressmen have

demanded that we reduce certain chemicals. I don't even think that they are dangerous. They also demand that we cut the cane green without burning it … they say the burning kills some small animals that live there. To us it came as a total surprise that they require us to reduce the areas that we burn by 12,500 hectares. They have never consulted us. They just did it like that.[9]

While there were clashes with the economic elite, there were also several examples of participation by the elite in dialogue with the government on elaboration of policies and their implementation. One example was the elaboration of the new water law. This was done in close consultation with ANEP, and with the support of FUSADES. Indeed, partly because of an exchange of plans and technological knowledge, FUSADES came to coincide with the government on the new law and it was approved also by the representatives of the economic elite.[10]

ANEP and other business associations also participated in the revision of the general national environmental policies. That resulted in a six-point action plan presented in May 2012, overlapping in many respects some of the other policies: Restoration of degraded ecosystems and landscapes, improved sanitation, integrated management of hydro-resources, integration of environmental issues in the territorial regulation, environmental responsibility and adaptation to climate change, and reduction of risk (MARN 2012b).

The contradictions the government faced in promoting economic productivity that is inclusive and addressing the country's extreme vulnerability to climate variability and change, were particularly evident in the case of Bajo Lempa.

The environmental degradation inherited from the old agricultural export model has magnified Bajo Lempa's vulnerability to climate variability and change, to the point of making it one of the most vulnerable areas throughout Central America. However, as a result of the high levels of organization and social capital of the population, there were important processes of transformation of productive and farming practices that favor small producers and strengthen local livelihoods while increasing the zone's resilience to climate change (examples include the cultivation and processing of organic cashew that is sold in niche international markets; the formation of the Permanent Roundtable of Local Actors of Bajo Lempa (MESPABAL) and the development of their own Strategic Plan for Territorial Development; and the first Community Plan for Sustainable Extraction in the Mangroves of Jiquilisco Bay).

Under the Funes government, new spaces for dialogue between territorial actors opened up with central government agencies that supported their initiatives. Nevertheless, Bajo Lempa found itself to also be a key region for new strategies of growth, investment and employment promoted by the government, i.e., the Development Strategy for the Coastal Marine Corridor, Partnership for Growth, and FOMILENIO II. These policy frameworks (particularly those driven through the US programs FOMILENIO II and the Partnership for Growth) favored the private sector that already had a significant presence in the territory in sectors such as sugar cane, and are expected to benefit substantially through the expansion of sugar cane, the logistical platform, mega projects of tourism, among other activities. The promotion of this kind of economic strategy will likely suffocate the local livelihood strategies and initiatives, as well as further exacerbate the vulnerability of Bajo Lempa and its population.

## Government–elite interaction: from dialogue to confrontation

Simultaneous with the formulation of the first governmental plans, the political right experienced its worst crisis in 20 years. The electoral defeat exacerbated the differences that had already become evident within ARENA during the Antonio Saca presidency (2004–09), between the party founders representing the old elites, and new sectors, represented by Saca and his preferred successor, the ARENA presidential candidate for the 2009 elections, Rodrigo Avila. The old elites, led by party founder Cristiani, managed to put their people back into COENA in September 2009 and sought loyalty from the ARENA group in the legislative assembly. The result of a long struggle between different factions was that 12 ARENA representatives to the Legislative Assembly left the party and formed their own, named the Grand Alliance for National Unity (*Gran Alianza por la Unidad Nacional* (GANA)), which acquired its legal status as a party in January 2010 (Fundaungo 2011) and was later presided over by Saca.

When the government started to discuss the most difficult issues with the elite representatives—a fiscal pact and new investments—it was faced with a split right wing. A new fiscal pact started to be discussed by CES in late 2010, but already in February 2011, ANEP withdrew from the discussions. One reason was that ANEP rejected corporate tax increases and rather argued for spending cuts and taxing the informal economy and to eliminate loopholes (FUSADES 2011). However, apart from the objections to the content of a new fiscal policy, the withdrawal was motivated by an intense lack of trust in the government. The ANEP representatives argued that the debates in CES were a smokescreen and that the government would introduce harsh tax increases no matter what the CES would agree on.

For a while the fissure of the right wing came to the rescue of the government. The discussion of a fiscal pact was re-launched in June 2011.[11] In spite of fierce opposition from business elites (Quintanilla 2011), it was passed in the Legislative Assembly in December 2011 with the support from GANA. However, the relations between the government and the ANEP elites seemed beyond mending. In the annual reports on the Funes administration produced by FUSADES, the chapters on the relationship between the government and the private sector in the first reports reflect largely a "war of words": a deep lack of confidence reflected in mutual accusations of intentions and actions. However, the report of the third year reports on a number of specific policy measures and political issues that contributed to a deteriorating climate, including a particular "violence tax" and governmental requirements for increased business transparency (FUSADES 2012).

The strained relationship with ANEP was a major challenge to the government's desire to increase economic growth and employment. As the government–business relations deteriorated, the private sector went on what the technical secretary of the presidency, Alexander Segovia, called an "investment-strike."[12] Increased private investments became even more urgent due to the inclusion of El Salvador in the Partnership for Growth (PFG) initiative launched by the Obama administration in 2010 (US Government, 2012). In July the main diagnosis of El Salvador from the PFG was made public, focusing on the high levels of crime and the low levels of productivity in the tradable sectors (USG-GOES 2011). This diagnosis was based on a number of different existing numbers and studies, and conversations and focus groups in El Salvador, but confined strictly to the elites: business and the upper skeletons of public administration (USG-GOES 2011, p. 1). No communities or social movements were consulted, and the emphasis was on unleashing the potential for the private sector to spur growth. Furthermore, while members of the Salvadoran group had argued for including vulnerability to climate change as a major challenge, this was flatly rejected by the US government and in the end the environment is only mentioned as a "risk factor" for increased economic growth (USG-GOES 2011, pp. 199–209).

In November the same year the Joint Action Plan 2011–15 was launched, emphasizing mutual understanding between the private sector and the government, based on transparency, communication and clear policies that support and generate innovation (USG-GOES, 2011).

In the joint declaration signed by El Salvador and the United States, the US government commits instead to mobilize a broad specter of instruments of assistance to strengthen the impact of the plan, including measures to leverage private capital, and call on the private sector to increase investment and assist national measures to create a climate for economic growth (USG-GOES, 2011b).

The PFG was to be the main framework for the follow-up of the Millennium Challenge Funds investment in El Salvador, the so-called FOMILENIO II. This was focused on the coastal areas, and a proposal for a broad-based project was developed by a diversity of actors including municipalities, communities and business elites, on a project of investments in human capital, tourism, infrastructure and logistical services. This also encompassed the area of Bajo Lempa. The government developed a carefully drafted plan with a thorough strategic environmental assessment for an improved management of natural resources in the sugar industry (including the reduction of burning), fisheries, protection of the mangroves, and laying the groundwork for sustainable tourism (MARN 2012c). A group of elite investors joined forces to plan a large-scale investment in tourism in the area. With a list of investors reading like a "who's who" of the Salvadoran elite, the *Asociación de Desarrolladores Turísticos Costero Marinos* (Promar) planned investments of US$2,000 million in the areas.[13] In order to become reality, it would have to be discussed with the government, but also, in accordance with the government's visions for governance, in dialogue with multiple actors, including the local governance mechanisms in Bajo Lempa.

However, the relationship between the government and ANEP was at that point so tense that the prospects of being able to develop such a mutual understanding with the private sector with ANEP as an interlocutor were bleak. In order to bypass ANEP the government convened instead a National Growth Council (*Consejo Nacional para el Crecimiento*) in November 2011, consisting of five governmental representatives and five of the country's richest businessmen: Roberto Murray Meza (President of Grupo Agrisal), Francisco de Sola (President of Grupo Homarca), Francisco Callejas (President of the supermarket chain Super Selectos), Juan Carlos Eserski (son of aforementioned Boris Eserski) and Ricardo Poma (President of the perhaps most powerful Salvadoran business group, Grupo Poma), jointly assumed to control around one third of the Salvadoran GDP.[14] The main purpose was to mobilize investments to the many projects envisaged in the five-year development plan and the PFG and to create a better climate for investments in general.

However, that did not happen. Again, the close, but increasingly complicated connections between the economic right and the political right hindered an improved relationship between business and the government. Around 2009, four of the five judges of the Constitutional Bench of the Supreme court started to act independently in a previously unknown manner and issued a series of court rulings that upset the political as well as economic elite. The rulings dismissed corrupt judges, hit down on the purchase of positions and rejected the government's transfer of funds between different ministries.

As a consequence, on June 2, 2012 all the right-wing parties (ARENA, PDC, PCN and GANA) joined forces to fast-track a reform to the Judicial Organization Law (decree 743) that would require unanimous rulings, thereby stopping the increasingly radical practice of the judges that had come to be known as "the fabulous four." The FMLN representatives voted against, but in spite of that President Funes sanctioned it and sent it to *El Diario Oficial* for publication the same day. This sparked off a strong reaction from a number of civil society organizations, led by ANEP, calling this a blow to Salvadoran democracy. ARENA founder Cristiani admitted that the main motive for the proposal was the fear that the "fabulous four" would make the Constitutional Bench repeal the Amnesty Law (Freedman 2012) that allowed many prominent members of the business and political elite to avoid persecution for war crimes. The constitutional crisis created hitherto unseen cleavages and alliances: ARENA and ANEP were for the first time in open, public conflict, while ARENA attempted to make FMLN join in on an effort to "repeal" the decree, something FMLN rejected, blaming ARENA for having brought themselves into the mess that they should also get out of. At the same time, the FMLN's disapproval of the Funes government increased, as did that of many left-wing civil society organizations.

As a result of the conflict, ANEP broke out of CES, and the five businessmen of the National Growth Council withdrew.[15] This happened in spite of the fact that the elite representatives integrating this council were all investors in PROMAR and would benefit heavily from the success of the initiative. Only under heavy pressure from the US ambassador did they return to the council, but the ANEP did not return to CES.[16]

The projects planned under the PROMAR were discussed in multi-stakeholder mechanisms established by non-governmental organizations such as the Latin American Center for Rural Dialogue's project on rural dialogue.[17] However, in interviews, the elite expressed that it was out of the question for them to participate in such interactive dialogue mechanisms as it was too associated with FMLN-controlled social organizations.[18]

## Conclusion: environmental governance in a context of structural inequality

The attempt by the Salvadoran government to include broad groups of society in a multi-stakeholder dialogue was done with the aim to establish new forms of governance of productive activities to make them more compatible with the grave environmental crisis that El Salvador found itself in. This crisis was a result of a combination of unsustainable production, particularly in agro-export sectors, and El Salvador's geographical location making it highly vulnerable to global climatic changes. It urgently had to include both national economic elites controlling capital for investments and marginal groups living in and off the most affected areas in such a dialogue. However, that dialogue proved everything but easy, and it sheds light on strengths and limitations of interactive governance in situations of deeply rooted structural inequality and weak state institutions.

One main conclusion is that the success of non-hierarchical interactive measures is hindered by the deep politicization and lack of a basic consensus about the desired development paths. This hinders a focus on the issues at stake, and allows various additional motives to come into play, in this case mainly political motives. The functioning of such governance mechanisms depends on a degree of confidence between the different stakeholders, and legitimacy of the actors backing such initiatives. This has been weak or absent in El Salvador due to the deep inequalities existing in the socio-economic system and the history of political polarization.

A second main conclusion is that, in contexts characterized by low growth and widespread poverty, it is impossible to analyze environmental governance separately from initiatives to strengthen growth and employment generation with a transformation of the productive apparatus. A sustainable and just use of natural resources including land, water and forest cannot be firmly established if it does not simultaneously provide livelihoods in rural areas as well as general employment. In the context of a structurally weak state, this requires that the government enters into direct dialogue with possible investors. However, in El Salvador, the government entered into these negotiations in a relatively weak position, and failed to simultaneously ensure investments and to regulate them in line with environmental impact assessments and general policies for a stronger and more inclusive form of environmental governance.

The situation in El Salvador is important also for understanding the viability of choosing a path of gradual reforms towards a more equitable and sustainable development model. El Salvador illustrates the profound difficulties with such a path, particularly in the context of the lack of governmental sources of income or access to capital independent of the economic elite. One could imagine that the country's rather accidental move away from natural resource dependency, due to the civil war and falling world prices, would facilitate the conversion to a more sustainable model. However, the combination of deep political antagonism and internationally embedded structural inequality has so far hampered such efforts.

## Notes

1  Boris Eserski is of the Eserski Araujo family, drawing its roots back to the landowning family of President Manuel Enrique Araujo (1911–13), and is related to Carlos Araujo Eserski, former president of ANEP and Walter Araujo, former president of ARENA and the Legislative Assembly, and current judge of the Supreme Electoral Court. See www.tse.gob.sv/index.php/organismo-colegiado/79-categorias-tse/magistrados/120.

2  Its lack of independence was proven when, among other cases, in 2005 the Probity Section of the court requested two domestic banks to supply information about the accounts of several former officials including ex-president Francisco Flores. The banks denied and filed a complaint to the Supreme Court, which in turn stripped the Probity Section of these powers (Wolf 2009, p. 444).

3  Interview, Emilio Espin, November 26, 2012.

4  This part is based on Cuéllar *et al.* (2013), commissioned for this study.

5  Encuesta de Hogares de propósitos Múltiple, 2008 and 2009, El Salvador.

6  Among the examples of the new technocrats was the leader of the economic team, Alex Segovia, with a PhD from Cambridge and a long trajectory of researching the economic structures of El Salvador and Central America generally. It was also true for the environmental team that was headed by the director of the respected research institution the Salvadoran Program for Research on Development and Environment (PRISMA), Herman Rosa, as minister of the environment, and the program coordinator for Heinrich Böll Foundation in El Salvador, Lina Pohl as vice minister. It was not a given that the post as the minister of environment should be given to Rosa; the environmental movements connected to the FMLN had rather favored the activist and director of the *Unidad Ecológica Salvadoreña* (UES), Angel Ibarra. See www.boell-latinoamerica.org/web/index-514.html.

7  See www.fmln.org.sv/oficial/index.php?option=com_content&view=article&id=122 &Itemid=618.

8  See www.imf.org/external/np/sec/pr/2010/pr1095.htm.

9  Interview, owner of sugar mills, San Salvador, November 16, 2012.

10 Interviews, high level governmental representative, November 15, 2012, and executive director of FUNDEMAS, November 15, 2012.

11 See www.elsalvador.com/mwedh/nota/nota_completa.asp?idCat=6374&idArt=5947245.

12 Personal communication.

13 See http://elmundo.com.sv/alistan-inversion-turistica-por-2000-mills.

14 Interview, Alfonso Goitia, Ministry of Economy, El Salvador, November 16, 2012.

15 See http://elmundo.com.sv/empresarios-se-van-de-asocio-por-crecimiento.

16 Interview, senior governmental representative, El Salvador, November 15, 2012.

17 See www.rimisp.org/proyectos/noticias_proy.php?id_proyecto=262&id_=1741.

18 Interviews, Salvadoran elite representatives, November 15–16, 2012.

# Bibliography

Acevedo, C., Barry, D. and Rosa, H. (1995) El Salvador's agricultural sector: Macroeconomic policy, agrarian change and the environment. *World Development*, 23(2): 2153–2172.

Artiga Gonzáles, A. (2004) *Elitismo competitivo: Dos décadas de elecciones en El Salvador 1998–2003*. UCA Editores, San Salvador.

Baloyra, E. (1989) *El Salvador en transición*. UCA Editores, San Salvador.

Barry, D. and Rosa, H. (1995) *El Salvador: Dinámica de la degradación ambiental*. PRISMA, San Salvador.

Bull, B. (2013) Diversified business groups and the transnationalisation of the El Salvadoran economy. *Journal of Latin American Studies*, 45(2): 265–295.

Bulmer-Thomas, B. (1987) *The Political Economy of Central America since 1920*. Cambridge University Press, Cambridge.

CEPAL (2010) *Anuario Estadístico de América Latina y el Caribe*. Comisión Económica para América Latina y el Caribe, Santiago de Chile.

CEPAL (2011) *La inversión extranjera directa en América Latina y el Caribe 2011*. Comisión Económica para América Latina y el Caribe, Santiago de Chile.

CEPAL (2012) *Panorama Social de América Latina*. Comisión Económica para América Latina y el Caribe, Santiago de Chile.

Colindres, E. (1977) *Fundamentos económicos de la burguesía salvadoreña*. UCA Editores, San Salvador.

Cuéllar, N., Luna, F., Díaz, O. and Kandel, S. (2013) *Gobernanza ambiental-territorial y desarrollo en El Salvador: El caso del Bajo Lempa*. Documento de Trabajo ENGOV No. 4, 2013.

Freedman, E. (2012) What's behind Decree 743? *Revista Envío* 368.

Fundaungo (2011) *El Salvador: Monografía de los Partidos Políticos 2011*. Fundación Dr. Guillermo Manuel Ungo, San Salvador.

FUSADES (2011) *Segundo año de gobierno de Presidente Funes: Apreciación general*. Fundación Salvadoreña para el Desarrollo Económico y Social, San Salvador.

FUSADES (2012) *Terceer año de gobierno de Presidente Funes: Apreciación general*. Fundación Salvadoreña para el Desarrollo Económico y Social, San Salvador.

Gammage, S. (2006) Exporting people and recruiting remittances: A development strategy for El Salvador? *Latin American Perspectives*, 33(6): 75–100.

Gobierno de El Salvador (2010a) *Plan quinquenal de desarrollo 2010–2014*. GOES, San Salvador.

Gobierno de El Salvador (2010b) *Plan Nacional de Desarrollo Productivo*. GOES, San Salvador.

Gobierno de El Salvador (2012) *El camino del cambio en El Salvador*. GOES, San Salvador.

Grupo Dialogo Rural (2012) *Memoria de Foro-Taller Agricultura Sostenible para la Restauración de Ecosistemas y Paisajes Rurales, 2012: 1*. RIMISP, Centro para el desarrollo rural, San Salvador.

Hecht, S. B., Kandel, S., Gomes, I., Cuéllar, N. and Rosa, H. (2006) Globalization, forest resurgence and environmental politics in El Salvador. *World Development*, 34: 308–323.

Koivumaeki, R.-I. (2010) Business economic experts and conservative party building in Latin America: The case of El Salvador. *Journal of Politics in Latin America*, 2(1): 76–106.

Lemus, E. (2014) La Milionaria Revolución de ALBA. *El Faro*, January 19, 2014, available at: www.elfaro.net/es/201401/noticias/14423 (accessed 30 July 2014).

MAG (2011) *Plan de Agricultura Familiar y Emprendedurismo Rural para la Seguridad Alimentaria y Nutricional 2011–2014*. La Libertad, San Salvador.

MARN (2012a) *Programa Nacional de Restauración de Ecosistemas y Paisajes Rurales*. Ministerio de Medio Ambiente y Recursos Naturales, San Salvador.

MARN (2012b) *Política Nacional de Medio Ambiente*. Ministerio de Medio Ambiente y Recursos Naturales, San Salvador.

MARN (2012c) *Evaluación Ambiental Estratégica de la Estrategia de Desarrollo para la Franja Costero Marina: Resumen de las Recomendaciones*. Ministerio de Medio Ambiente y Recursos Naturales, San Salvador.

Mejía, A. (2009) Partidos gastaron $15 mills en un año de prosetilismo, La Prensa Gráfica, available at: www.laprensagrafica.com/el-salvador/politica/19020-partidos-gastaron-15-mlls-en-un-ano-de-proselitismo (accessed 25 September 2014).

Moreno, I. (1998) Ley del Medio Ambiente: en el ojo de la tormenta política. *Revista Envío*, 193, April, available at: www.envio.org.ni/articulo/355 (accessed 30 July 2014).

Paige, J. M. (1997) *Coffee and Power: Revolution and the Rise of Democracy in Central America*. Harvard University Press, Cambridge, MA.

Paniagua, C. R. (2002) *El bloque empresarial hegemónico salvadoreño* (vol. 645–646). Universidad centroamericana José Simeón Cañas, El Salvador.

Quintanilla, L. (2011) ANEP urge que el gobierno controle el despilfarro. *La Prensa Gráfica*, August 31.

Rockwell, R. and Janus, N. (2005) *Media Power in Central America*. University of Illinois Press, Chicago, IL.

Rosa, H. (2008) *Trayectorias del cambio económico de El Salvador: Una perspectiva desde las fuentes de divisas*. PRISMA, San Salvador.

Segovia, A. (2002) *Transformación estructural y reforma económica en El Salvador: El funcionamiento económico de los noventa y sus efectos sobre el crecimiento la pobreza y la distribución de ingreso*. F&G Editores, Guatemala.

Solimano, A. and Allendes, C. (2007) *Migraciones internacionales remesas y el desarrollo económico: la experiencia Latinoamericana*. Comisión Económica para América Latina y el Caribe, Santiago de Chile.

Towers, M. and Borzutzky. S, (2004) The socioeconomic effects of dollarization in El Salvador. *Latin American Politics and Society*, 46(3): 29–54.

US Government (2012) *Partnership for Growth: A US Government Fact Sheet*. March 27, Washington DC.

USG-GOES (2011a) *Pacto por el Crecimiento Análisis de Restricciones Equipo Técnico Conjunto Washington–San Salvador*. US Government–Gobierno de El Salvador.

USG-GOES (2011b) *Asocio para el Crecimiento El Salvador–Estados Unidos Plan de Acción Conjunto 2011–2015 y Declaración Conjunta de Principios*. United States Government–Gobierno de El Salvador.

Utting, Peter (1991) *The Social Origins and Impact of Deforestation in Central America*. United Nations Research Institute for Social Development, Geneva.

Williams, R. G. (1986) *Export Agriculture and the Crisis in Central America*. University of North Carolina Press, Columbia, NC.

Williams, R. G. (1994) *States and Social Evolution: Coffee and the Rise of National Governments in Central America*. University of North Carolina Press, Columbia, NC.

Wilson, E. A. (1978) La crisis de integración nacional en El Salvador, in R. Menjívar and G. Véjar (eds), *El Salvador de 1840 á 1935*. UCA Editores, San Salvador, 151–241.

Wolf, S. (2009) Subverting democracy: Elite rule and the limits to political participation in post-war El Salvador. *Journal of Latin American Studies*, 41: 429–465.

# 4 Bolivia

## Emerging and traditional elites and the governance of the soy sector

*Marte Høiby and Joaquín Zenteno Hopp*

## Introduction

The Bolivian presidential election won by Evo Morales in 2006 is perhaps the most emblematic event of Latin America's recent governmental political shifts. A new social group came to power together with the Morales government, forming an emerging elite that contested the power of the previous traditional elite known for its control over Bolivia's economic resources. While in the eastern lowlands of the country control over agricultural activity had historically secured the economic power of the local traditional elite, the new government was now in a position to regulate such activity and thus defy their influence. Consequently, the shift gave rise to several conflicts that escalated throughout the first years of what has become known as the *Proceso de Cambio* (Process of Change). Yet during recent times the two elites have found common ground in aspects concerning environmental governance and agricultural development.

Our findings indicate that the approval of the new constitution in 2009 signified the beginning of a new political dynamic between the emerging (political) elite and the traditional (economic) elite. A common interest in the direction of agricultural development—large landholdings and use of genetically modified (GM) soy—has become their meeting point. As a result, and despite the contrasting discourse of the Morales government, the two elites are allowing large landholdings to continue and encourage GM soy production.

Given that the increasing use of land for soy cultivation is a well-known environmental problem in Bolivia, the regulation of landholdings and the use of GM crops are critically important when addressing environmental governance in the country. On the one hand, the use of GM soy has been shown to have a lower environmental impact than previous conventional soy produced on the same land due to the implications of agro-chemicals. On the other hand, the productivity and cost efficiency of the GM soy model poses a threat to the forest areas by encouraging the expansion of monoculture production. Hence, the main concern is the unregulated future expansion of the agricultural frontier supported by the agreement between the two elites and thus the lack of a social group with political power to abate negative environmental impacts.

Based on numbers from the Vice Ministry of Rural Development in 2013 and as shown in Figure 4.1, the cultivation of soy covers a total area of about 1.18 million hectares (95 percent of the department of Santa Cruz), accounts for the production of 2.6 million tons per year, and employs around 100,000 people. Only approximately 20 percent is exported as seed, and the rest is exported as semi-processed products such as soybean oil and soybean meal. The total value of the soy exports in 2013 were about US$1.12 billion, the majority of which are sold in the Andean market. Bolivia has no direct tax on soy but its exportation is regulated by the central government through exportation bounds given once the domestic market has been fulfilled.

The data used for the research of this chapter consist of a secondary literature review, including news reports, governmental documents and semi-structured interviews with key actors. The interviewees are representatives from the elites identified during research, including governmental officials, academic professionals and recognized non-governmental organizations as well as high-level representatives of the soy industry, including farmers and business associations and associates. The interviews were conducted during the first trimester of 2013 in the city of Santa Cruz de la Sierra and in the soy fields in northern parts of the Santa Cruz department.

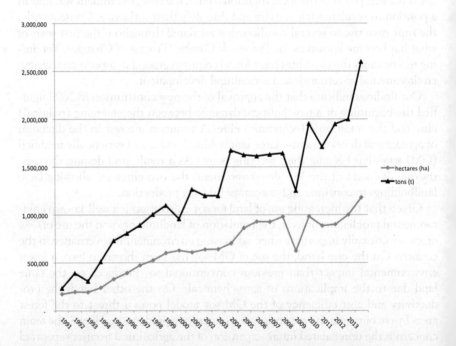

*Figure 4.1* Evolution of soy production and area in Santa Cruz, Bolivia, 1990–2013

Source: Based on data published by Zeballos (2012) and consultations with ANAPO's President Demetrio Perez and General Manager Rolando Zabala in 2013.

## The elites of the soy sector—who are they?

In this chapter we refer to two main groups of elites which we have termed "traditional elites" and "emerging elites." Each one of these elites includes several other (sub)elites and are defined by their power over different natural resources as shown in Figure 4.2. While the main resource of the emerging elites is their position in a political movement that is supported democratically by a clear majority, the main resource of the traditional elites is their capital, which is based on their ownership over extensive productive lands.

The traditional elite includes members of Santa Cruz society who have historically controlled land, capital and political power, but also includes new actors, especially Brazilian landholders. An important group within the traditional elite is formed by individuals who are involved in the soy industry; we refer to them as the "soy elite." Based on the definition outlined in Chapter 2, the soy elite is defined as such based on their control of land and economic resources related to agribusiness for soy production. Other resources controlled by the soy elite are networks, technology and knowledge related to soy production and industrialization.

Several emerging (sub)elites have also appeared in Bolivia during recent times (Ayo, 2012). One group consists of persons who hold strategic positions, like politicians at the highest level of government and individuals next to them: Evo Morales and his closest allies in and around the government. Ayo calls them the "strategic elite." Another emerging (sub)elite is formed by influential persons outside the government such as those who contribute with finances (e.g., the banks), individuals who represent the national government in a specific

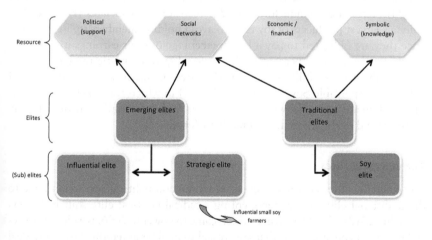

*Figure 4.2* Visual representation of the elites studied in this chapter (light grey) and their resources (dark grey). Note that the "emerging elites" and the "traditional elites" could include other (sub)elites not shown in the diagram

Source: Authors' elaboration.

area (e.g., local politicians from the *Movimiento al Socialismo* party in a specific municipality) and social organizations closely linked to the government. Ayo labels them the "influential elite." Besides their political power acquired through a democratic system, another important resource of the emerging elites (strategic and influential) is their well-established social networks formed through their membership in grass-roots organizations.

An interesting group that has arisen with the empowerment of the Morales administration consists of small farmers who have gained modest access to land and capital with the cultivation of soy. Many of them have achieved great success in their production and have become leaders at the local level. This has enabled them to hold positions such as mayors or heads of associations through which they have gained political influence in the central government, given that most of them are members of the *Movimiento al Socialismo* (Movement Towards Socialism, abbreviated as MAS) party. We call them "influential small soy farmers" and we categorize them as part of the strategic (sub)elite and thus part of the emerging elites. For clarification, these are the only actors within the soy sector who belong to the emerging elites.

The soy producers' biggest and most important association—the Oilseed and Wheat Producers Association (ANAPO)—has become a space in which members of the traditional elite and the emerging elite interact. This is because ANAPO has representatives both from the soy elite and among the influential small soy farmers. While the association has historically represented the traditional elites of Santa Cruz, its number of associates has increased and today the majority of its members can be identified as part of the influential small soy farmers. ANAPO encompasses about 14,000 producers of which 80 percent are small soy farmers owning approximately 50 hectares, while its largest producers own more than 1,000 hectares and account for about 2 percent of the associates (Pérez, 2007). Bolivia's largest producers of soy tend to avoid holding membership in ANAPO since they are obligated to pay a large percentage of their earnings in fees. The association generates 9 percent of the national gross domestic product (GDP), and has about US$1 billion in productive investment. It is part of the Round Table on Responsible Soy Association (RTRS) in which they exchange knowledge and create networks with soy producers and industrialists in neighboring countries and in the international market (Zeballos, 2012).

### The emerging elites

The emerging elites are often seen as an ethnic and political opposition force to the traditional elite, and as representing a radical political elite shift in Bolivia (Chaplin, 2010). The MAS party, which came to power in 2006, is a cluster of several grass-roots organizations that are critical to neoliberal reform. The main ideal that provides the different groups within MAS political identity is based on the premises of *Buen Vivir* ("Good Living"). *Buen Vivir* is an evolving concept based on indigenous worldviews and values; it is a pluralistic concept that includes a critique of the ideas of Western development and an alternative view of development and well-being in which the two can only be achieved in tandem, and in local communities, all with respect for cultural diversity and nature. In this way, the concept focuses on social groups that have been traditionally excluded in Bolivian history, most of whom are impoverished indigenous peoples.

The main motive that encouraged today's emerging elites to aim for a political shift has probably been their experience with neoliberal reforms since the mid 1980s. Even though the country had economically hit bottom during the first half of the 1980s after a chaotic period of military regimes and then the collapse of the center-left *Unidad Democrática y Popular* (UDP) government, the president that came to power in 1985 decided to implement a series of urgent changes towards economic liberalization. With the new reforms, the country got back on its feet as inflation reduced from 66 percent in 1986 to 17 percent in 1989, but the poor rural segments of society felt abandoned by the authorities as there was no possibility of maintaining the social benefits that the UDP party had announced. Social bonds were suspended, a massive closure of state owned mines caused unemployment to skyrocket, and cheap food imports resulted in a radical fall in the price of products traditionally sold by small-scale farmers. Thus, major rural poor social groups were forced to migrate to urban centers that could not offer adequate basic services, creating even further discontent (Kaup, 2013).

The emerging elites include individuals who used to represent or continue representing major national grass-roots organizations, the most important of which are the Bolivian Central Labor Union (COB), the Confederation of Rural Workers Association (CSUTCB) and the Six Coca Production Federations. They also consist of representatives from indigenous organizations such as the National Council of Ayllus and Markas from Qullasuyu (CONAMAQ), the Confederation of Intercultural Communities of Bolivia (CSCIB), the Confederation of Peasant Women "Bartolina Sisa" and the Confederation of Indigenous Peoples of Bolivia (CIDOB), all related to the National Coordinator for Change (CONALCAM). Furthermore, it has representatives from some urban social groups, such as several urban neighborhood councils and even from some sectors of the middle class, mainly from the western highlands.

Even though the above-mentioned organizations have a long history, their political empowerment only began during the mid 1990s as an effect of a law known as "Popular Participation" introduced by President Sánchez de Lozada in 1994. The law was designed to decentralize 20 percent of the national budget in all municipalities and it therefore encouraged local authorities and organizations to participate independently. The idea was to create a financial system that could attend to local needs more efficiently, but Chaplin (2010) argues that it was also made to politically undermine the main national social organizations by providing local leaders financial independence from authorities of the national movements. However, contrary to expectations, the new flow of money stimulated these national social movements since they already had a strong territorial basis and well-organized representation to which local leaders felt very committed. As a result, the representatives of the national movements and organizations began to participate in national politics and were empowered without the need of depending on the traditional political parties.

Finally, the emerging elites in Bolivia have a well-recognized international image due to their radical position in international forums. Their discourse is based on confronting capitalist forces forged by imperialistic countries—mainly referring to the United States—and they encourage other developing countries to also seek cultural and economic liberation. In this sense, their most recognized actions with respect to the environment are criticisms to global inconsistencies on environmental justice. The Morales government is thus seen as an example in the international sphere as a leader of environmental justice. In the same sense, but with respect to agricultural development, the government maintains a clear anti-genetically modified organism (GMO) discourse; a position that receives its greatest support from the Centre for Biosafety (GenØk), a research institution based in Norway.[1]

## The traditional elites

The traditional elites of Santa Cruz consist of members of local families belonging to the upper class. Although they mainly derive their income from the land, Plata (2008) argues that they can be characterized as business oriented. Thus, it is the commercial side of agricultural production that they value most. Their origins and power are linked to the commercialization of rubber in the late 1800s. The cultural values of these elite are in part explained by their historical association with mine owners who were based in the cities of the Andean highlands and who were the leading national elite at the end of the nineteenth century (Soruco, 2008). A common strategy among people who invested in rubber was to get involved in the business to earn money and connect with networks that could eventually enable them to invest in mining in the Andean highlands. Therefore, the use of land was already from the beginning influenced by a resource extraction mentality.

Since colonial times, the traditional elite has consisted of a significant foreign presence, and they have been appreciated by the local Santa Cruz society due to their crucial role in the rubber boom. The boom attracted mainly Europeans who were willing to invest and thus were well received by the local society. The foreigners used their commercial networks to maintain contact with the outside world, which was particularly valued, as the eastern areas of Bolivia had historically received little attention from the government. Around 70 years later, soy was introduced as a strategic way to continue attracting foreign investment and ensure relations with the international market and economic independence from the Bolivian government.

The soy elite emerged in the 1980s, and proved distinct from elites in other economic sectors due to its ability to survive and make a profit during the period of hyperinflation that Bolivia suffered between the years 1982 and 1985 (Pérez, 2007). They obtained their power mainly through land acquisition after the 1952 revolution and especially during Banzer's dictatorship in the 1970s. Nowadays, members of the soy elite have large, good quality landholdings in the rural Santa Cruz department. They mainly run their businesses from the department's capital city, Santa Cruz de la Sierra, where they often manage several other businesses simultaneously.

Most of the foreigners in Bolivia's soy elite today are Brazilians, but there are also many Argentineans, Colombians and Venezuelans (Urioste, 2011). There is also an already integrated group of Japanese small producers that arrived in the 1950s, and some isolated colonies of Mennonite immigrants that arrived in the 1960s who came from Mexico (Pérez, 2007). The Mennonites are not considered as part of the soy elite even though they hold an important portion of soy production, as shown in Figure 4.3, because of their self-imposed isolation from society, which means they have little influence on any political affair, both locally and nationally. Argentinean presence is increasing at a high rate, but they usually have temporary business interests and thus tend to only lease land.

During the 1980s Brazilians who were already involved in the soy business in Brazil became involved in Bolivia's soy industry as they were attracted by the low price of lands and lack of regulations. They have nowadays become fully integrated with the local elites, given that many have married into local families and are now in their second generation. Since their arrival, they have been recognized as bringing capital, technology and agronomic technology, and they are known for having the highest yields in soybean production (Mackey, 2011).

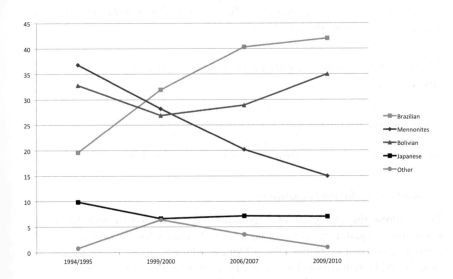

*Figure 4.3* Percentage area of cultivated soy in Bolivia (mainly Santa Cruz) by nationality or origin[2]

Source: Urioste (2011) and consultations with ANAPO's President Demetrio Perez and General Manager Rolando Zabala in 2013.

Additionally, Brazilians are appreciated because they are considered to be open-minded.[3] It should be added that on past occasions some Brazilian large-scale producers have been representatives on ANAPO's board, which reflects the extent of Brazilian participation in negotiations and decision-making, and thus governance of the sector.

Many Brazilians own and cultivate land in both Santa Cruz department and the Brazilian states of Mato Grosso and Mato Grosso do Sul, and travel back and forth between their businesses. They keep close relationships with institutions such as the Brazilian Enterprise for Agricultural Research Institution (EMBRAPA) and the Mato Grosso Foundation, a leading body working to improve agricultural production technologies in Brazil. However, the Bolivian Institute for Commercial Exports (IBCE) states that there has been a small decline in Brazilian investment possibly due to skepticism towards the Morales government discourse on sovereignty and legal uncertainty of the land titling process.[4]

Foreign activity in Bolivia's soy sector includes increased investment in companies that process and export soy, including transportation and market services. Some companies specialize in processing and exportation. The industrial products are the most competitive aspect of the Bolivian soy sector in the international market (Zeballos, 2012). Even though the capacity to process products in Bolivia is recognized as having the fastest growing industrialization rate in the region, the number of companies in Bolivia has decreased. Today they amount to only six companies in total, of which one is Peruvian (Fino), one American (ADM: Archer Daniels Midland Company), one European, one Bolivian–Venezuelan (previously Colombian) and two other smaller ones. The companies have been buying each other and therefore becoming fewer, especially during the last five to six years.

## The interaction between elites and their influence on governance

In the official discourse the traditional and emerging elites are often in opposition. However, in concrete policy making, these groups have shown that they can relate to each other in a rather pragmatic way. In the following, we discuss how this interaction began and what it meant in terms of environmental governance.

### Negotiations of the new constitution

To readdress the challenge of large landholdings owned by individuals and ensure more equal distribution of land for Bolivians, a land reform was initially promoted as a major priority by the Morales administration. It proclaimed that land should be redistributed to those who work it and need it the most. In 2006 the government launched a law named the Community Reorientation of the Agrarian Reform Law, in which large landholdings were considered an issue in urgent need for change. During past dictatorships, large areas of land had been given to people from the traditional elite of the lowland region as a strategy to encourage colonization and thus development in those areas (Pérez, 2007).

The governments of that time justified this action by stating the importance of promoting agricultural production among those who could demonstrate having the tools, skills and knowhow to perform the needed work. Even though this argument probably had some merit in a society where material access and education were not available to all, it was clearly biased to benefit the traditional elite and not the small-scale farmers of the region.

Nevertheless, in spite of calls for redistribution, the new constitution approved in 2009 by the MAS government did not challenge large landholdings, but instead gave legal rights to large landholders and endorsed future large landholdings, in contradiction to the stated intentions. Even though article 398 states that no person or associate can own more than 5,000 hectares, the constitution has other articles that enable owners of larger plots of land to maintain their property and even expand. This is mainly a result of the way in which the constitution is applied and the definition of the terms in which it was written. Katia Ferrufino, an independent Bolivian social–environmental researcher argues that: "The document that shows the greatest advancements and biggest contradictions of the Morales administration is ironically the document for which the government has fought the most and bases all its actions: the new constitution." This has several implications. First, article 399 in the new constitution declares that the new laws—as in the instance of large landholding restrictions—can only be applied from the date the constitution was ratified (January 2009). This implies that all large landholdings established before 2009 are indirectly legalized given that technically the law can only be applied to legal procedures which began from 2009 onwards. Thus, the government's attempt to ensure land redistribution instead resulted in endorsement of large landholdings. Second, article 315 states that there is no limit to the number of associates who together can administrate a larger piece of land, and provides no regulation of ways in which individual landholders can administrate land together. Consequently, a person who owns larger lands than permitted can distribute their holdings among members of their trust categorized as associates, each of which has an individual 5,000 hectare limit, and all without inhibiting the original landowner from continuing with business as usual. Such inconsistency in the law is mainly a result of the process of making the new constitution.

The articles referred to above were negotiated between the government and the political representatives of the traditional elite who lead the opposition. Articles 399 and 315 were included as a result of the negotiation even though more than 80 percent of the population had agreed through a national referendum to abolish large landholdings. Land rights are at the core of the traditional elites' interest since control over land has been their main power resource, and thus became the opposition's main focus in the negotiations. Although Morales won the national election, the opposition in Parliament was significant enough to force the government to include the addressed articles if the constitution was to be approved.

Nonetheless, the approval of the new constitution was a milestone for the Morales administration which had been struggling with internal dissent as well as a nationwide social conflict in the previous years. The first years of the Morales government were characterized by the direct confrontation between the government and several department leaders, including that of Santa Cruz. Each of them demanded their autonomy from the state and together they eventually formed what was called the Media Luna Region. One of the most contentious issues was that the Media Luna Region, which was led by the traditional elite based in the city of Santa Cruz de la Sierra, saw the Morales government as an obstacle for their activities linked to export of agricultural commodities. Since the most important of such commodities for this region is soy, the soy elite became an important social group, challenging the government from the very beginning.

Although tensions continued, the approval of the new constitution represented an example of another way in which both factions could achieve their political interests. After the approval of the new constitution and especially after Morales won the presidential election for a second term in December 2009, the opposition became increasingly divided and politically weak. The traditional elite was forced to search for new political strategies and thus adapt to a reality in which they could either continue to confront a government more directly or try to find common ground to negotiate their interests. Nowadays, even though there is still tension between the traditional elite and the emerging elite, the two factions have reached consensus and even cooperate on several issues. One of the results of such alignment has been the rapid increase in GM soy production.

### GM soy: the new consensus among the two elites

GM soy was first introduced in Bolivia illegally by the soy elite in the mid 1990s. It was brought from neighboring countries, mainly from Brazil but originally from Argentina, where GM soy had just been legalized as part of a technological package for agricultural development. The soy elite argued that Bolivia would never be able to compete in the international market without a conversion to GM soy, and that by not legalizing it the government would be provoking the emergence of an illegal market. Despite their clear and strong influence on government politics from the 1990s and until 2005 during the presidency of Rodríguez Veltzé, the soy elite was finally able to convince the government to legalize GM soy. However, legalization was criticized by several civil society groups as it did not follow the normal legal procedures, but was validated as a Supreme Decree. Nevertheless, the law only authorized the cultivation of GM soy for exportation and not for domestic use, and genetically modified production was only legalized for the production of soy and not other crops (Zeballos, 2012).

During the first years in government, the Morales administration was recognized for its efforts to support small soy farmers by ensuring their independence from agricultural companies managed by the traditional elite and linked to the international GM soy market. As a result, the state-owned Company for the Support of Food Production (EMAPA) was created, aiming to encourage the production of conventional soy during its first years of operation. Based on an agreement with Venezuela in 2006, EMAPA encouraged small-scale farmers to cultivate either organic or conventional soy. However, cultivating organic soy turned out to be almost impossible due to biological competition; besides, EMAPA was unable to deliver credits and supplies in time, causing big losses for farmers and thus creating distrust among small farmers in the market for conventional soy.

In an interview, Georgina Catacora, a Bolivian exchange researcher from SEED-GenØk, Norway, stated:

> Nowadays, [Bolivian] small-scale farmers grow GM soy because they do not have any other option ... Soy industrial companies, which almost all are in the hands of the elite, tend to keep small soy farmers in debt. The credits that they provide come with strict conditions, which are more favorable to the companies ... [However], the government has not been able to provide the needed infrastructure to maintain an alternative market.

The use of GM soy became increasingly popular as it was more cost efficient, easier to handle in the field and prices in the international market went up without differentiating between conventional or GM soy.[5] Furthermore, the supply companies and industries of the traditional elite in the GM soy market became known for their efficiency (delivering credits, supplying materials and giving technical support) and thus attracted almost all producers over time. As seen in the graph in Figure 4.4, by 2011 GM soy produced in Bolivia had reached

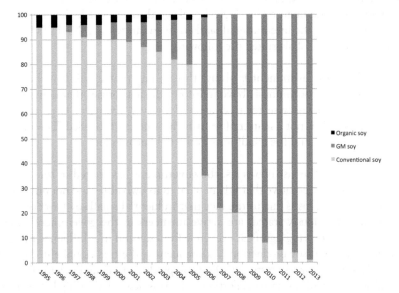

*Figure 4.4* Percentage distribution of different types of soy planted in Bolivia, 1995–2013

Source: Based on data published by Zeballos (2012) and consultations with ANAPO's President Demetrio Perez and General Manager Rolando Zabala in 2013.

92 percent of the total (Zeballos, 2012). Nowadays, even though some soy is marketed and sold under the label of conventional soy, the leaders of ANAPO state that GM soy has virtually replaced the remainder of conventional soy production due to the unchecked incursion of GM soy seeds into conventional soy fields.[6]

Article 409 in the new constitution states that all production, import and commercialization of GMOs will be regulated by law, which implies that GMOs are legal and their use depends on further governmental decision. As a first effort, the government created Law 144 for Communal Productive Revolution during 2011 with the aim of prohibiting the use of GMOs in crops. However, the prohibition is only for species that are native to Bolivia, thus it does not affect the use of GM soy, as soy is originally from China. Nevertheless, in 2012 the government launched a new law known as the Mother Earth Framework Law. This law was among other things designed to specifically prohibit all GM crops in Bolivia. However, the law is not entirely clear as to what that means. It states: "There shall be actions to gradually eliminate the use of those GM crops already authorized in the country." The word "gradually" provides flexibility and thus implies that there will not be a direct and concrete action to eliminate the use of GM crops, meaning that the law can allow it until the government decides not to.

Probably one of the reasons why GM soy is situated in perpetual legal limbo is because the government needs it as a political strategy to create space for negotiation with the traditional elite, and especially the soy elite. Besides land legislation, the legal status of GM soy is of crucial importance to the soy sector as it represents the main technological package through which they have been able to compete in the international market. In an interview, ANAPO's General Manager Rolando Zabala stated the following:

> The Morales government is always threatening that it will ban the use of GM soy. We continuously have to inform the authorities that doing so will cause the entire soy sector to collapse. However, sooner or later, they will realize that it is not a matter of wanting it or not. It is needed. The international context and the conditions in the field demand it.

However, during the last two years, the government has started to see GM soy production as an alternative that is beneficial to its own allies and not only to the traditional elite. This is due to the fact that influential small soy farmers, many of whom, as previously stated, are active members in the government's MAS party, are now receiving significant revenue from soy and thus influence the government to support soy production.[7] Consequently, the traditional elite benefits indirectly since their interests regarding soy production coincide with those of the influential small soy farmers. Furthermore, this new relationship between the influential small soy farmers (i.e., emerging elite) and the soy elite (i.e., traditional elite) has created the opportunity to exchange and thus understand each other's reality in a more comprehensive way.

The new relationship between the soy elite and the influential small soy farmers unites the traditional elites and emerging elites and enables a better organized soy sector to create new political strategies and thus find creative ways to influence policy making. For instance, ANAPO, which used to symbolize the traditional elite's power in agriculture, appointed an indigenous small soy farmer as its president in 2009. The president, Mr. Demetrio Pérez, is a migrant from the Bolivian Andes who became successful and gained influence through soy production. His designation contrasts with ANAPO's history of white European descendent leaders and is likely a strategic move, since Pérez is ethnically and socially closer to Evo Morales than ANAPO's previous leaders. Mr. Pérez, who is now in his second term, has been successful in creating a close relationship between ANAPO and the MAS government. ANAPO now has open access to the presidential palace and has frequent meetings with high ranking officials of the government.[8] As a result, ANAPO is increasingly becoming the main channel for the traditional elite to approach the government.

Another example of how the soy elite has taken direct part in the governance of the sector is the case of Mr. Reynaldo Chávez, one of Bolivia's five largest soy producers and the only one of them who is Bolivian by origin (the other four are Brazilian). Mr. Chávez was General Coordinator of the Program for Food Security Support in 2010. His position was under the direct guidance of the Ministry of Rural Development and Land, and thus had a strategic office within policy planning for rural affairs. In this political position, Mr. Chávez exercised an important role in the decision-making procedures of rural and agricultural development, while at the same time managing his own soy production. In an interview carried out for this research, he was asked whether his landholdings and production had complications for his position during that time, and responded:

> That was one of the reasons why I had to quit. I left the position because of the internal conflicts and focus on my business ... Even though I am no longer in that position, I still have very close contact with the Minister [of Rural Development and Land], she is one of my really good friends.

It is not clear to what extent members of the traditional elite are involved with the Morales administration. Cases such as Mr. Chávez's are seen as exceptions, but inclusion of new influential agro-industrial actors within the governmental sphere is increasing. One of the opposition's main critics of the Morales cabinet is that it lacks qualified professionals with technical expertise for agricultural development, since most of the people in high positions come from grass-roots organizations and small-scale farming, and usually have not had the opportunity for higher education. This might be one reason why the MAS government has seen the need to attract members of the traditional elite who usually have competitive academic credentials and more experience with agribusiness and agro-technology.[9]

## Environmental consequences of the new consensus: effects of the recent GM soy boom

The two most popular arguments used *against* GM soy cultivation are alleged negative environmental impacts (deforestation, biodiversity loss, soil erosion, and soil and water contamination, among others) and health risks (mainly physiological malfunctions). The arguments *supporting* GM soy are that it allows for more efficient production, higher economic gains and less environmental and health damage when compared to monocultures of conventional crops (Smale et al., 2012). Since most critics of GM soy are based in social organizations (RALLT, 2013), they are often accused of being only ideologically motivated and not scientifically informed. Those who support the production of GM soy are criticized for only considering studies that are financed by private companies, and not acknowledging the experience of rural communities who are unable to benefit from the GM soy business.

Given the lack of studies on Bolivia, most of the negative critiques of GM crops have been adopted from other countries such as Brazil, where social groups and environmental organizations have led a strong campaign against GMOs during the past decade. However, at least for the case of Bolivia, this perspective ignores an important fact about the context in which GM soy was introduced. While soy cultivation indeed is today's main cause of environmental impacts in the rural areas of Santa Cruz, most of the negative consequences were not originally caused by GM soy, but by conventional soy. This fact is important to address, given that the conversion to GM soy might have meant different environmental impacts for soy production than if it had not been introduced.

Soy production has been the main driver of environmental degradation in Bolivia since the mid 1990s. From the beginning of the soy boom, the deforestation rate has fluctuated between 200,000 and 350,000 hectares per year (Pedraza, 2011). Between 2000 and 2012, a forested area of 1,388,903 hectares was lost to agricultural activity—mainly soy production—in Santa Cruz department (FAN, 2012). The rapid expansion of soy cultivation is due to its economic benefits. One hectare of soy is on average 20 times more valuable than one hectare of forest cover within the conditions of the Bolivian market (Arias, 2013). A study published by the United Nations Development Programme (UNDP, 2008) shows that the agro-industrial actors involved in soy (soy elite) appear to be the group with the highest deforestation rate since the late 1990s, as seen in Figure 4.5. The study states that even though the graph only shows the rates until year 2000, the tendency among the agricultural industry is still the same, while other groups might have changed (such as Andean migrants, whose rate has likely increased).

Even though GM soy was grown illegally since the mid 1990s, it only became a significant portion of the total production after it was legalized a decade later, as shown in Figure 4.3. This means that most of the environmental impacts caused by soy during the 1990s, when the expansion rate of agricultural land peaked, were the result of conventional soy production and not GM soy. Environmental degradation of GM soy can only be affirmed after 2009, when it finally represented the

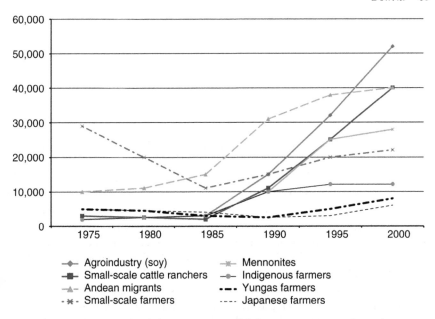

*Figure 4.5* Evolution of the deforestation rate of different economic and social groups in Bolivia (in hectares)

Source: UNDP (2008).

vast majority of soy production (90 percent), and thus became the main driver of agricultural expansion.

Nowadays, it is difficult to determine whether the expansion of cultivated land would have been the same without the introduction of GM soy. In 2009 higher profits from GM soy due to its high profitability may have motivated some farmers to expand further into the forest. However, economic motives for expansion are perhaps more related to steadily increasing soy prices in the international market than the advantages of GM soy cultivation per se. Thus, most new agricultural land cultivated with soy may have been soy regardless of the introduction of the GM variety.

The main concern about GM soy production is the negative environmental effects caused by Roundup Ready, an herbicide containing the chemical named glyphosate, produced by the chemical and agricultural biotechnology company, Monsanto. The most recognized studies against glyphosate were conducted by Séralini *et al.* (2012) and Antoniou *et al.* (2010). Both state that glyphosate can cause several kinds of physiological malfunctions in humans and animals. However, these studies have been criticized for not following scientific procedures and ignoring overwhelming scientific data of contradictory findings by several internationally recognized authors and institutions as compiled by Chassy and Brookes (2012) and the European Food Safety Authority (EFSA, 2012).

The World Health Organization (2010) considers glyphosate to have toxicity level III, meaning that it is slightly toxic but not dangerous to humans.

When comparing herbicide use, the production of conventional soy has greater negative environmental effects than GM soy (Bindraban *et al.*, 2009). First, this is due to the fact that conventional soy needs larger amounts of herbicides—a minimum of four to five rounds of chemical spray—while GM soy demands maximum three (Rovea, 2012). Second, measured by the likelihood of causing acute hazards in people, the herbicides used for GM soy are less dangerous than those used for conventional soy (see Table 4.1). Consequently, the introduction of GM soy implies a lesser environmental impact in terms of agrochemical toxins released than if soy would have continued to be produced only by conventional practices.

However, the term "acute hazard" in Table 4.1 only refers to those symptoms that are felt instantaneously or after short-duration exposure; in other words it does not consider consequences of long-term exposure.[10] It is also important to mention that Roundup Ready contains a series of other chemicals in smaller amounts also identified as toxic, but that are not well researched (Salazar and Aldana, 2011). Nevertheless, glyphosate is constantly watched by social and health organizations, which is positive given that it is a pesticide in increasing use across the globe. Yet, the problem is that the overwhelming attention on glyphosate tends to disregard other more toxic herbicides, such as paraquat, bentazon, 2,4-D (a major ingredient in Agent Orange) or trifluralin, which are all used for conventional soy without any restriction.

In any case, the concern points to the fact that over time producers are pressured to use more amounts of herbicide than originally prescribed as they are challenged by weeds that develop resistance to herbicides, either glyphosate or otherwise (Benbrook, 2012). However, the president of ANAPO, Mr. Demetrio Peres, argues that weeds develop resistance mainly because of wrong agricultural practices. If herbicides were used as prescribed, the problem would not be so great. Therefore, overuse of glyphosate can be harmful, just as with any other herbicide, and thus farmers need training in order to learn proper use.

*Table 4.1* World Health Organization classification of pesticides by hazard in percentage

| | Very hazardous | Hazardous | Moderately hazardous | Slightly hazardous | Unlikely acute hazard | Total |
|---|---|---|---|---|---|---|
| Conventional soy | 0.0 | 0.0 | 24.6 | 22.2 | 51.6 | 100 |
| GM soy | 0.0 | 0.5 | 13.1 | 13.1 | 73.3 | 100 |

Source: Paz-Ybarnegaray and Fernández-Montaño (2009).

Another issue is the practice known as "no-till" agriculture. GM soy does not require the farmer to till the soil, meaning that there is no need for mechanical intervention on the ground, as is often the case with conventional production. This is normally positive for the soil as no-till practice limits risk of erosion and further disruption of the soil's structure. Those who promote the use of GM soy often refer to the no-till practice as a positive aspect of GMOs. However, the no-till practice was already a very well used technique in conventional production during the 1990s in South America (Bindraban *et al.*, 2009). Therefore, while marketed as an opportunity to avoid tilling, it is not clear whether GM soy has made a difference in this regard in Santa Cruz when compared to recent conventional practices.

Finally, Bolivian soy cultivators gain an extra US$196 per hectare on their GM soy than they would if using conventional soy (ISAAA, 2013). If considering such net returns with the approximately one million hectares of GM soy produced in 2012, the benefits in total are around US$200 million. This surplus comes from a 30 percent increase in yield and 22 percent savings on herbicide costs. Yet, not all producers in Santa Cruz experience the technical and financial advantages of GM production, usually due to inadequate training and limited access to supplies and networks. For instance, small farmers tend to have limited access to credit, seeds and machinery.[11]

## Conclusions

Bolivia's political shift has not meant a major change in agricultural practice in the country's eastern lowlands. The main interests of the soy elite have been maintained while simultaneously meeting the interests of the emerging elite—despite their popular discourse. The GM soy model has become the main element for common ground between the two elites, which has enabled a reconciliation materialized through ANAPO. Therefore, this institution has turned into a strategic meeting place for multiple aspects of decision making for future agricultural development and thus environmental governance. Furthermore, even though the conversion of areas produced by conventional soy to GM soy means decreased use of pesticides (at least in the short term), it has certainly not meant a more sustainable production for the long run given its encouragement to expand the agricultural frontier over forested areas.

The alliance between the two elites was publicly established on July 11, 2013 when the agro-industrial leaders in Santa Cruz and the government agreed on critical decisions for the next decade. They agreed that the country's agricultural frontier should be expanded from the current 3 million hectares of productive land to 13 million hectares in 2025 (Fundación Tierra, 2013). Such an expansion was based on calculations of needed land to secure food production and secure sufficient land for the exportation of agricultural commodities. The agro-industrial elite committed to invest 3 billion dollars before 2025 and addressed its support for the government in its effort to accomplish the 13 pillars of the "Patriotic Agenda 2025."

As future expansion of the agricultural frontier is likely to be cultivated with GM soy, the discussion about the shift from conventional to GM becomes less relevant. Simultaneously it raises the debate on whether GM productivity for global demand can justify such expansion of the agricultural frontier. It can be worrisome, considering the increasing rate of deforestation. This is where the arguments supporting GM use for the benefit of the environment become contradictory. More efficiency, higher productivity and increased profits are unlikely to limit its expansion, and thus it presents an environmental threat. Consequently, the need for territorial regulation of agricultural activities, specifically in areas where GM soy is produced, is urgent. However, if the different political elites agree on a more intense production of soy, how much regulation can there be? Moreover, the real risk is if the government's double discourse strategy continues, because if so, there will be no specific guidance for proper land use.

In any case, if the soy sector is able to successfully produce soy with proper care for natural resources, the positive effects over time could be many. Increased income from small-scale soy farmers can benefit local society and thus the entire country through proper use of revenues, promoting equality. In the case that the traditional elites and the government do not find common ground and fail to avoid new conflicts, the tension could reduce business and development opportunities for the soy sector. The traditional elites will presumably continue to use their economic power to challenge the government using their capability to decide over the natural resources in their territory, while the government will continue using its popularity to abate any opposition. Nonetheless, as the new presidential elections approach in December 2014, it is possible that the traditional elites will decide to cooperate with the Morales government, which at the moment seems likely to be re-elected for five more years.

## Notes

1  Information provided by Maria Mercedes Roca, Professor at Zamorano University. Date of interview: January, 2013. Santa Cruz, Bolivia.
2  Note that these numbers do not consider Argentinean activity since they represent owned, not leased land.
3  In an interview, Mr. Reynaldo Chavez, a Bolivian landholder who produces 50,000 hectares/year, stated that "We use a technological package that was introduced by the Brazilians, our neighbors ... The Brazilians are very helpful and supportive. Even though they gather in somewhat closed societies, they are open-minded."
4  Information provided by Gary Antonio Rodríguez Álvarez, General Manager, IBCE. Date of interview: February, 2013. Santa Cruz, Bolivia.
5  Information provided by Miguel Ángel, Crespo, General Manager, PROBIOMA. Date of interview: February, 2013. Santa Cruz, Bolivia.
6  Such incursion usually happens during the transportation of seeds.
7  Information provided by Georgina Catacora, Researcher at GenØk. Date of interview: March, 2013. Florianopolis, Brazil.
8  Information provided by Demetrio Pérez, President of ANAPO. Date of interview: January, 2013. Santa Cruz, Bolivia.
9  Information provided by Reynaldo Chavez Gutierrez. Large scale producer. Date of interview: February, 2013. Santa Cruz, Bolivia.

10  See www.epa.gov/oswer/riskassessment/rcra_acute.htm.
11  Information provided by Miguel Ángel, Crespo, General Manager, PROBIOMA. Date of interview: February, 2013. Santa Cruz, Bolivia.

## References

Antoniou, M., Brack, P., Carrasco, A., Fagan, J., Habib, M., Kageyama, P., Leifert, C., Onofre Nodari, R. and Pengue, W. (2010) *GM SOY Sustainable? Responsible?* GLS Gemeinschaftsbank GARGE Gentechnik-frei Bochum, Germany.

Arias, S. (2013) Tierra agroindustrial aporta 20 veces más que la forestal. *Los Tiempos*, November 15.

Ayo, D. (2012) Nuevas élites económicas y su inserción en la política. Working Paper No. 01. Foro de Desarrollo Friedrich Ebert Stiftung Fundación Boliviana para la Democracia Multipartidaria, La Paz, Bolivia.

Benbrook, C. M. (2012) Impacts of genetically engineered crops on pesticide use in the US—the first sixteen years. *Environmental Sciences Europe*, available at www.enveurope.com/content/24/1/24.

Bindraban, P. S., Franke, A. C., Ferraro, D. O., Ghersa, C. M., Lotz, L. A. P., Nepomuceno, A., Smulders, M. J. M. and Vande Wiel, C. C. M. (2009) *GM-Related Sustainability: Agro-ecological Impacts, Risks and Opportunities of Soy Production in Argentina and Brazil.* Plant Research International, Wageningen University.

Chaplin, A. (2010) *Movimientos sociales en Bolivia: De la fuerza al poder.* Oxford University Press and *Community Development Journal*, Oxford, UK.

Chassy, B. and Brookes, G. (2012) A critical assessment of the paper "GM Soy: Sustainable? Responsible?". University of Illinois and PG Economics UK.

EFSA—European Food Safety Authority (2012) Review of the Séralini *et al.* (2012) publication on a 2-year rodent feeding study with glyphosate formulations and GM maize. NK603 Food and Chemical Toxicology.

FAN—Fundación Amigos de la Naturaleza-Bolivia (2012) Mapa de deforestación de las tierras bajas y yungas de Bolivia. Asociación para la Biología de la Conservación, La Paz, Bolivia.

Fundación Tierra (2013) *Estudios de caso sobre tierra y producción de alimentos en Bolivia.* Informe Fundación TIERRA 2012, La Paz, Bolivia.

ISAAA—The International Service for the Acquisition of Agri-biotech Applications (2013) Biotech Facts & Trends, Bolivia.

Kaup, B. Z. (2013) *Market Justice: Political Economy Struggle in Bolivia.* Cambridge University Press, New York.

Mackey, L. (2011) *Legitimating Foreignization in Bolivia: Brazilian Agriculture and the Relations of Conflict and Consent in Santa Cruz, Bolivia.* Department of Planning, University of California, Los Angeles, CA.

Paz-Ybarnegaray, R. P. and Fernández-Montaño, W. (2009) *Best Practices for Assessing the Social and Economic Impact of Using GM Crops by Small Farmers: The Bolivian Case Using Glyphosate-Resistant Soybean.* Cochabamba, Bolivia.

Pedraza, R. (2011) *Serie de Investigación de estado ambiental Informe de estado ambiental del departamento de Santa Cruz 2010.* Lida de Defensa del Medio Ambiente LIDEMA, La Paz, Bolivia.

Pérez, M. (2007) *No Todo Grano que Brilla es Oro Un análisis de la soya en Bolivia.* CEDLA, La Paz, Bolivia.

Plata, W. (2008) *El Discurso Autonomista de las Élites de Santa Cruz: Los Barones del Oriente El poder en Santa Cruz ayer y hoy.* Fundación TIERRA, Santa Cruz, Bolivia, 101–166.

RALLT—Network for a Transgenic Free Latin America (2013) At almost two decades from the introduction of GM crops in Latin America GM Free Latin America Open Letter to High Commissioner for Human Rights. Special Procedures of the United Nations.

Rovea, A. (2012) Estudio comparativo de la soja convencional y la genéticamente modificada para Argentina, Brasil, Paraguay y Uruguay Evolución y agronomía. Secretaría de Agricultura, Ganadería y Pesca, IICA Reporte de consultoría, Buenos Aires, Argentina.

Salazar, N. J. and Aldana, M. L. (2011) Herbicida Glifosato: Usos, toxicidad y regulación. *Revista de Ciencias Biológicas y de la Salud*, Universidad de Sonora, 23–28.

Séralini, G. E., Clair, E., Mesnage, R., Gress, E., Defarge, N., Malatesta, M., Hennequin, D. and Spiroux de Vendômois, J. (2012) Long term toxicity of a Roundup herbicide and a Roundup-tolerant genetically modified maize. *Food and Chemical Toxicology*, 50, 4221–4231.

Smale, M., Zambrano, P., Paz-Ybarnegaray, R. and Fernández-Montaño, F. (2012) A case of resistance: Herbicide-tolerant soybeans in Bolivia AgBioForum. *The Journal of Agrobiotechnology Management and Economics*, available at www.agbioforum.org/v15n2/v15n2a07-smale.htm.

Soruco, X. (2008) *De la Goma a la Soya: El Proyecto Histórico de la Élite Cruceña Los Barones del Oriente El poder en Santa Cruz ayer y hoy.* Fundación TIERRA, Santa Cruz, Bolivia, 1–95.

UNDP—United Nations Development Program (2008) Informe Temático sobre Desarrollo Humano: La otra frontera Usos alternativos de los recursos naturales en Bolivia.

Urioste, M. (2011) *Concentration and "Foreignisation" of Land in Bolivia.* Fundación TIERRA, La Paz, Bolivia.

World Health Organization (2010) The WHO recommended classification of pesticides by hazard and guidelines to classification: 2009 International Program on Chemistry and Safety IPCS Cooperative agreement: FAO, UNEP, ILO, UNIDO, UNITAR, WHO and OECD.

Zeballos, H. (2012) *Bolivia: Desarrollo del Sector Oleaginoso 1980–2010: Comercio Exterior n-7.* Instituto Boliviano de Comercio Exterior (IBCE), Santa Cruz, Bolivia.

# 5 Argentina

## Government–agribusiness elite dynamics and its consequences for environmental governance

*Joaquín Zenteno Hopp, Eivind Hanche-Olsen and Héctor Sejenovich*

## Introduction

The debate about environmental aspects of the genetically modified (GM) soy production model in Argentina has been weak, given the overwhelming public acceptance of the technological package as a development strategy. The biotechnology hegemony thesis presented by Newell (2009) states that such a situation is due to the dominance of an agribusiness elite that has effectively excluded opposition, especially environmental considerations, through persuading public opinion at all levels. Moreover, the argument of the existence of such hegemony is based on how the agribusiness elite use their resources (material, institutional and discursive) to influence the Argentinean government.

The biotechnology hegemony thesis, however, overlooks significant aspects about the agribusiness elites' features. First, it does not address properly the variety and thus difference between different subgroups of elites within the agribusiness elite. And thus, second, it does not reflect the range of dynamics that exist between these elites as they interact with the government. By presenting a more nuanced analysis of the agribusiness elite, several aspects about the dynamics created by the interaction of different actors in the environmental governance of the soy sector are made visible and their differences are better addressed.

Our findings show that it is possible to distinguish interesting attitudes, discourses and/or type of decisions about which and when certain subgroups of the agribusiness elite have a different position on the environmental debate. Furthermore, we find different points of consensus that have been developed between the different elites within the agribusiness elite and the government about key issues related to the soy sector. We thus offer a more detailed perspective allowing an analysis about crucial features of environmental governance related to GM soy production in Argentina.

This chapter will focus specifically on the relationship between the Kirchner administrations and the elites related to the GM soy model. The arguments presented here are based on a review of secondary sources and on fieldwork conducted in the region of Santa Fe during 2012. The research is supported by interviews with researchers located in Buenos Aires and representatives of Argentinean agricultural organizations.

## The importance and the development of the GM soy model

Over the last two decades, Argentinean agriculture has gone through a profound transformation resulting in an explosive expansion of cultivation of GM soy (Figure 5.1). GM soy was introduced in the country in 1996 and came with a technological package that enabled farmers to produce soy in a cheaper and less labor-intensive way, and with high profitability. It soon expanded from the Pampa region to large parts of the country, currently occupying approximately 22 million hectares which is between 50 and 60 percent of all the cultivated land in Argentina (USDA, 2013).

The production of GM soy generates approximately one tenth of the GDP and one fourth of the nation's export value (Loman, 2013). The main places to which GM soy is exported are the European Union and Asia. About 80 percent of the total production is industrialized soybean oil and soybean meal; just 18 percent is exported as soybean, and the remaining 2 percent is exported as other derivatives. From these exports, the government receives through taxes 35 percent of the income from grain and 32 percent from soybean oil (Calvo *et al.*, 2011).

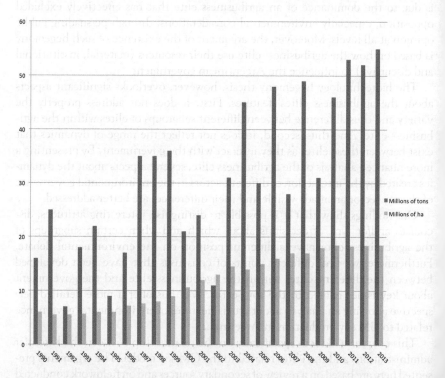

*Figure 5.1* Evolution of soy production in million tons (without differentiating GM soy and non-GM), and area of expansion of soy production in Argentina

Source: Authors' own compilation, based on IICA (2013) and ArgenBio (2013).

Even though Argentina is the third largest exporter of soybean in the world, it is number one in exporting soybean oil with 4.3 million tons, and number one in soybean meal exports with 30.4 million tons (USDA, 2013).

As Figure 5.2 shows, the conversion from conventional soy to GM soy was completed in less than two decades. Trigo (2011) states that the conversion to the GM soy model generated a net value of US$65,435 million for Argentina between 1996 and 2010 due to savings in costs and higher profitability. Furthermore, it has enabled consumers to save US$89,000 billion due to its capability to reduce the price of foods made with soy.

The GM soy model consists of the use of soy seeds that have been genetically modified to survive a herbicide known as Roundup Ready that kills all other plants, allowing the soy plant to grow without virtually any competition for space, nutrients, water or sun. There is therefore no need to plough or harrow the soil for weed control, which is why the GM soy producers consider the no-till method as part of the model. Conventional soy, on the other hand, refers to the production of soy using any available method that assures a profitable production without having to use GM seeds. It consequently involves the use of different types of agrochemicals, soil management techniques and mechanization.

## The diversity of elites in the GM soy model

We use the diagram presented in Figure 5.3 to identify different clusters of actors with varying degrees of power in the soy sector by distinguishing the actors who

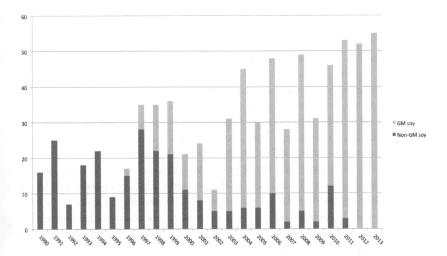

*Figure 5.2* Evolution of GM soy and conventional soy in Argentina in millions of tons and presented as percentage of the total amount

Source: Authors' own compilation, based on ArgenBio (2013).

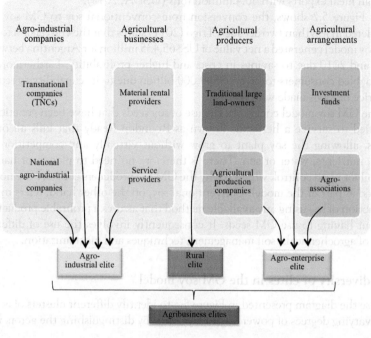

*Figure 5.3* Elites formed by the combination of different groups (darker squares) belonging to different agricultural sectors related to the soy industry in Argentina

Source: Author's own compilation, based on Bustamante and Maldonado (2009).

are recognized as the most influential in each group. As shown in the figure, each sector and its associated actors can be defined by its control over different kinds of resources (either economic, political, organizational, symbolic or social networks, as discussed in Chapter 2), allowing a useful classification of elites involved in the soy industry in Argentina. For instance, the agro-industrial companies are known for their major investments in property assets and material goods, either for processing or developing inputs. The agricultural businesses are well known for their extended social networks given that they provide services to entities of all sizes and locations in the country. The agricultural producers are mainly known for their land acquisitions, either because they are owners or because they are bounded to them by management contracts with landowners. Finally, the agricultural arrangements are known for their high investments in the management of large-scale production.

The definitions of the three groups of elites shown in Figure 5.3 ("agro-industrial elite," "rural elite" and "agro-enterprise elite") are related to how the addressed resources are demarcated for each agricultural sector. However, this does not mean that such resources are the only elements that characterize each elite, but rather serve as indicators to identify them. Thus, as will be discussed further in this section, each elite is characterized by a complex combination of different resources. The plural term "agribusiness elites" refers to all the elites related to the GM soy industry, which means the sum of the three addressed elites.

The "agro-industrial elite" is formed by transnational companies (TNCs) or national firms dedicated to agricultural activities, either distributing inputs, processing grains, transporting agricultural products and/or exporting agricultural commodities. The resources that define them as an elite are their capacity to invest large funds in industrial production, their large national and international networks, and their specialized knowledge related to their activity in agro-industrial processes. Their political power is generally recognized, given that they have a long relationship with the government, beginning with the neoliberal reforms of Menem in the 1990s, which is why the biotechnology hegemony thesis tends to refer to them as the main group of power behind the GM soy sector.[1]

Foreign companies have traditionally played an important role in the development of the agricultural sector in Argentina through the import of machinery, seeds and herbicides.[2] Therefore, it is common to believe that the agro-industrial elite is only formed by TNCs, but this is not true as national companies also have a large presence. As shown in Figure 5.4, even though three of the largest companies dedicated to industrialization of soybean oil production are TNCs, national agro-industrial companies have an important share in the market. In the soybean oil sector, national companies are responsible for more than half of the soy industrialization in the country and have a high number of industrial facilities (Schavarzer and Tavosnanska, 2007). Their economic growth has been stable and they are among the clusters within the soy sector that were most benefited by recent governments. In any case, both transnational and national companies are allied with private biotechnology firms, large national commercial banks and some Argentinean state institutions (Loredo, 2013).

An important characteristic of the agro-industrial elite is its overwhelming influence on the media for marketing purposes. Their impact on society is illustrated by how they are able to convince the media (television, newspapers and radio) to back up their positions. Based on a study of the two main newspapers of the country (*La Nación* and *El Clarín*), Newell (2009) argues that the media continuously address the advantages of biotechnology use, especially as a result of the TNC lobby. The media backs up the companies' positions in the main debates and discredits those who present counter arguments. There are very few newspapers that present the other side of the soy discussion; just *Página 12* and its associate magazine *Veintitrés* have presented some critical views (Motta and Alasino, 2013).

Since the agro-industrial elite is a heterogeneous group, their approach towards sustainable practices can vary and therefore their ability to adopt new practices might be more flexible than what is usually believed. Their search for lower impact products, logistical efficiency or any other environmentally friendly practice depends on several factors such as national legislation, interests of customers and producers or other market related matters. Consequently, besides the

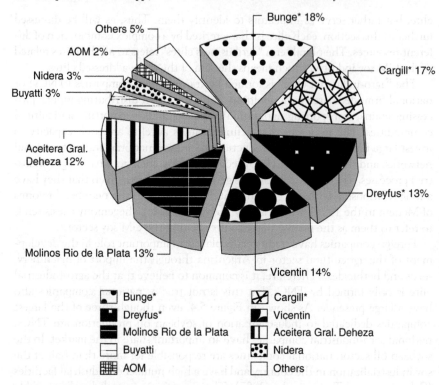

*Figure 5.4* Companies dedicated to soybean oil production and exportation, presented as a percentage of the whole sector

Source: Based on Schavarzer and Tavosnanska (2007) and CIARA (2011).

firms that specialize in the GM soy model, the agro-industrial elite does not necessarily depend on it and can therefore adapt to new circumstances if the market demands it and the profits are appealing.

Major associations representing the interests of the agro-industrial elite are the Argentine Forum of Biotechnology (FAB), the Argentine Seed Association (ASA) and the Association of the Production Chain for Soy (ACSOJA). All these associations are formed by major national companies and TNCs, but also include governmental institutions such as the National Institute for Agricultural Technology (INTA). The main idea behind all these associations is to integrate the production chain into the expansion of soy consumption, enhance research and discuss the use of new technological advancements. These associations are also important due to their direct role in representing the agro-industrial elite in meetings with governmental officials (Greenpeace, 2004).

The term "rural elite" refers to the traditionally powerful groups in rural Argentina that have owned large portions of land for several generations, mostly in the Pampa region, but also in other areas. During the nineteenth and first half of the twentieth centuries, large landowners were recognized as the major socio-economic elite of Argentina. The main entity representing them was the *Sociedad Rural Argentina* (SRA, or Rural Society of Argentina), created in 1866 by the most powerful landlords of the country, consisting of about 344 families who owned the entire Pampa region—about 11 million hectares in total. Controlling such large amounts of land allowed them to accumulate considerable capital from the export of agricultural commodities, mainly to the United Kingdom. Since then the rural elite has continually tried to influence the political scene in different ways, supporting some governments and dictatorships or directly confronting others. However, the economic power of the rural elite was to some extent limited between the 1940s and the 1990s when soy production strengthened the rural sector once again (Tedesco and Picardi de Sastre, 2001).

As expected, the general interest of the rural elite is to maintain their land-ownership, since it is their main resource and source of power. However, the GM soy model remains within their interests in condition to their land ownership rather than due to the advantages of the GM soy package per se. Thus, they may have a stronger tendency to consider environmental issues since they depend on the productivity of their land. Their reasons for using the GM soy model are not only based on economic concerns but also due to the sustainability of their practice for long-term investments.

Nonetheless, an interesting aspect when analyzing the characteristics of agricultural landowners, from small-scale to large-scale farmers is not only that the production of GM soy is more common, but also the level of dependency on a third party land manager (Moreno, 2011). This is because most of today's land is not managed by landowners themselves, but by a third party known as agricultural producers who either rent from landowners or serve as contractors that manage the land. Whereas years ago the countryside was dominated by large landowners and peasants, today these third party agricultural producers are among the most important economic groups (Barsky and Fernández, 2008).[3] Thus, while land ownership has not become more concentrated during the soy boom, there has been a shift in the management of land. The development of a larger market of lands for rent has contributed to make these arrangements more common.

Consequently, the most important actors with economic and political power in present-day rural Argentina are agricultural producers utilizing a management model in which several individuals or companies have different roles in the system, from renting land from landowners, to administering external investments and managing the total production (Benchimol, 2008). This group is commonly referred to as "agro-enterprise"; however, it is difficult to define since there is no legal definition of it, and so it can have a great variety of forms. In general, agro-enterprises combine several agreements where landowners, contractors and investment brokers are involved. For example, the agreements take the form of investment funds, agro-associations (in Spanish known as "pools de siembra"), financial trust coalitions, and simple contract alliances, among others. At present, agro-enterprises are responsible for about 70 percent of total grain production and are known for their expansion into other provinces of Argentina since land is usually 20 to 50 percent cheaper in the northern part of the country compared to the Pampa region (Barri and Wahren, 2009).

Thus, the term "agro-enterprise elite" refers to a new group of people who control the major entities involved in a type of business that rents several pieces of land for large soy production, this enables them to control most of the productive land at present and thus obtain higher benefits from soy exports without owning the land. The main resource that defines the agro-enterprise elite is the capital that they are able to invest in large-scale GM soy production. Through these capital investments the agro-enterprise elite is able to exert considerable influence over production decisions taking place in large-scale landholdings. Thus the relationship between this elite and the land is mediated through their investments in land rent and production. As shown in Figure 5.3, the agro-enterprise elite is composed of the agricultural arrangements sector and agricultural production companies from the agricultural producers sector.

Some of the most recognized groups that form part of the agro-enterprise elite are Cresud, Adecoagro, Los Grobo Group, Lartirigoyen, El Tejar, Cazenave & Asoc., MSU, Olmedo and Liag, which combined manage more than a million hectares of land planted with soy. Most agro-enterprises are formed by university-educated people who are well connected to the agribusiness sector, and are recognized for their productivity and high technical capacity. They have wide access to information about market prices, trends and the newest technology in the agricultural sector. The agro-enterprises work through what is known as network agriculture, meaning that they tend to be connected within synchronized social systems, which are an advantage for the professional management of the business (Murphy and Grosso, 2012).

The agro-enterprise elite has been criticized for not having direct contact with rural areas since they only administer the lands as a commodity, while leaving the production in charge of local workers. They have also been accused of resembling the management pattern of mining activities since they tend to have a narrow investment–extraction–profit mentality, without direct attachment to the implied natural resources or the need to address long-term agricultural production (FNC, 2008). It is clear that the agro-enterprise elite are completely dependent on large-scale monocropping of GM soy—the main source of their current power. Consequently, and especially because they do not depend directly on the land on which they produce, they are not concerned with sustainability.

Both the agro-enterprise elite and the rural elite are together involved in several of the same associations. In many cases this is due to the fact that several individuals of the agro-enterprise elite have close social ties to the rural elite, either because of family or business relationships. As seen in Figure 5.5, the most recognized associations in which the agro-enterprise elite participate are the Argentinean No-Till Farm Association (AAPRESID) and the Argentinean Association of Regional Consortiums for Agricultural Experimentation (AACREA). Pérez (2013) states that AAPRESID has had a major role in driving agricultural producers to become business entities by promoting professionalism

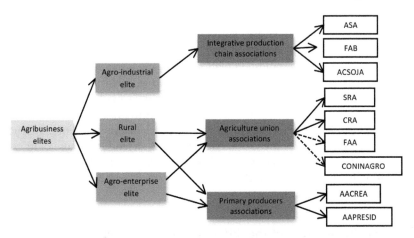

*Figure 5.5* Associations of political importance for GM soy production in Argentina and their relation to the different elites; FAA and CONINAGRO (dotted arrows) are not considered to be directly related to the agribusiness elites, as will be explained later in this section

Source: Authors' own elaboration.

and entrepreneurship. Nevertheless, it must be mentioned as well that some individuals of the agro-enterprise elite are also becoming part of the agro-industrial elite. For instance Gustavo Grobocopatel, popularly known as the "Soy King" and owner of Los Grobo Group, is one of the individuals who has great experience inventing in agricultural companies and is now owner of Bioceres, a major biotechnology firm.

The political participation of many powerful stakeholders from the sectors related to the production of GM soy, and thus all the addressed elites, is formally performed through agricultural unions. Thus, the main agricultural unions of Argentina at present are few and known to have great political influence. They have clear characteristics that differentiate them, but the social antagonism at the beginning of the twentieth century in which they were founded has now diminished and has become less evident (Tedesco and Picardi de Sastre, 2001). The previously mentioned SRA and the Rural Confederation of Argentina (CRA) are known to have the wealthiest landowners or managers, and are therefore formed by the rural elite and the agro-enterprise elite. Two other important unions are the Agrarian Federation of Argentina (FAA) and the Inter-Cooperative Agrarian Confederation (CONINAGRO), which are known to have small- and medium-scale capital; however, some individuals of the agro-enterprise elite are more involved with these associations than with SRA or CRA due to their family and social backgrounds. These four associations have proven capable of mobilizing enormous amounts of people and resources throughout the entire country, allowing them independence and affording them influence when any political or economic decision is being made.

Given that the addressed unions are not unique to an elite but rather formed by a combination of them and several non-elite groups, their approach towards the environment is based on the political agenda of the moment. This means that they do not have a pre-established platform as many other social organizations have. Environmental issues, for instance, are seen as themes for consideration rather than a main focus. All of the associations are in favor of the GM soy model because of the immediate advantages they represent to producers, members and industries regardless of being part of an elite or not. However, the unions as such do not depend directly on the GM model, thus they defend it because of its current importance to the market but not because they are directly associated with it. Their political strategies can therefore change once there are other aspects to consider in future circumstances.

## The changing position of the different agribusiness elites before the Kirchner administrations

Large-scale production of soy was initially led by the rural elite and was the result of a process of agricultural intensification, in Argentina known as *agriculturización* or "agriculturization", where, in addition to the introduction of technology for agricultural production, livestock range was converted into agricultural lands. *Agriculturización* was needed due to the effect of national economic restraints, the development of the Green Revolution and the lack of agricultural subsidies during the 1970s and 1980s (Vara *et al.*, 2012). Soy was a good alternative for such an intensification process because, even though prices were not high, it allowed producers to intercrop wheat in the same land during the same season, since both crops can be produced one after the other, thus providing higher income in a shorter time. Thus when the 1990s came, soy production was already important in Argentina, but it was not until the mid 1990s and parallel to the introduction of GM soy, that production of soy took off, as seen in Figure 5.1.

When the neoliberal government of Carlos Menem took power in Argentina in 1989, it took over a country with high debts and a great need to enhance industrialization schemes. The loans given to the military junta during the 1980s by the World Bank, IMF and Club de Paris and the financial chaos that emerged after the first period of democracy between 1983 and 1989, generated several financial disturbances. The central idea of Menem's government was based on the notion that the only way to get out of debt was to exploit the country's natural resources for exportation and fill the gap left by the decline in manufacturing of goods during the 1970s with agricultural production. Thus, in 1991 the agribusiness model was created by the deregularization of agricultural production by decree 2284/91.[4]

During Menem's administration, export taxes were eliminated and special export facilities were given to Southern Common Market (MERCOSUR) countries. Therefore, through the 1990s, the agro-industrial elite became a close ally of the government as large companies were encouraged to invest and expect a future with greater opportunities. In the same way, but not only because of investment openings, the rural elite saw Menem as a new opportunity for securing their interest in land. The introduction of the GM soy model strengthened these relations as it provided both elites with opportunities to secure their economic power to maintain their resources over time (Calvo *et al.*, 2011). However, the GM soy model was also praised because of important environmental factors.

When the GM soy model was introduced by the rural elite, it was presented as a means to decrease the environmental impacts caused by the production of conventional soy. This was urgent given that during the 1980s the main problem for agriculture in all of Argentina, especially in the Pampa region, was soil erosion due to poor soil management practices (Pincen *et al.*, 2010). GM soy was encouraged since it minimizes manipulation of the soil. The amount of soil cover loss by no-till is only 2 tons per hectare, while soil degradation from conventional soy production with plowing can reach as much as 19–30 tons per hectare (Del Río, 2012).

The GM soy model was also introduced because even though it is entirely based on the use of an herbicide (glyphosate), it prevents the use of other agrochemicals applied in conventional production and known to be more toxic (Bindraban *et al.*, 2009). Moreover, conventional soy needs larger amounts of herbicides—a minimum of four to five rounds of chemical spray—while GM soy demands a maximum of three (Rovea, 2012). As Figure 5.6 shows, the use of other herbicides for conventional soy production (paraquat, bentazon, 2,4-D or trifluralin) decreased over time as GM soy became more popular. However, GM

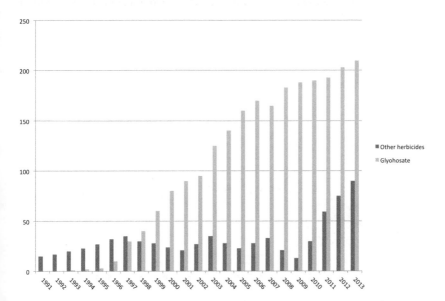

*Figure 5.6* Evolution of the consumption of glyphosate in Argentina in millions of liters

Source: Based on data taken from Ramirez (2010); Trigo (2011); Moltoni (2012).

soy production has recently shown the need for other herbicides besides glypho-sate due to the development of resistance of competing weeds.[5]

At the end of Menem's administration in 1999 the relationship between the rural elite and the government changed. To mitigate the economic crisis caused by the increase of the national debt, Argentina tried to focus on increasing the production of agricultural commodities for the international market, but the rural elite did not have the resources—either technical or economic—to boost soy pro-duction to fulfill the level required by the government. This opened an opportunity for the emergence of the agro-enterprise elite, given the advantages that this group had in terms of finances, contacts and reduced costs due to technology use and the possibility to manage larger-scale production. In some occasions, as Cristina Fernández de Kirchner once mentioned in a public speech, the profitability of the agro-enterprise elite could sometimes be as high as 30 percent per year.[6]

The GM soy model provided a unique opportunity for economic empow-erment to all producers, but especially to the agro-enterprise elite, because of several reasons. First, profits of GM soy increased because it enables 15 percent savings when compared to conventional soy production (Del Río, 2012). Seed prices were kept down since Monsanto was prevented from patenting their seeds because the original gene had already been released by a third company. Furthermore, the price of glyphosate decreased from US$10 per liter in 1990 to US$3 per liter in 2000 due to the end of the patent contract (Penna and Lema, 2003). Second, while production costs for GM soy were low, soy prices at the international market increased without distinction between GM soy and con-ventional soy. Soy prices have mainly increased, as seen in Figure 5.7; the highest

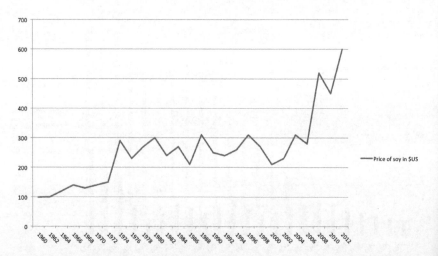

*Figure 5.7* Evolution of the international soybean price

Source: Based on data taken from MINAGRI (2011).

price of soy occurred the last week of July 2012, reaching US$618 per ton—about three times the price in 2000. Thus, the total benefit from the reduction of production costs due to the shift from conventional to GM soy from 1996 until 2011 had been US$3,519 million (Trigo, 2011).

During the beginning of the 2000s and as the crisis got worse, the government was unable to focus on the agricultural sector and let many agricultural support programs decline, even though it had once been portrayed as the main strategic element for economic growth. The budget of INTA was reduced to a point that it became financially unmanageable; the two main programs for the agricultural sector, known as Rural Change and Agriculture Social Program, were neglected (Barsky and Fernández, 2008). Thus, the soy sector was left alone to develop without much control from the authorities and thus all the agribusiness elites were strengthened. As a result, and because of the great revenues from agricultural commodities, the agro-enterprise elite became particularly powerful since it was able to expand as small- and medium-scale farmers were forced to sell their lands due to the crisis.

## Dynamism between elites and their first encounters with the Kirchner governments

Richardson (2009) suggests that the inauguration of the Kirchner era in 2003 with president Néstor Kirchner meant the beginning of an export-oriented populist era. This new political orientation favored the urban population through taxation of the increasing production and export of agricultural commodities, particularly GM soy. In contrast to the old populism in Argentina which rejected the rural sector, the Kirchner governments are increasingly dependent on income from agricultural production to carry out their redistributive policies and for securing support from the popular segment of the urban population. Therefore, the elites related to the GM soy sector have a very different relationship with the government than in previous years. However, such a relationship varies from one type of elite to another.

One of the first moves of Néstor Kirchner was a deal with the IMF in which 40 percent of the total repayment of the economic crisis would come from taxes on exports of soy and its derivatives (Joensen *et al.*, 2005). The government declared that the idea was to use a tax on the exportation of soy to finance poverty reduction strategies in the country, but the main procedures to do this were not clear, thus, a sense of distrust emerged among the entire soy sector, uniting all the elites against the government. However, this unification was broken when Néstor rejected the intellectual property rights law that would have given the agro-industrial elite the right to control their seeds and demand royalties. However, after strong pressuring from the agricultural union associations, the government chose to support Argentinean producers and adopted Law 20247, known as the Seeds Law, which allowed farmers to store and continue reproducing their own seeds. This enabled the creation of the seed black market, known in Argentina as "bolsa blanca." As seen in Figure 5.8, this initiative permitted

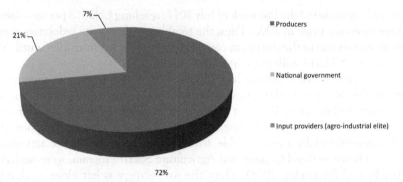

7%

21%

■ Producers

■ National government

■ Input providers (agro-industrial elite)

72%

*Figure 5.8* Distribution of cumulative benefits generated by GM soy from 1996 until 2010

Source: Based on data taken from Trigo (2011).

producers (especially the agro-enterprise elite) to obtain most of the commercial benefits of GM soy in previous years (Trigo, 2011).

Nonetheless, the government of Néstor Kirchner did favor the agro-industrial elite on some occasions. For instance, as soy became a tactical element for development, a boom of soybean industries emerged to the point that the total amount of soy produced in the country was not enough for the industry, forcing them to import soy from neighboring countries. Thus, Néstor's government created decree 2147/06,[7] which enabled transitory importation of goods, subject to a process of industrial improvement, with a tax benefit. All imports that were obtained for export duties, such as soybeans, had to only pay (when exporting) the added value of what they had paid when imported. These policies mainly favored big processing companies and thus created important alliances between the agro-industrial elite and the Kirchner government.[8]

The contrasting elite-government interaction described above created a new political context for Cristina Fernández de Kirchner's administration when she began her first term in 2008. Before taking office, there was an expectation that the Fernández government would lead more proactive agricultural policies, particularly to protect small farmers and peasants. However, her government has continued with the same agricultural model as the previous governments as seen in the Strategic Agro-Food Plan for 2020, which is based on increasing the production of GM soy to 70 million tons. Nevertheless, her government has introduced several initiatives intending clearly to control the elites as a political force, but at the same time, it has proposed creative alternatives to generate a new type of relationship with them. However, these new options have not been able to develop enough and are seen by critics as the result of a double discourse that the government creates just to gain temporary political support.

Soon after Cristina Fernández de Kirchner began her first term, a major conflict emerged between the government and the four main agricultural unions (SRA, CRA, CONINAGRO and FAA). The conflict emerged due to the government's intention to impose a system of mobile taxes where the export tax for soy could have reached up to 50 percent over time. So, the agricultural associations created the *Mesa de Enlace* (liaison committee of agricultural landowners) to oppose such a measure and imposed what later became known as the "lock-out empresario." The agribusiness elites (mainly represented by SRA and CRA) protested side by side with non-elite agricultural groups consisting of smaller farmers represented by cooperatives and national federations (CONINAGRO and FAA). They all stated that the measure would discourage investments and thus limit the economic growth that the country needed. This was an important political move that enabled the unions to gain the needed power over the government, even though the political views among the producers were very heterogeneous. The smaller ones worried about their livelihoods, while the larger ones rejected being used as a "milking cow" by the government. This was one of the very few historical moments in which Argentinean elites and non-elites related to the agricultural lands were able to cooperate with each other.

In reaction, Cristina Fernández de Kirchner responded by accusing the protesters of trying to limit the power of the government by force and thus increase the influence of the agribusiness elites in governmental issues. The government stated that there was an urgent need to control the *sojización* (soyization) of the country since it was displacing other crops and so increasing food prices. The president justified her position by saying that the government had to find new sources to pay for the external debt of Argentina (about US$52 billion) between 2008 and 2011 (Lazzari and Simonetta, 2008). After several months of direct confrontation, the congress made a final decision against the government, signifying a major gain for the agribusiness elites. Yet, the political power of Cristina Fernández de Kirchner did not necessarily diminish as expected, but rather she maintained her popularity and managed to still take a great portion of the income from soy production. Arbolave (2013) states that the state can currently take from producers 93 percent of their total income obtained from soy production through adding existing taxes: export duties tax, property tax, income tax, diesel tax, value added tax and leasing tax.

Since 2008 the agro-enterprise elite along with the rural elite have remained hostile toward the government. Probably one of the most critical moments was during 2012 and 2013 when the government started to accuse the agro-enterprise elite of "hiding" their production while waiting for better conditions to appear in the market. The government's need for motivating all producers—especially the agro-enterprise elite—to not store their beans was because of the economic imbalance it creates for the state when the benefits do not maintain continuous economic growth. The reason why many producers preferred to hold back their harvest (about 30 percent) was due to the regulation of the dollar exchange market for exportation. During 2013 exporting soy producers were formally given 3.3 pesos per dollar when exchanging currency, while the dollar in commercial banks (known as the "blue dollar") was valued at 5.8 pesos and 8.4 pesos in the internal black market. This meant that the import costs ended up being extremely high for soy producers, pressuring producers to wait until the government was not able to maintain the exchange regulation regime (Wurgaft, 2013).

The differentiation of exchange value is due to the taxes that the government imposes as a way to avoid the economic collapse that Argentina could face soon.

Regardless of the troubled relations described above, the most important governmental institutions for agriculture decisions have become more independent from Fernández de Kirchner's administration, which some critics say has enabled the agribusiness elites to have a greater opportunity to exert influence (Robin, 2008). The regulatory process for the use of biotechnology in agriculture has been reorganized and has included a number of public and private actors with interest in the sector. The Biotechnology Directory that was previously a technical committee for the National Advisory Commission on Agricultural Biotechnology (CONABIA) was assigned a more independent role and is now able to make major decisions without having to maneuver politically. CONABIA is now a multi-sector body with the representation of public and private organizations. Consequently, it serves as a forum for the exchange of opinions and decision making among the government and the agro-industrial elite. However, the agro-industrial elite does not directly participate representing their firms, but rather associations such as FAB or ASA.

Another important change has been the creation of the Ministry of Agriculture, Livestock and Fishery (MINAGRI), which used to be the Secretariat of Agriculture, Livestock, Fisheries and Food until 2009. This decision has permitted the restructuring of agricultural matters within the administration. On the one hand it has meant the opportunity to include representatives of agricultural sectors previously excluded and on the other hand it has elevated agricultural politics to become more influential on a national level. This decision seems to have been made strategically to fulfill Fernández de Kirchner's promise of supporting underprivileged sectors of rural society and pave the way for a closer relationship with the agribusiness elites, mainly the agro-industrial elite.

## The dynamic between elites and their new counterparts in Cristina Fernández de Kirchner's administration

The political reorganization that the government has initiated might quickly change its relationship with the agro-business elites. For instance, a possible new law for renting land might restrain the profits of the agro-enterprise elite by increasing the requirements for renting land. Furthermore, a new Seed Law, designed by MINAGRI, will enable private companies to patent their seeds and charge farmers directly without the intervention of the government. Thus, the share of total benefits will be reduced for the agro-enterprise elite, decreasing their economic influence at a national level, while economically bolstering the agro-industrial elite. The aim of the law is to incentivize research for better seeds so that Argentinean producers become more competitive. However, data obtained from Wikileaks reveals the involvement of the US Embassy in supporting the interests of TNCs in Argentina, particularly Monsanto (O'Donnell, 2011).

Monsanto has already begun the construction of a new plant, to be opened in 2014, and the investment of more than US$125 million in Argentina.

Moreover, Monsanto has already introduced a new GM soy named "Intacta RR2 Pro" which is expected to be 11 percent more productive than previous GM soy. Furthermore, Bayer CropScience stated that it will introduce LibertyLink soy or "LL soy" which uses a new type of herbicide (glufosinate ammonium). Trigo (2011) estimates that the general benefits of the new GM crops could be between US$1.586 million and US$3.668 million by 2022. This would certainly provide the government with a substantial incentive that cannot be ignored, and could also create dependency on the agro-industrial elite in the long term. However, TNCs are not the only potential beneficiaries, since Bioceres (a national company owned by the Grobo Group as mentioned previously), will launch a new soy seed resistant to drought on the international market by 2015–17, the royalties of which would be of major benefit to the state.

The new incentives for biofuel production from the production of GM soy might have several interesting effects. Act 26093[9] is designed to regulate and promote the production and sustainable use of biofuels for the next 15 years. The law establishes that all diesel produced in Argentina must include at least 5 percent biodiesel, which is equivalent to 650,000 tons of oil, and thus secures an internal market for soy production. Moreover, when exporting biodiesel from soy, the exporter has the right to reclaim an amount equivalent to 2.5 percent on top of the export price (the current biodiesel export tax is only 20 percent). This initiative will directly benefit the agro-enterprise and rural elites and will most likely force the agro-industrial elite to invest in the biodiesel market (Giancola *et al.*, 2010).

Regarding environmental legislation, there is no law at the federal level that regulates environmental impacts of the GM soy model. All initiatives are started at the municipal level and are therefore dependent on local actions. This can be partially explained by the lack of requirements from importers, of which China is the most important. In 2010 the Environmental Lawyers Association of Argentina (AADEAA) proposed a short-term ban on glyphosate after publications by Professor Andrés Carrasco from the University of Buenos Aires Medical School showed how the chemical had negative health impacts. However, the study was considered by Chassy and Brookes (2012) as misleading due to lack of evidence; a book which compiles several research analyses done by INTA supports this critic (Camino and Aparicio, 2010). Yet Robin (2008) states that these kinds of studies are a result of the agribusiness elite lobby trying to restrain any effort against their interests. In any case, besides the agro-enterprise elite and some representatives of the agro-industrial elite, a limitation on glyphosate use could also mean a business opportunity for other sectors the agro-industrial elite is involved in. For instance, major companies that specialize in selling chemicals used by conventional soy would be interested in limiting the GM soy model. Similarly, companies that sell or rent machines would also benefit, given that the GM soy model considerably reduces the need for tractors.

Nonetheless, the most important government accomplishment regarding limiting the environmental impact of GM soy expansion has been the Forest Law. Its success has even been addressed by major critics of the GM soy model, such as Greenpeace Argentina (Mendoza, 2011). The law, also known as Minimal Budget for Environmental Protection of Native Forests N.-26631, was proposed to control agricultural advancements as a way to tackle the quick and unorganized expansion of soy. However, it does not directly target GM production, but rather the protection of the remaining forest cover through land management schemes. Therefore, the law does not threaten any of the resources of the agribusiness elite. Nevertheless, it conserves certain areas and provides a protection framework for small-scale farmers and indigenous communities.

## Towards sustainability?

Throughout this chapter, we have seen that the various agribusiness elites have developed differentially before and during the Kirchner administrations. While the agro-industrial elite was empowered during the 1990s with the Menem Administration, the rural elite took the opportunity to maintain its interests without having to play a major role in politics. Furthermore, even though the agro-enterprise elite had already begun to form with the introduction of GM soy, its rise to prominence only occurred after the economic crisis of the early 2000s. Moreover, on one hand we have seen that currently the agro-industrial elite seem to have a closer relationship with the Kirchner administration given its constant lobbying and mutual dependency with the government. On the other hand, we have seen that the agro-enterprise elite and rural elite have maintained a more independent relationship with the government given that they are more related to the international market, are less regulated and currently have a tense relationship with Fernández de Kirchner's administration.

An analysis of the diversity and dynamics of the different powerful groups within the Argentinian agribusiness elites has enabled us to understand better why debate about the environmental impacts of GM soy has been lacking. For instance, we have seen that the GM soy model was introduced to tackle environmental problems of specific interest to the rural elite. Thus, from the beginning, it already had an advantage over environmental counterarguments. We have also seen that the increasing economic power of the agro-enterprise elite is based not on recognizing the environmental implications of the GM soy model, since it would lead to more government control, which explains their efforts to downplay the debate. Finally, besides those who represent firms that are part of the GM soy model, we have seen that the agro-industrial elite does not depend on the GM soy model per se but tends to restrain the environmental debate due to economic initiatives supported by the government.

To close, we have seen that with Cristina Fernández de Kirchner, major governmental institutions for agricultural matters in Argentina have become more inclusive of new actors in the agricultural sector than with previous governments. However, this process has been changing lately as a result of the political pressures caused by the current economic problems, making the government less confrontational with the interests of the agribusiness elite. The fact that the agro-enterprise elite continues to grow exponentially in economic power and that the agro-industrial elite is resuming participation in political matters both prove this. Nonetheless, achieving more sustainable agricultural development might depend more on how the practices of the agro-enterprise elite are regulated. Given that the agro-industrial elite and rural elite are either more flexible or depend more on long-term perspectives, they will potentially fare better than the agro-enterprise elite when it comes to technological changes if the GM soy model is replaced by another model in the future.

## Notes

1  Information obtained from Teubal, M. Researcher the National Scientific and Technical Research Council (CONICET), interviewed November 19, 2012.
2  Information obtained from Barsky, O. Researcher for CONICET and the Latin American Faculty of Social Science (FLACSO), interviewed November 2, 2012.
3  Information obtained from M. Dávila, PhD stipend about agro-politics, interviewed November 7, 2012.
4  "Deregulation of Domestic Trade Decree for Goods and Services and Foreign Trade."
5  The surprising increase of glyphosate as seen in the graph is mainly due to the expansion of GM soy, not because there is an increasing demand per hectare.
6  Speech by Cristina Fernández de Kirchner at the World Food Summit, Italy, 2008.
7  Decree for Temporary Import of Goods.
8  Information obtained from M. Dávila, PhD stipend about agro-politics, interviewed November 7, 2012.
9  The Regulation and Promotion of Sustainable Production and Use of Biofuels Law.

## References

Arbolave, M. R. (2013) Los impuestos que paga la soja 2013/14. *Márgenes Agropecuarios*, November.
ArgenBio Consejo Argentina para la Información y el Desarrollo de Biotecnología (2013) Information about production of soy in Argentina, available at: www.argenbio.org (accessed November 12, 2013).
Barri, F. and Wahren, J. (2009) *El modelo sojero de desarrollo en la Argentina: tensiones y conflictos en la era del neocolonialismo de los agronegocios y el cientificismo-tecnológico.* Centro de Ecología y Recursos Naturales Renovables UNC Grupo de Estudios Rurales—Gino Germani Research Institute, Buenos Aires.
Barsky, O. and Fernández, L. (2008) *Cambio técnico y transformaciones sociales en el agro extrapampeano.* Editorial Teseo, Buenos Aires.
Benchimol, P. (2008) La concentracion de la tierra, latifundios y agro-societies. *Página 12* digital newspaper, available at: www.pagina12.com.ar/diario/suplementos/cash/17-3460-2008-04-20.html (accessed November 16, 2013).
Bindraban, P. S., Franke, A. C., Ferraro, D. O., Ghersa, C. M., Lotz, L. A. P., Nepomuceno, A., Smulders, M. J. M. and vande Wiel, C. C. M. (2009) GM-related sustainability: agro-ecological impacts, risks and opportunities of soy production in Argentina and Brazil. Plant Research International, Wageningen University.
Bustamante, M. and Maldonado, G. I. (2009) Actores Sociales en el Agro Pampeano Argentino Hoy, Algunos Aportes para su Tipificación BIBLID. *Cuadernos Geográficos*, 44 (2009–1), 171–191, Granada, Spain.

Calvo, S., Salvador, M. L., Giancola, S., Iturrioz, G., Covacevich, M., and Iglesias, D. (2011) Causes and consequences of the expansion of soybean in Argentina National University of Córdoba National Institute of Agricultural Technology. INTA, Cordoba, Argentina.

Camino, M. and Aparicio, V. (2010) *Aspectos ambientales del uso de glifosato estacion experimental agropeciaria*. Balcarce, Argentina.

Chassy, B. and Brookes, G. (2012) A critical assessment of the paper 'GM Soy: Sustainable? Responsible?'. University of Illinois and PG Economics, UK.

CIARA (Cámara Industrial de Aceites de la República Argentina) (2011) Estadísticas de soja, available at: www.ciaracec.com.ar/estadísticas (accessed September 14, 2013).

Del Río, J. (2012) Análisis comparativo de costos de la soja convencional y genéticamente modificada para Argentina, Brasil, Paraguay y Uruguay. Secretaría de Agricultura Ganadería y Pesca de Argentina, IICA Reporte de consultoría, Buenos Aires.

FNC (Frente Nacional Campesino) (2008) Un campo más ancho de lo que parece Los productores invisibles. *Página 12* digital newspaper, June 3, available at: www.pagina12.com.ar/diario/elpais/subnotas/105361-33160-2008-06-03.html (accessed September 13, 2013.

Giancola, S., Salvador, L., Covacevich, M., Iturrioz, G. (2010) Análisis de la cadena de soja en la Argentina. *Estudios Socioeconómicos de los Sistemas Agroalimentarios y Agro-industriales No. 3*, INTA, Buenos Aires.

Greenpeace (2004) Lavagna, el empleado del Mes de Monsanto, available at: www.greenpeace.org/argentina/es/noticias/lavagna-el-empleado-del-mes-d (accessed November 17, 2013).

IICA (Inter-American Institute for Cooperation on Agriculture) (2013) Informacion about produccion de soja en Argentina, available at: www.iica.int/Esp/regiones/sur/argentina/Paginas/default.aspx (accessed November 6, 2013).

Joensen, L., Semino, S. and Paul, H. (2005) *Argentina: A Case Study on the Impact of Genetically Engineered Soya*. Report for the Gaia Foundation, London.

Lazzari, G. and Simonetta, M. (2008) *Economía K: ¿Cómo llegamos? ¿Cómo estamos? ¿A dónde vamos?* Fundación Atlas, Buenos Aires.

Loman, H. (2013) Country Report Argentina Rabobank, available at: https://economics.rabobank.com/publications/2013/october/country/report/argentina (accessed January 21, 2014).

Loredo, V. G. (2013) Not a pretty girl: transgenic soy turns fifteen. General thoughts and unknown consequences: the case of Santiago del Estero. *Astrolabio Nueva Epoca 10*, 420–458, Buenos Aires.

Mendoza, C. (2011) Bosques en Argentina, desplazados por la soja DW Deutsche Welle, available at: http://dw.de/p/10nFu (accessed October 2013).

MINAGRI (Ministerio de Agricultura, Ganadería y Pesca) (2011) *Informes agricultura*. MINAGRI, Buenos Aires.

Moltoni, L. (2012) *Evolución del Mercado de Herbicidas en Argentina*. INTA National Institute of Agricultural Technology, Buenos Aires, Argentina, available at: http://inta.gob.ar/documentos/economia-y-desarrollo-agroindustrial-boletin-1-2-.-evolucion-del-mercado-en-argentina/at_multi_download/file/INTA-%20Econom%C3%ADa%20y%20desarrollo%20agroind-%20Boletin1-2.pdf (accessed September 25, 2014).

Moreno, M. (2011) La estructura de vínculos socio-productivos en el agro pampeano: El partido de Pehuajó 2010. Final degree project, Universidad Naciónal de La Plata Facultad de Humanidades Ciencias de la Educación La Plata, Argentina.

Motta, R. and Alasino, N. (2013) Medios y política en la Argentina: Las disputas interpretativas sobre la soja transgénica y el glifosato. Universidad Libre de Berlín and Universidad Nacional de Rosario. *Question*, 1, 38. Rosario, Argentina.

Murphy, A. and Grosso, S. (2012) Impactos socio-territoriales del avance de un frente agropecuario. *VII Jornadas de Sociología de la Universidad Nacional de La Plata Argentina en el escenario latinoamericano actual: debates desde las ciencias sociales*. La Plata, Argentina.

Newell, P. (2009) Bio-hegemony: The political economy of agricultural biotechnology in Argentina. *Journal of Latin American Studies*, 41, 27–57.

O'Donnell, S. (2011) *Argenleaks: Los cables de Wikileaks sobre la Argentina, de la A a la Z*. Editorial Sudamericana, Buenos Aires.

Penna, J. and Lema, D. (2003) Adoption of herbicide tolerant soybeans in Argentina: An economic analysis, in N. Kalaitzandonake (ed.), *The Economic and Environmental Impacts of Agbiotech A Global Perspective*. Kluwer Academic/Plenum Publishers, New York, 203–222.

Pérez, N. (2013) 20 años de pensar y repensar la sociología. Nuevos desafíos académicos, científicos y políticos para el siglo XXI. *1 a 6 de Julio de 2013 X Jornadas de sociología de la UBA*, Buenos Aires.

Pincen, D., Viglizzo, E. F., Carreño, L. V. and Frank, F. C. (2010) La relación soja-ecología-ambiente entre el mito y la realidad, in E. F. Viglizzo and E. Jobbágy (eds) *Expansión de la Frontera Agropecuaria en Argentina y su Impacto Ecológico-Ambiental*. Ediciones INTA, Buenos Aires, 53–63.

Ramirez, O. J. (2010) *Perception of the risk of the agribusiness sector in connection with the agricultural use of pesticides: Transgenic soy in Argentina's Pampa*. Centro de Estudios Interdisciplinarios de la Universidad Naciónal de Rosario, Argentina. *Ambiente y Desarrollo*, XIV(26), Bogotá.

Richardson, N. (2009) Export-oriented populism: Commodities and coalitions in Argentina studies. *Comparative International Development*, 44(3), 228–255.

Robin, M. M. (2008) El mundo según Monsanto: de la dioxina a los OGM: una multinacional que les desea lo mejor. Editorial *Península*, Barcelona.

Rovea, A. (2012) Estudio comparativo de la soja convencional y la genéticamente modificada para Argentina, Brasil, Paraguay y Uruguay. Evolución y agronomía Secretaría de Agricultura, Ganadería y Pesca IICA Reporte de consultoría, Buenos Aires.

Schavarzer, J. and Tavosnanska, A. (2007) El complejo sojero argentino evolución y perspectivas. Centro de Estudios y Perspectivas de la Argentina Universidad de Buenos Aires Facultad de Ciencias Económicas Documento de trabajo no. 10, Buenos Aires.

Tedesco, L. and Picardi de Sastre, M. S. (2001) Historia económica del sector agropecuario argentino en los años '90. *III Jornadas Agrarias y Agroindustriales Universidad Nacional de Buenos Aires*, Argentina.

Trigo, E. (2011) *Fifteen Years of Genetically Modified Crops in Argentine Agriculture*. Consejo Argentino para la Información y el Desarrollo de la Biotecnología (Argentine Council for Information and Development of Biotechnology). ArgenBio, Buenos Aires.

USDA (United States Department of Agriculture) (2013) USDA Agricultural Projections to 2022. Office of the Chief Economist World Agricultural Outlook Board US Department of Agriculture. Prepared by the Interagency Agricultural Projections Committee Long-term Projections Report OCE-20, 13(1), 105, Washington, DC.

Vara, A. M., Piaz, A., Arancibia, F. (2012) Biotecnología agrícola y "sojización" en la Argentina: controversia pública, construcción de consenso y ampliación del marco regulatorio. *Política & Sociedad de Florianópolis*, 11(20), Florianópolis, Brazil, 135–170.

Wurgaft, R. (2013) Argentina amenaza con aplicar la Ley Antiterrorista a los productores de soja in El MundoEs, available at: www.elmundo.es/america/2013/03/25/argentina/1364233032.html (accessed October 6, 2013).

# 6 Ecuador

## Changing biosafety frames and new political forces in Correa's government

*Pablo Andrade and Joaquín Zenteno Hopp*

## Introduction

In the 2008 constitution, initiated by the first administration of Rafael Correa and his Alianza País (*Patria Altiva I Soberana*) movement, the cultivation of genetically modified organisms (GMOs) was banned. However, shortly before the end of his second term in September 2012, the president announced his interest in changing the constitutional provision. Activist groups and some other social groups reacted with strong criticism at this announcement and in general to the new political changes proclaimed by Correa. Thus, the question of how one might explain such a reversal of policy arises. As we will show in this chapter, the conduct of the president is not erratic, but the result of new power relations emerging within the Ecuadorian government.

Taken as a whole, the development project of the Correa administration is a state-run program of rapid economic change under a sociopolitical process of transformation called Revolución Ciudadana ("Citizen Revolution") (SENPLADES, 2013). This political project is a response to the decline of a party system that only managed to satisfy the interests of its members and not those of society in general. The central concept guiding this transformation is *Buen Vivir* ("Good Living"), which refers to the building of a united, accountable, and reciprocal society living in harmony with nature.[1] Additionally, Alianza País's political project is based on two assumptions: the change must be led by experts working for the state, and the best guide to these experts' decision-making is scientific knowledge.

With this backdrop, thus, the main question of this chapter is *what accounts for President Correa's new perspective towards GMOs?* We find that it is due to the emergence of scientific actors recognized as experts on biosafety in Ecuador. We see that this has occurred in parallel to an increase in the political authoritarianism of Correa and a loss of political power of individuals and environmental organizations known for their anti-GMO stance. We conclude that these new dynamics are due to the rise and thus influence of young professionals becoming key players in defining strategies to achieve the diversification of the productive matrix in Ecuador. Therefore, based on their knowledge as a symbolic resource and as outlined in Chapter 2, we argue that such young professionals can be considered a new technocratic elite given that they stand in a privileged position to influence decisions with key environmental implications.[2]

This inquiry is based on 17 in-depth semi-structured interviews and another 11 pilot interviews. The fieldwork was done in December 2013 in the city of Quito and the interviewees were chosen from various sectors: government, academia and independent. The study is also supported by an extensive literature review.

## The Revolución Ciudadana and the political decline of the greens

Despite the apparent political continuity of the Revolución Ciudadana, the current Ecuadorian government is not the same it was when elected in 2006. Between 2007 and 2008, Correa urged a quick and radical reform of the constitution, which achieved nothing short of a complete transformation of the government; a transformation that was reinforced and legitimized by the elections of 2009 and 2013, in which Correa was re-elected as president both times. Although some of the actors from the 2007–13 period still hold high-level government positions, Correa along with Alianza País are still in power and *el Buen Vivir* as a philosophical fundament continues to legitimize government's decisions, the governmental model is not the same. The practical approach of Correa's development policy has changed markedly, especially since 2013.

A branch of political science explains such changes as the result of "the transformation of the ruling coalition" (Leftwich, 2000, 4). Simply put, there are two major sets of factors that can explain the change of the ruling party depending on how they win or lose control over various power resources—which also corresponds to the definition of elites given in Chapter 2. The first instance of change occurs when a new group of elites gain power because their resources have increased as a result of the economic policies pursued by a government in a certain period. If this is true and the emergent group achieves enough clout to become an actor whose interests must be taken into account, then the ruling coalition changes to incorporate the new group. In the second instance, a group that was part of the original coalition government loses the resources that supported their power, and therefore their interests are no longer partially or totally relevant to other groups in the coalition government. It is necessary to note, however, that both processes can occur simultaneously or as a combination of the two; thus our distinction is purely didactic.

The development plan that the Ecuadorian government sponsored between 2009 and 2013 sought a rapid diversification of the Ecuadorian economy to spur a thriving industrial sector (SENPLADES, 2013). To accomplish this goal, the government adopted a strategy of "selective import substitution"—in other words, the creation of an industrial sector that would satisfy domestic demand. If this goal had been achieved in four years, then the industrial sector should have been at the forefront by now, but this is not the case. According to the National Secretariat of Planning and Development (SENPLADES), not only did the industrial sector not grow, but it actually fell to below 1990 levels.[3] What did grow since 2009 was the tertiary sector, including trade, services and especially construction (Figure 6.1).

Accordingly, it is assumed that the change in development policy of the current administration is not due to the emergence of a new group of interests. The key factor appears instead to be a change in the composition of the political elite and their relationship to social groups during the past few years of the Correa administration. In particular, we can assume that the shift towards the possible introduction of GMOs must be related to the potential loss of political power of a major group within the initial ruling coalition.

Development policies adopted by the government during its early years had a strong environmental bias. The government's initial anti-GMO approach was the result of the power it had at that time, supported by a group of actors with interests and demands reflecting social and rural movements (indigenous and peasant) allied with urban environmental organizations and intellectuals. For simplicity, we refer to this group as "the greens" (not to be confused with any environmentalist Green Party in Europe or North America). The greens are the group that lost their ability to direct government policy, and was replaced by a new governing elite as of 2013.

The greens originated in the evolution of Ecuadorian politics between 1978 and 2005. Since 1990, the indigenous movement has demanded a diverse set of rights that are still in conflict with the existence of a development model based on oil drilling in the Ecuadorian Amazon. During the 1990s the indigenous movement

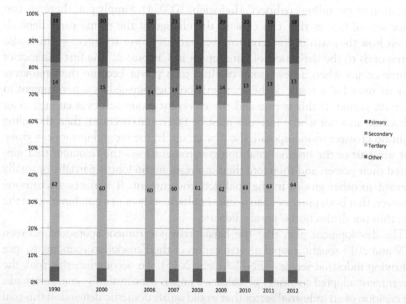

*Figure 6.1* Evolution of economic sectors in Ecuador, 2006–12

Source: Based on data taken from SENPLADES (2013).

and political party—called Pachakutik—found allies in the urban elite, especially intellectuals, politicians and environmentally minded non-governmental organizations (NGOs). During that decade, indigenous politics were highly successful, achieving political representation and even state control briefly in 2002. However, this experience leading the government turned out to be disastrous for the party and movement.

In 2005, relations between indigenous peoples and the urban environmentalist elite changed. The latter, by becoming the dominant of the two partners, developed an ideology that, while retaining indigenous demands, now couched them in the language of deep ecology. At this time the greens appeared as a more or less cohesive group. The political turmoil that the 2006 elections produced provided an opportunity for the greens to create alliances with other politically active segments of the urban middle class. This was the origin of *Patria Altiva I Soberana* (PAIS), the electoral movement that brought Correa to power in 2006 (Basabe *et al.*, 2012).

In 2007, PAIS won a referendum to convene a constitutional assembly. In the election of representatives to the assembly, the greens increased their power, gaining control of key positions in the body including the assembly's president, which was filled by their best-known leader, Alberto Acosta. The committee in charge of designing Ecuador's new development model, Comisión 7 and the natural resources committee, Comisión 5 were directed and controlled by notorious green leaders. The legislative agenda of the greens was simple and successful, granting significant protection in the Constitution to the country's ecosystems. Among these protections were mechanisms to halt expansion of oil extraction and GMO-based agri-business, while promoting long-term conservation (Andrade, 2012).

Although the coalition met its goal, the price was high. Correa and other members of his administration made clear their dissatisfaction with the economic model established in the constitution, such as the intention to base the government on a mechanism of broad citizen participation. In the President's vision of this project, a strong state is needed with the insertion of Ecuador into the global economy—not the anti-capitalist model promoted by the greens. Additionally, the mechanisms for deliberation and citizen participation implied the need for a long political timeline, which Correa saw as conflicting with the need for rapid change and hampering the effectiveness of his leadership. The conflict between the president and the green coalition was resolved in favor of Correa when he, through internal pressuring, forced the resignation of the president of the assembly in June 2008.

The influence of the greens declined even further in the elections of 2008 (constitutional referendum) and 2009 (presidential elections). As the 2009 general election polling data indicate, the greens were unable to expand their electoral support. However, they retained enough power within the executive branch by leading some key ministries during the remaining period of the administration to block the most blatant anti-environmental initiatives from the president and other members of the government. But the situation became even more difficult for the greens in the 2013 elections. The most radical faction of their coalition rejoined the indigenous movement to compete against Correa in the election. The coalition candidate, Alberto Acosta, scored an extremely low vote and his party earned only three representatives in the legislature. Finally, the last visible leader of the greens in the central government, the Secretary of National Planning and Development, resigned a few weeks after the elections due to internal differences with Correa on the handling of the Yasuni ITT Initiative.[4]

## The struggle for power over the politics of biosafety

The importance of biosafety in politics stems from the broad spectrum of alternatives it presents for development projects, including nutritional, economic and health benefits. However, it also includes risk factors due to its economic impact and implications for cultural and ethical concerns (Qaim, 2010; Braun, 2011). In this chapter we refer to biosafety (not to be confused with biosecurity) as the "wide range of measures, policies and procedures that deal with preserving biological integrity, while minimizing the potential negative effects or risks that *biotechnology* could eventually pose for the environment or human health" (IICA, 2013, 1–2, original emphasis). Consequently, we focus specifically on the effects of biotechnology defined as "any technological application that uses biological systems, living organisms or their derivatives, to make or modify products or processes for specific uses" (CDB, 1992, 2–3). Thus biotechnology can have several applications from fermentation to hybridization, cell or tissue culture, molecular marking, biological pest control, and transgenesis among many others. Transgenesis particularly refers to the production of GMOs—organisms whose DNA has been altered through genetic engineering. This technology is not exclusive to the agricultural sector since it is also widely used in industrial processes and medicine.

With the exception of the banana industry, Ecuador is not known for large-scale agriculture, but rather is recognized internationally for its rich biodiversity. As a result, the issue of biosafety only gained momentum in Ecuador with the emergence of the environmental debate in the international arena that was in vogue during the early 1990s. Accordingly, from the outset the Ecuadorian focus on biotechnology developed around the potential risks to the country's biodiversity and not on the potential for national development (Albornoz, 2013).

Although Ecuador ratified the Convention on Biological Diversity in 1992, biosafety was never on the agenda of any national entity, whether governmental or independent until the early 2000s. Only after Ecuador ratified the Cartagena Protocol in 2003 did the government take interest in regulating biosafety. As part of the ratification, a project was created to form a commission to regulate the issue of national biosafety. The initiative established a restrictive and precautionary environmental discourse within the traditional environmentalist perspective, but despite having logistical and financial support from the United Nations Development Programme (UNDP) and the Global Environment Facility (GEF), it never materialized for political reasons. In an interview, Maria de Lourdes Torres, Associate Dean and Coordinator of Biotechnology at the Universidad

San Francisco de Quito, explains: "The subject never had sufficient economic significance of direct benefit to the state … There was always deep uncertainty among decision makers due to lack of information. [Moreover] the lobby of anti-GMO groups in Ecuador is very strong."

The Correa administration is the first government to make important decisions on biosafety, mainly due to pressure from the greens but also to demonstrate its ability to comply with international commitments. At the beginning of the Revolución Ciudadana and within a discourse of respect for *Pachamama*—"Mother Earth" in Quichua—GMOs were categorized by the political elite of the green as a manifestation of the capitalist system and therefore an instrument of colonization (Acosta, 2008). The clearest manifestation of this is in the formulation of the constitution where Article 401 declares Ecuador free of transgenic crops and seeds. In addition, Article 15 of Title II of the constitution bans GMOs along with chemical, biological and nuclear weapons, strategically framing them as negative and dangerous. Note, however, that in the same article, the prohibition of GMOs is conditional, specifically in cases in which "it is found that GMOs are harmful to human health or threaten food sovereignty or ecosystems." In other words, it opens the possibility that if GMOs can be proven as non-hazardous, technically there would be no prohibition, especially in relation to research and experimentation.

In a personal interview with Alberto Acosta, former president of the constitutional assembly and now a professor at the Latin American Faculty of Social Sciences (FLACSO) Ecuador, he states: "Our greatest achievement was the development of the process to approve the introduction of GMOs … It was established that the approval of a GMOs should be made by the National Congress rather than be an exclusively Executive decision." Consequently and according to María Amparo Albán, executive director of ACD Consulting,[5] this provision implies a technical inability to approve GMOs:

> [T]his clause established a bureaucratic barrier that is difficult to overcome because the Legislature does not have the tools to generate rules, since its only function is to authorize them, which therefore disables almost any real option to achieve approval.

A study published by the Ministry of Environment (2008) shows that the political power of the greens on the issue of biosafety is primarily based on its popularity in civil society. The data shows that almost 60 percent of the Ecuadorian population believes that GMOs have a negative connotation for health. However, the same study concluded that 79 percent of the population does not know what biotechnology is, 81 percent do not know what biosafety is and 73 percent do not know what a GMO is. The greens generally emphasize the need to protect nature from potential genetic contamination or from impacts caused by agricultural practices required for the production of transgenic crops. Similarly, they denounce the potential incursion of foreign companies or corporations that may displace small producers and/or affect the domestic market. Finally, they question the actual benefits if a cost/benefit analysis is made. Ana Lucia Bravo, an independent consultant from Acción Ecológica, states: "The requirements for developing GMOs appropriate for local conditions tend to demand a lot of time, resources and qualified personnel, because their application becomes difficult, unrealistic and inadequate especially compared to alternatives such as agroecological ones."

Much of the society's negative perception of GMOs is due to the strong anti-GMO campaign of environmental organizations. While there is no entity in Ecuador that openly promotes the introduction of GMOs since they are banned, there is constant anti-GMO propaganda in the media.[6] Also, aside from being respected for their political success during the early years of the Correa government, these groups and individuals maintain a discourse of fear and uncertainty about the potential effects of GMOs, as expressed in the book compiled by Bravo and Vogliano (2012). They justify their position with scientific studies, such as the study done by Séralini *et al.* (2012), which claimed that lab rats developed cancer and physiological deformations from eating GMO corn. It is worth noting, however, that the study has been widely discredited by the scientific community (EFSA, 2012; *Economist*, 2013). In contrast, most scientific research on the health impacts of GMOs has not found evidence to support Séralini *et al.*'s findings (Nicolia *et al.*, 2013).

Aside from potential health impacts, the major argument of anti-GMO groups and individuals is that a clear need permitting the use of GMOs in Ecuador has not yet been identified, as Elizabeth Bravo from Acción Ecológica, echoes: "With the exception of bananas, the identification of a specific cultivar in which a genetically modified version could result in a clear advantage for the production or marketing in Ecuador is very unclear." The most important crop in this regard could be potatoes since it is an important food crop and its production is decreasing due to the effects of climate change. However, it is difficult to consider a genetically modified (GM) version in Ecuador since the potato is native to the Andes, and as such there is international pressure to protect it from any possible genetic risk (Bravo and Vogliano, 2012).[7] Another option could be cacao due to its commercially strategic importance, but a GM version could be counterproductive because most of it is sold to Europe where the public has an aversion to GM products. As for the production of soy or corn, for which there are already very successful GM varieties, Ecuador already has a stable import market for these products. The only successful initiative so far has been by the Ecuadorian Biotechnology Research Center (CIBE) with the development of GM bananas resistant to an important foliar disease called black Sigatoka, which has been of great benefit to Ecuador's banana industry (REDU, 2013).

The main anti-GMO entities in Ecuador are Acción Ecológica and the Plurinational and Intercultural Conference on Food Sovereignty (COPISA). The first is a recognized NGO with a long and important presence in Ecuador and the second is an autonomous civic body attached to the government to propose policies on food safety decisions. While there are several international organizations that support these organizations, such as SwissAid and GenØk Norway,[8] they are also supported by organizations such as Friends of the Earth, Misereor IHR Hilfswerk, Rallt, Global Greengrants Fund and Greenpeace.

This relationship between international and local entities is one of the most important factors that allow Ecuadorian NGOs to stay updated and keep their economic independence from the government.

However, in parallel to the decline of the political power of the greens, Ecuadorian environmental NGOs known for their great importance during the 1990s have lost political force in recent years. The explanation is largely due to the decay of the financial support of international aid agencies to NGOs over the past decade as well as the redefinition of priorities of governments and organizations with an interest in environmental issues. Since Ecuador has shown positive growth in almost all development indicators since 2001 and has had a clear economic success on taxation, it tends to be considered a lower-priority country on the international aid agenda. Consequently, green NGOs have become limited in their ability to maintain the same capacity for action in terms of producing activist materials (i.e. literature, reports, etc.), funding participation workshops and providing competitive wages to their employees.

Even though Figure 6.2 presents two graphs with different amounts, it enables to see the contrasting evolution (arrows) of income between International Aid to Ecuador (mainly NGOs) versus the Ecuadorian State. While the financial weakening of NGOs was unfolding, the Correa government was gaining greater financial power due to three main factors: (1) the new system of internal revenue taxation, (2) the renegotiation of contracts with oil companies, and (3) the increase of oil prices in recent years (Viteri, 2012). Furthermore, Correa's focus on sovereignty has created an effort to include strategic issues such as the environment on the government agenda. Correa's justification for this is that no independent government entity has the democratic legitimacy to make decisions about sovereign natural resources. In an interview with María Amparo Albán, executive director of ACD Consulting, she stated that:

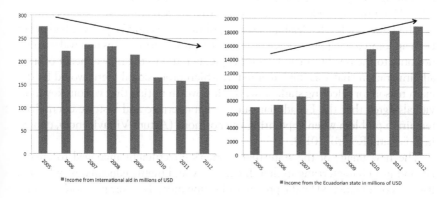

*Figure 6.2* Evolution of Ecuadorian environmental NGO income sources from international aid and the Ecuadorian state, 2005–12

Source: Based on data taken from OECD (2013) and FME (2013).

This new reality means that there is a restructuring in Ecuadorian environmental governance, thus a redefinition of environmental priorities and moreover the relation of these to social issues ... Civil society groups that had once had the opportunity to participate more actively now see themselves as dependent on the spaces granted and/or authorized by the government.

Consequently, the government has managed to expand its presence gradually and thus impose their agenda on previously independent sectors (Pachano, 2012). The most important initiative that demonstrates the state's consolidation of political power is Decree 16 issued in May 2013. The decree requires that all independent entities define their activities in coordination with the government and not guided by foreign entities, whether international organizations or cooperating governments. It is also required that any organization must be assigned to a government institution for oversight, restricting the organizations' ability to operate independently within the frame of Ecuadorian law. Moreover, this exposes organizations to a sort of summary trial in which judges have the power to disable them from using normal defense procedures, leaving the constitutional court as the only alternative to repeal a decision. This gives the government the legal power to pressure any entity that becomes a political threat. The most important instance showcasing this new political dynamic was the closure of Pachamama Alliance in December 2013.

### The influence of young professionals in Correa's government

The Revolución Ciudadana implied a renewal of the political elite in Ecuador, since the failure of the political party system that was previously in charge in the country was one of the main reasons that Correa was able to run in the 2006 elections (Verdesoto, 2007). An interesting example of this renewal appears upon examining the profile of the people involved in the Constituent Assembly of 2007. Diamint and Tedesco (2011) reveal that 80 percent of the assembly members had never held a leadership post in a political party and 76 percent had never been appointed to a public office by popular representation. This renewal was due not only to the need to include new people, but also to the new concept of state administration that was implemented in which professional merit would be the main reason for selecting staff. However, it is worth noting that various key individuals agree that the Ecuadorian state's characteristic and historic clientelism remains a problem when appointing key positions (Arturo Villavicencio, quoted in Rojas and Rosero, 2013).

The new image of the state that Correa's government managed to create, beyond just characterizing itself as having new and highly educated people, sees itself as complemented by the presence of young officials in key positions (besides being more gender equal). Some of the most well-known examples of such people are presented in Table 6.1. It is worth noting that the list of individuals here is from 2014, so young people under 40 years old who were appointed to key government positions in previous years were not considered. If we should include

*Table 6.1* Some of the young professionals under 40 years old holding key positions in the Correa government in January 2014

| Name | Position | Age |
| --- | --- | --- |
| Viviana Bonilla | Governor of Guayas State 2012–13 | 28 |
| Andrés Factos | Project Director Biosafety Implementation Regulatory Framework | 29 |
| Gabriela Rivadeneira Burbano | President of the National Assembly | 30 |
| Carla Zambrano | Under Secretary of Zone 5 of the National Secretariat of Planning and Development (SENPLADES) | 31 |
| Ximena Amoroso | Director of the Internal Revenue Service | 33 |
| Héctor Rodríguez Chávez | Director of the Yachay EP (*Ciudad del Conocimiento*) | 33 |
| Patricio Rivera Yánez | Coordinating Minister of Political Economy | 34 |
| Silvana Vallejo Páez | Vice Minister of Rural Development | 34 |
| Álvaro Armijos León | Vice Minister of Information and Communication Technology | 35 |
| Diego Martínez Vinueza | President of the Directorate of the Central Bank of Ecuador | 35 |
| Fausto Herrera Nicolalde | Minister of Finance | 35 |
| José Rosero Moncayo | Executive Director of the National Institute of Statistics and the Census (INEC) | 35 |
| Víctor Hugo Villacrés Endara | Sub-director General of the Central Bank of Ecuador | 36 |
| Cecilia Vaca Jones | Coordinating Minister of Social Development | 38 |
| Mateo Patricio Villalba Andrade | Director General of the Central Bank of Ecuador | 38 |
| Gabriela Rosero Moncayo | Technical Secretary of International Aid | 38 |
| Lorena Tapia Nuñez | Minister of the Environment | 38 |
| René Ramírez Gallegos | National Secretary of Higher Education, Science and Technology and Innovation | 39 |
| Guillaume Long | Coordinating Minister of Human Talent | 39 |
| Rafael Poveda Bonilla | Coordinating Minister of Strategic Sectors | 39 |

Source: Produced by the authors.

them, the list of young people in key positions since 2007 and defined as less than 40 years old, should include people who today are 47 to 48 years old.

An interesting fact upon reviewing the vital statistics of the majority of the young people named in Table 6.1 is that in general their political career is related in one way or another to SENPLADES. In this sense, SENPLADES would appear to act as a strategic center for training and recruitment of young professionals, a few years after which they transfer to other state institutions. As an institution, SENPLADES was already formed in 2004, but its strategic role for the government began in 2007, given that it is defined as the main office for strategic thinking of the Citizen Revolution. As Carolina Báez, information advisor of SENPLADES, commented: "The reason that other state institutes recruit staff from our offices is due to the fact that in SENPLADES the essence of the conviction that drives our present government is forged: *El Buen Vivir*."

According to information provided by SENPLADES, today 71 percent of all the employees that work for the Secretariat are under 40 years old and three-quarters have higher education. It is therefore interesting to know in detail the profile of people working at SENPLADES and above all those in key positions, as Figure 6.3 shows. Of all the authorities in the Secretariat from 2007 to present, the vast majority were born in the 1970s and 1980s. Moreover, two-thirds of the

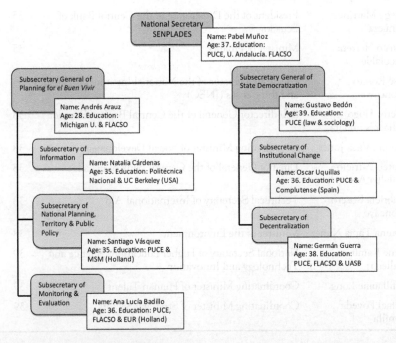

*Figure 6.3* SENPLADES officials 2014

Source: Produced by the authors based on data obtained from SENPLADES (2014).

present officials in SENPLADES come either from the Latin American Social Sciences Institute (FLASCO Ecuador) or the Pontifical Catholic University of Ecuador (PUCE). It is also interesting to note that 80 percent of the employees are sociologists, economists or mathematicians, and the main country abroad in which they have studied is Spain, although the Netherlands is also notable and to a lesser extent the US.

The role of young professionals in the planning of *el Buen Vivir* is considered vital due to their orientation towards the future and their advanced technical–academic knowledge of the potential of future technologies. In relation to the definition of an elite done in Chapter 2, these are individuals with privileged political positions, socio-economic resources and well-established academic social networks—therefore they show the traits of a technocratic elite. The presence of young professionals in key positions is not a unique characteristic of SENPLADES, since the same pattern is seen in almost all governmental institutions, especially the Central Bank of Ecuador and the Coordinating Ministries.

The main project of SENPLADES is the National Plan for Good Living 2013–17 (PNBV) in which the philosophical inspiration of the Revolución Ciudadana are established. One of the main features of this document, as in the previous version of PNBV (2009–13), is the strategic focus on what is termed "bio-knowledge"[9] as the basic element for achieving change in Ecuador's production complex. In both versions, bio-knowledge is established as the alternative to achieve three primary objectives of the Revolución Ciudadana: economic independence, food sovereignty, and environmental sustainability. It is with this logic that biotechnology is presented as an interesting alternative. In an interview with Eduardo Morillo, leader of the National Department of Biotechnology at the National Institute of Agricultural and Fisheries Research, he stated: "Biotechnology is a practical application of bio-knowledge—it is an option for achieving an economy sustained by finite resources, capable of generating food through more efficient means while conserving existing biodiversity."

Despite being a proposal presented by SENPLADES, the leading entity for the development of biotechnology in Ecuador is the National Secretariat of Higher Education, Science, Technology and Innovation (SENESCYT). The main reason why SENESCYT is given this responsibility is that the development of biotechnology in the country was always based in universities, and thus the academic sector. Thus, biotechnology turns into an entity in which the political theory of SENPLADES converges with the practical–scientific approach of SENESCYT. Note, however, that even though this shows the government's ability to complement policy making with scientific advancement, it can also lead to the mixing of knowledge and policy production.

The most important result of this effort is the "City of Knowledge" or "Yachay," embodying the idea of creating a center of development for bio-knowledge, serving as a practical–strategic entity to achieve the main objectives presented by *el Buen Vivir*. Yachay is a planned city where there is currently an environment of technological innovation that combines the best ideas, human talent and the best infrastructure. In addition to housing the Research University of Experimental

Technology, the idea is also for it to serve as a space to host international high-tech companies. The ultimate aim of using biotechnology is to make products generated from biological and genetic information, as bio-prospecting, bio-production and bio-commerce for export, and via this generate an economy based on finite resources as an innovative application of "Green Economy." Aside from biotechnology, the proposed fields of research to be developed at Yachay are nanoscience, petrochemistry, renewable energy, and information and communication technology.

Within the context of biotechnology development promulgated by Correa's government, a few important critiques have surfaced to analyze. First, the purely scientific linear model proposed by SENESCYT does not allow space for the local know-how that SENPLADES demands. It is argued that this is due to the fact that the model depends solely on technological advancement in other countries without considering the potential for human capital present within Ecuador. Second, it is predicted that there will be a conflict over the vision of the use of biotechnology between different state institutions themselves. With reference to this, María Belén Albornoz, professor at FLACSO Ecuador, commented:

> Biotechnology, characterized as a conservation tool by the Ministry of Environment and the Ministry of Heritage Conservation [*Ministerio de Conservación del Patrimonio*], clashes directly with the vision of the Coordinating Ministry for Production, Employment and Competitiveness and the Vice President, who see biotechnology (above all GMOs) as a source of innovation and business.

According to the technical scientific discourse of those who are around Correa, GMOs are the most promising alternative that exists today to develop products that aim to attain the initiatives set forth by Yachay. It is due to this situation that the need of various government actors to reconsider the impact of using GMOs in the country has arisen. In turn, this need to reconsider GMOs is exactly what is forcing an evaluation of the issue of national biosafety. Although biosafety regulation in Ecuador is established in the 2008 constitution, the successful repackaging of the issue of biotechnology by the new technocratic youth elite and its application specifically in GMOs is in the end the pressure that was needed for this shift in attitude to occur. As a result, the government decided to establish a second phase of the initiative started previously in 2003 and to form a commission dedicated to regulating biosafety. Anchored within the Ministry of Environment and newly funded by GEF and UNDP, the initiative known as the Biosafety Implementation Regulatory Framework (IMRB), is created with the purpose of forming the stated commission.

Due to the loss of political power by the green elite and the re-emergence of the need to evaluate the impact of GMOs, Correa turned to a new group of experts to advise him on the potentials and real risks of using GMOs. Thus, the president called a private meeting with scientists known for experience and knowledge about biotechnology, who for years had concluded that GMOs could potentially serve as a viable alternative for development if considered case by case and not following into generalizations. The main people present at the meeting were: Dr. Eduardo Morillo, leader of the Biotechnology Department at the National Autonomous Institute of Agricultural and Fisheries Research (INIAP); Dr. César Paz and Miño, dean of the Institute of Biomedical Research at the Universidad de las Américas; and Dr. María de Lourdes Torres, associate dean and biotechnology coordinator at the College of Biological and Environmental Sciences, Universidad San Francisco de Quito.

Similarly and in the same period, President Correa made various trips to different biotechnology research and experimentation centers in different countries (Brazil, USA, EU and South Korea) to inform himself of the potentials and risks of GMOs. As a result, Correa commented during his *sabatina*—Saturday speech—number 287 in September 2012 that the prohibition of GMOs under the constitution was "a mistake" and he regretted not having had "the firmness" to oppose that clause supported by "the childish environmentalism" of the greens (*El Comercio*, 2012).

## Biosafety regulation and environmental governance

From the start of the first legal discussions, biosafety regulation in Ecuador fell within the parameters of environmental governance. This was due to the fact that in Book IV of the Unified Text of Secondary Legislation (TULAS) from 2003, the Ministry of Environment was established as the principal body for addressing biosafety. Thus, in response to the ratification of the Cartagena Protocol in 2003 and in line with the Convention on Biological Diversity, the issue of biosafety began to fall under the National Biodiversity Policy and Strategy. This view is reinforced by the focus of the constitution, since the protection of nature is established as a cross-cutting principal. Consequently, laws such as the Environmental Management Act, the Agriculture and Fisheries Support and Development Act, the Agrarian Development Act, the Seeds Act and the Plant Protection Act respond to the issue of biosafety within a framework of environmental governance (Crespo, 2009).

The formulation and application of these laws include the participation of different entities, creating a complex multisectoral dynamic, even though it is not governed by a regulatory framework. Bodies such as the Ministry of Agriculture, Livestock, Aquaculture and Fisheries, the Ministry of Health, the Ministry of Foreign Trade, among others, all have a strong connection with the issue. Similarly, representatives of the productive, environmental, academic, civic and rural sectors are linked both directly and indirectly. The existing dynamic between all these actors is so complex that the lack of systematic regulation begins to be felt in various ways. In an interview with Freddy Proaño, head of biotechnology at the Ecuadorian Network of Universities and Polytechnic Schools for Research and Graduate Studies (REDU), he states: "The most notable effect of the lack of [biosafety] regulation is that some government agencies begin implementing important laws without the necessary coordination with other institutions, causing large inconsistencies."

The most striking case is the measure carried out to label GMOs issued by the Ministry of Industry and Productivity and the Coordinating Ministry for Production, Employment and Competition in October 2013. Various analysts agree that this law, beyond conforming to the constitution, has no basis for technical application. In an interview with Germán Romo, spokesperson for biotechnology use and Scientific Advisor to the Ecuadorian Council of Industries and Production, he signals the following:

> [A]lmost no international company has information about whether their product has GMOs or not … this is due to the large amount of fluctuations along the chain of production which makes it very difficult to control. … Requiring companies to carry out their respective analyses will end up affecting consumers with higher prices at the local market.

Similarly, in an interview with Andrés Factos, biotechnology engineer specialized in aspects about regulation, he comments on other inconsistencies: "Very probably many small food companies will be unable to compete with companies with economic power due to the new requirements for entering the Ecuadorian market created by labeling."

Thus, the importance and urgency of Ecuador to form a technical commission to regulate the issue of biosafety cannot be overstated. Moreover, the regulation of biosafety in Ecuador represents a great opportunity to finally frame biotechnology as an option compatible with biodiversity conservation. Since there is clear internal pressure favoring adoption of strict regulation of GMOs in Ecuador, if they are legalized, it is most probable that only certain types of crops will be allowed. In other words, the challenge is to define the necessary criteria to determine which types of GMOs are needed and for what. In an interview with Julio Escobar, Biotechnology and Biosafety Specialist from the Inter-American Institute for Cooperation on Agriculture (IICA) in Ecuador, he states: "If the GMOs that are approved are specifically utilized for subsistence crops, this could mean a great boon for sectors which are currently economically depressed."

The reason why local use of biotechnology represents an opportunity for biodiversity conservation is its ability to develop technological packages with diversified gene variability, besides being better customized to local needs and risks. GMO crops do not necessarily need to be introduced by big corporations or depend on chemical inputs, as in the best-known cases of RR Soybean or BT Corn, along with the chemical Roundup Ready, all sold by Monsanto. Instead, they can be designed by non-profit organizations, public or not, to simply improve performance or nutritional values of certain key crops without competing with or damaging other crops. Big corporations can and should be regulated as a way to enable this type of development. Furthermore, GMOs represent an opportunity to allow a more efficient bioremediation in case of oil or chemical spills and to decrease the effect of waste from industrial activities. Thus, biotechnology development could control pollution sources while conserving the environment and biodiversity.

## Final comments

Throughout this chapter we have seen how young professionals, defined as a new technocratic elite, have a direct relationship with environmental governance in Ecuador because their influence has started changing perceptions toward biosecurity governance. However, this process is difficult to distinguish from the projects undertaken by the government's development model, which is no longer led by the greens. In this way, and in line with the hypothesis posited in this book, we see that the dynamic between the emergence of a new elite (young technocrats) and the decline of another (the greens), explains why Correa revived the issue of GMOs. However, it should be noted that this does not necessarily represent a political turn away from sustainability. Rather the regulation of biotechnology could have positive environmental repercussions, besides having an effect on important economic sectors.

However, while young professionals enjoy more important positions in government, current laws tend to be designed to be more and more dependent on the president. In this sense, the most interesting illustrative case is Correa's decision to introduce GMOs. Even though the process of approval depends on the National Assembly as previously mentioned, the president is the only authority qualified to issue justification for the need to introduce GMOs or not. Although the requirements for the basis of this declaration can be adjusted under the rule of law, the constitution states that such measures are always subject to the authority of the president.

The tendency of the government to take precedence over the rights of citizen participation can adversely affect the development of biotechnology regulation. It could be the case that the majority of society does not see the introduction of GMOs by the government favorably because of the lack of a public, comprehensive and informed discussion about it. Consequently, it is important to support initiatives such as REDU for research on uses and impacts of GMOs (REDU, 2013). By the same token, it is important to include alternative information from independent parties through public forums. In short, the moment in which Ecuador currently finds itself represents a great opportunity to reach a consensus on the type of regulation required for biotechnology, which would signify a step forward toward *el Buen Vivir*.

## Notes

1  *El Buen Vivir* is a transformational concept taken from the indigenous Andean and Amazonian cosmovision, and is presented as an alternative to neoliberalism.
2  In this chapter, environmental governance refers to the definition from Chapter 1, but as understood from the perspective of the political dynamics of biosafety regulation.
3  The contribution of industry to GDP in 2012 was just 12.8 percent, while in 1990 it was 14.1 percent. Even more interestingly, in 2008—before the execution of the *Plan Nacional para el Buen Vivir* from 2009–13—the contribution was 14.1 percent.
4  This was a project that proposed to not exploit a certain amount of oil to conserve the environmental integrity of the Amazonian Yasuní National Park in exchange for international compensation equaling at least half of the total value of estimated revenue.

5 ACD Consulting is a well-known private consultancy specialized in environmental affairs.

6 The only initiative attempting to depict an impartial view towards GMOs was accomplished on the radio by the Ministry of the Environment at the end of 2013. It is worth mentioning that the advertisement was removed after various groups accused it of being illegal.

7 Ecuador covers an important area of the Andes where potatoes is a native crop. Although not scientifically proven, it is believed that GMO crops could pass genes to native crops through gene flow and thus reduce genetic diversity.

8 GenØk is a biosafety research center known internationally for proposing an adverse vision about the environmental and health impacts of GMOs.

9 "Bio-knowledge" is a combination of scientific and traditional knowledge and applications that society has developed in relation to complex systems from the natural world (SENPLADES, 2013).

# References

Acosta, A. (2008) *Un sello de calidad y coherencia para el Buen Vivir Libre de transgénicos.* ALAI América Latina en Movimiento Quito, Ecuador.

Albornoz, M. B. (2013) La biotecnología y su paradoja del buen vivir. *Universitas Humanística*, 76, 235–251. FLACSO Quito, Ecuador.

Andrade, P. (2012) En el reino (de lo) imaginario: los intelectuales ecuatorianos en la creación de la Constitución de 2008. *Ecuador Debate*, 85. Quito, Ecuador.

Basabe, S., Pachano, S. and Acosta, A. (2012) Ecuador: democracia inconclusa, in M. Cameron and J. P. Luna (eds), *Democracia en la Región Andina*. IEP Lima, Peru, 165–196.

Braun, B. (2011) Global disorder: Biopolitics and the molecularization of life, in R. Peet, P. Robbins, M. Watts (eds), *Global Political Ecology*. Routledge, London, 389–411.

Bravo, E. and Vogliano, S. (2012) *Cien razones para declarar al Ecuador libre de transgénicos.* Swissaid and Acción Ecológica Quito, Ecuador.

CDB (Convenio sobre Diversidad Biológica) (1992) *Convenio sobre Diversidad Biológica. Secretaria del Convenio sobre Diversidad Biológica.* United Nations, New York.

Crespo, R. (2009) Armonización de la propuesta de reglamentación sobre la Bioseguridad de Organismos Genéticamente Modificados acorde con la constitución vigente Proyecto: implementación del marco nacional de Bioseguridad. Dirección Nacional de Biodiversidad Ministerio del Ambiente Quito, Ecuador.

Diamint, R. and Tedesco, L. (2011) ¿Quién educa a los políticos? Cambios y continuidades en Argentina y Ecuador tras el grito "que se vayan todos." Real Instituto Elcano (ari) Open Society Institute de Washington DC.

*Economist* (2013) Smelling a rat: GM maize, health and the Séralini affair. Vol. 409 no. 8865, December 7–13, p. 75, London.

EFSA (European Food Safety Authority) (2012) Review of the Séralini et al. (2012) publication on a 2-year rodent feeding study with glyphosate formulations and GM maize. NK603 Food and Chemical Toxicology, Parma, Italy.

El Comercio (2012) Resume del Enlace ciudadano 287 desde Nayón available at: www.elcomercio.com/sociedad/Presidente-hablo-denuncia-Huaoranis-enlace_0_766123404.html (accessed October 2012).

FME (Financial Ministry of Ecuador) (2013) Ecuadorian State Income, available at: www.finanzas.gob.ec/ (accessed February 2014).

IICA (Instituto Interamericano de Cooperación para la Agricultura) (2013) Marco Estratégico del Área de Biotecnología y Bioseguridad del IICA: 2013 Programa de Innovación para la Productividad y la Competitividad. San José, Costa Rica.

Leftwich, A. (2000) *States of Development on the Primacy of Politics in Development*. Polity, Cambridge.

Ministry of Environment (2008) Estudio de Percepción Pública sobre organismos genéticamente modificados. MARKET SA 48 Quito, Ecuador.

Nicolia, A., Manzo, A., Veronesi, F. and Rosellini, D. (2013) An *Overview of the Last Ten Years of Genetically Engineered Crop Safety Research: Critical Reviews in Biotechnology*. Informa HealthCare, USA.

OECD (Organization for Economic Cooperation and Development) (2013) Evolution of International Aid Income, available at: http://stats.oecd.org (accessed February 2014).

Pachano, S. (2012) RC – R'C'= 0 Rafael Correa, in S. Mantilla and S. Mejía (ed.), *Balance de la Revolución Ciudadana*. Centro Latinoamericano de Estudios Políticos, Editorial Planta del Ecuador, SA Quito, Ecuador, 43–74.

Qaim, M. (2010) Benefits of genetically modified crops for the poor: Household income, nutrition, and health. *New Biotechnology*, 27(5), 552–557.

REDU (Red Ecuatoriana de Universidades y Escuelas Politécnicas para Investigación y Posgrados) (2013) *Pronunciamiento de la Red Ecuatoriana de Universidades y Escuelas Politécnicas para Investigación y Posgrados sobre la Investigación y Uso de los Transgénicos*. Quito, Ecuador.

Rojas, C. and Rosero, M. (2013) Arturo Villavicencio (personal interview), La meritocracia sólo funciona para el servidor público del nivel inferior. *El Comercio* newspaper, available at: www.elcomercio.com/politica/meritocracia-funciona-servidor-publico-inferior_0_846515420.html (accessed January 2014).

SENPLADES (Secretaria Nacional de Planificación y Desarrollo) (2013) Plan Nacional del Buen Vivir República del Ecuador Consejo Nacional de Planificación, p. 295. Quito, Ecuador.

SENPLADES (Secretaria Nacional de Planificación y Desarrollo) (2014) Profile of officials, available at: www.planificacion.gob.ec/ (accessed February 2014).

Séralini, G. E., Clair, E., Mesnage, R., Gress, E., Defarge, N., Malatesta, M. Hennequin, D. and Spiroux de Vendômois, J. (2012) Long term toxicity of a Roundup herbicide and a Roundup-tolerant genetically modified maize. *Food and Chemical Toxicology*, 50, 4221–4231.

Verdesoto, L. (2007) El nacimiento de una nueva clase política en el Ecuador: Taller de Análisis de Coyuntura. *Revista de Ciencias Sociales*, 28, 13–21, Facultad Latinoamericana de Ciencias Sociales–Sede Académica de Ecuador (FLACSO) Quito, Ecuador.

Viteri, M. E. (2012) Recursos para la eficiencia fiscal contra la injusticia social, in S. Mantilla and S. Mejía (eds), *Rafael Correa Balance de la Revolución Ciudadana*. Centro Latinoamericano de Estudios Políticos Editorial Planta del Ecuador SA, Quito, Ecuador, 349–372.

# Part 2

# Mining

Part 2

Mining

# 7 New elites around South America's strategic resources

*Barbara Hogenboom*

## Introduction

Since the turn of the century, various rapid and unforeseen changes have produced important shifts in the actors, discourses, interests, power relations and institutions that influence the governance of oil, gas and mining in South America. For instance, few would have predicted Bolivia to elect an indigenous ex-union leader for president, who would then choose his first Labour Day in office to renationalize the gas and oil sector, and use the extra revenues for redistribution. Similarly, the speedy economic rise of China had already come as a surprise, but no one would have expected that within just a few years Chinese companies and banks would bring major oil-related investments and loans to the region. Another unexpected development is the boom of the global commodity markets, which has been remarkably large and long. These new economic and political conditions have been a strong force behind the massively expanding extraction of the region's valuable minerals including both metals and fossil fuels. As both the value and the volumes of the exploitation and exports of mineral reserves have risen, the economic importance of these extractive sectors is basically back to pre-1980s levels. Next to this renewed economic centrality, extractive activities are also back at the centre of political debate and social struggle. The notion of oil, gas and metals being strategic resources that require stronger state scrutiny has regained relevance, most strongly under leftist governments. Simultaneously, new policies and the increase of extractive projects have led to criticism and resistance from a range of groups, including those who lose certain privileges and those whose livelihoods and territories are negatively affected.

However, the arrival of new political and economic actors does not necessarily imply a shift in elites (see Chapter 2 of this volume), nor does the increased profitability and centrality of extractive activities necessarily lead to a more sustainable and equitable use of mineral reserves. While the overall tendency may correctly be labelled as 'more state control' in South America's strategic sectors, the changing roles and interdependencies between old and new actors and elites deserve greater attention and nuance. This chapter looks from a panoramic stance at the arrival of new actors who affect the ways in which oil, gas and metal minerals in South America are used and managed, and discusses to what extent this involves a shift of elites. Its objective is to provide an overview of the main developments that are relevant for the governance of these so-called strategic resources. In the following section, on national changes, this is done by analysing the changing attitudes towards these resources in Venezuela, Bolivia, Ecuador and Brazil. Then, in the section on international elites, the focus is on changes affecting the region as a whole, such as the growing importance of Chinese actors. The subsequent section studies recent resource-related trends of regionalization. Finally, we will discuss and conclude with how elite shifts around oil, gas and mining influence environmental governance in South America.[1]

## Shifting national actors and elites around strategic resources

Since its insertion in the world system, minerals have been crucial in South America's political processes and imaginaries. After centuries of foreign exploitation of its metals, and later on oil, in the twentieth century most countries created state companies to gain more control over extraction activities and revenues. After a trend of oil nationalizations, such as in Bolivia (1937 and 1969), Mexico (1938) and Venezuela (a 50/50 split of oil revenues between the public and the private sector in 1943, and nationalization in 1976), a nationalization trend in mining took off: Brazil, for instance, created the state company Companhia Vale do Rio Doce (1942), tin was nationalized in Bolivia (1952), and copper was nationalized in Peru (late 1960s) and in Chile (1971). While fitting in the development model of import substitution industrialization (ISI), the nationalization wave was strongly influenced by anti-imperialist sentiments and popular and labour resistance against foreign companies exploiting workers and nature. In the 1980s and 1990s, the political and economic tide turned. Neoliberal regimes and technocrats came to power whereas busting world market prices for minerals further deepened the region's economic crisis. Under the Washington Consensus, the mining, oil and gas sectors also had to follow the recipe of privatization, deregulation and liberalization to attract new foreign direct investment. Despite previous problems with large state-owned oil and mining companies, such as corruption and inefficiency, there was a popular sense of injustice about the privatizations, and a fear that the nation's natural endowments would no longer benefit the people. In that context, local protests against projects of multinational mining and oil companies hooked up with the wider mobilization against neoliberal policies as well as the rising indigenous movements. As a result, the governance of mining and oil and gas extraction ended up in the core of social and political contestation of neoliberal policies.

As discussed in Chapter 1, from the late 1990s onwards, numerous national elections in South America were won by candidates and parties from the Left who promised they would make a real change to politics and policies. A characteristic of several of the new leaders is their non-elite background and 'bottom-up' political career. Presidents such as Lula and Morales come from poor families and first led unions (of steelworkers and coca-farmers, respectively), which later created political parties. Chávez also came from a humble background, but he made a career through the army, a trajectory that resembles the path to politics made by traditional populists, such as Juan Perón in the 1940s. Leftist regimes succeeded in winning elections due to ties with social movements, an echoing of widespread criticism of the limited depth of democracy under neoliberal regimes, and proposals for more participatory politics. Moreover, they promised to make development more equitable, and favoured greater state control over oil, gas and mining in order to redistribute the mineral revenues. In addition, both in ethnicity and gender, politicians have gradually come to be somewhat more representative of the make-up of their societies. After the region-wide rise of indigenous movements and parties, it was for the first time in Bolivia, in 2005, that presidential elections were won by an indigenous candidate. As we will see, along with their growing political visibility and participation has come more attention to indigenous values and views on how to live in harmony with nature, but this has hardly resulted in policy reforms for greater sustainability.

Once in office, leftist regimes implemented new economic measures, especially in the extractive sectors. The discourse of oil, gas and mining being strategic resources that require special treatment and extra state scrutiny thus reappeared in the highest political circles. While state ownership of subsoil resources had not been given up by their predecessors, the new governments claimed that extraction should be better controlled and should primarily serve the nation and national development. On the day of President Morales's decree of gas and oil nationalization, for instance, he declared that with this new law the wealth of hydrocarbons 'returned into the hands of the nation', and he called on the private companies to 'respect this decision of the Bolivian people' (*El País*, 2 May 2006). After two decades of deregulation, liberalization and privatization, new policies involved reregulation (through reforms of legal codes, laws and constitutions), 'retaxation' and sometimes also renationalization. However, the extent of these changes differs: while Venezuela, Bolivia and Ecuador experienced what could be called post-neoliberal economic restructuring of their extractive sectors, in countries such as Brazil, Peru and Chile left-leaning presidents introduced much less policy change. Nevertheless, the new governments generally expanded the budgets for social programmes. Since for most countries the primary sector is the main single source of public sector revenues, these market and policy shifts have been crucial to accommodate these increased social expenditures. In Venezuela, oil revenues accounted for 66 per cent of fiscal income in 2005, while in Chile copper revenues accounted for 33 per cent in 2006 (CEPAL 2008).[2] Fiscal revenues from oil, gas and mining as a percentage of gross domestic product (GDP) increased substantially from the beginning to the end of the 2000s. In Bolivia and Ecuador the increase was particularly high, from 5.1 to 10.1 per cent and from 7.2 to 12.9 per cent, respectively (ECLAC 2013). Taken together, the high commodity prices produced greater state revenues, and created positive conditions for those states that also wanted to capture a greater share of revenues for the public sector.

## Venezuela

In Venezuela, at the start of his presidency, Hugo Chávez (1999–2013) announced that he was leading a Bolivarian Revolution that would make a break with the long-standing patterns of socio-economic and political inequality. Indeed, a profound shift took place in the setting of groups that influenced decision making, in particular with respect to oil. In 2001, Venezuela adopted a new law on oil that strengthened the central state's control over the oil sector, and established that all joint operations have to count with a majority share for state-owned company Venezuelan Petroleum (PDVSA). In effect, 33 joint ventures with multinational corporations operating in the Orinoco basin had to be renegotiated. While international media criticized the reform, most multinational companies (MNCs) accepted the new situation, with the exception of ENI and Total which ended their investments, and Exxon-Mobil and ConocoPhillips which made an international complaint. In the following years, the share of PDVSA in these joint ventures went up to 78 per cent, while the royalties for foreign oil companies increased from 1 to 30 per cent, and taxes from 34 to 50 per cent. This renationalization of control and revenues clearly hurt foreign companies, but booming oil prices partly alleviated the pain. Furthermore, state control over oil is internationally quite common and multinationals may always opt to lower the investments or leave a country altogether.

National political and economic elites responded strongly to Chávez's oil policies, especially to his steps to gain control over the management and revenues of PDVSA. In 2002 and 2003 Venezuela experienced a series of protests and oil strikes, led by opposition parties and the managers and (unionized) workers of PDVSA. These mobilizations counted with substantial support from groups who were critical of the centralizing institutional tendencies under Chávez (Corrales and Penfold 2011). Simultaneously, Chávez and his populist policies and new institutions remained very popular, especially among the poor, and he continued to gain majority support in a series of elections and referenda (Philip and Panizza 2011). Next to growth due to booming oil markets, the central state's budget increased substantially and new health care, education and food programmes (*misiones*) as well as support systems for cooperatives reached poor citizens. Between 1998 and 2006, the central state's spending increased from 21 to 30 per cent of GDP. Real social spending per person even tripled in this period as in addition to the state also PDVSA made direct contributions to this cause, reaching as high as 7 per cent of GDP in 2006. Venezuela's poverty rate dropped from 44 to 28 per cent (Weisbrot and Sandoval 2008), even though a considerable part of these extra expenditures leaked away due to inefficiency and errors (Philip and Panizza 2011), and the lack of transparency and reliable data prevent a full assessment of the social and economic results of Chávez's redistributive policies (Corrales and Penfold 2011). Still, while at first his oil policies were nationally and internationally viewed as radical, soon afterwards other South American countries experienced political changes that resulted in similar reforms in the extractive industries.

## Bolivia

In Bolivia, protests in the early 2000s had shown the widespread popular discontent with neoliberal policies, especially on issues combining social inequality and natural resource use. In 2000, large groups mobilized against the privatization of water (including rain water) in Cochabamba. In 2003, mass mobilizations and violent confrontations with the military police in La Paz turned into a 'gas war' (or 'October war'/*guerra de octubre*), which forced President Gonzalo Sánchez de Lozado to leave the presidential palace and the country. The immediate case was the government plan for gas policy reforms, which fed in with outrage about poverty, marginalization and discrimination. These developments paved the way for the 2005 election of Evo Morales of the *Movimiento al Socialismo* (MAS). In 2006, on the symbolic date of May 1, Labour Day, Morales announced a decree to raise the public sector's take of profits in Bolivia's two largest natural gas fields from 18 to 82 per cent, thereby turning the balance between public and private sector revenues upside down. This presidential decision was widely broadcasted with images of Morales and the army 'repossessioning' a gas installation. The state-owned company Bolivian Fiscal Oilfields (YPFB) regained tasks lost through privatization, and production-sharing contracts with multinational corporations were replaced by servicing contracts (see the following section for the reaction of foreign investors). Indeed, important social programmes have been financed by the new direct tax on hydrocarbon profits: *Bono Juancito Pinto*, which provides a bonus to poor families who send their children to primary school, and *Renta Dignidad*, which provides a pension to poor elderly people (Hinojosa 2009).

Bolivia's governmental shift evidently changed the balance of power between various influential groups. New gas policies together with new policies on ownership and distribution of land were a source of strong resentment among national and subnational elites, who were not willing to give up property, privileges and power. From 2006 to 2008, influential economic groups within the more developed (*media luna*) provinces fiercely resisted new national policies and threatened to seek autonomy from the central state. Morales's attempt to partly re-centralize the decentralized distribution of public revenues from the gas and mining operations was another sting for the opposition. However, since the implementation of the new constitution in 2008, which involved some compromises from both sides, the call for autonomy has weakened. This rather progressive constitution, formulated by an elected constitutional assembly, prioritizes redistribution and better living standards for the poor. It also established Bolivia as a plurinational state, acknowledging the plurality of peoples within the national territory. On natural resource governance, it mentions simultaneously the rights of indigenous peoples within their territories, and more power of the central government, signifying that the Bolivian people are in control of these resources (see also Chapter 4). Nevertheless, the central government and indigenous groups have recently clashed over a few large projects (e.g. gas extraction and the Isiboro Sécure National Park and Indigenous Territory (TIPNIS) highway) that affect natural resource use.

## Ecuador

In Ecuador, under President Rafael Correa (since 2007), some similar political shifts and policy reforms occurred. The entry of a leftist president was also quite surprising in Ecuador, but compared to Venezuela and Bolivia there was less of a strongly established and institutionalized political elite that had to be dealt with. In his first year in office, Correa decreed to raise the state's share of windfall oil profits from 50 to 99 per cent. Aided by the global oil boom and Ecuador's dollar economy, expanding state revenues allowed Correa, among other things, to double welfare payments to poor households, subsidize electricity for poor households, and make a range of (emergency) investments in education, health, micro-credits and infrastructure. Like Chávez, Correa has been known for his verbal attacks on foreign capital (for instance, when Ecuador defaulted on its foreign debts in 2008) and identifies with Socialism of the twenty-first century, but he also stresses that this new socialism has to be aware of the importance of the market, which should function in the service of the citizens.[3] President Correa has been able to secure major electoral support for his regime, and for his policies of more state control over the oil sector and the emerging mining sector. However, in 2008 Catherine Conaghan (2008) already conceptualized his rule as a plebiscitary presidency in which Correa's decrees, charisma and 'playing the media' have rendered the National Congress irrelevant.

Despite the absence of an old political elite effectively resisting Correa's reforms, the recent governance of Ecuador's oil and mining has been rather conflictive. In 2010, the National Assembly approved legislation to allow only for servicing contracts in the oil sector, as a result of which the contracts with MNCs had to be renegotiated. In this case, four out of nine companies did not come to a new agreement and ended their operations, leaving the oil sector predominantly (for about three quarters) to Ecuador's state companies (including one joint venture with PDVSA). Even proponents of more state control on oil extraction have criticized the reform and renegotiation. Alberto Acosta (2011), who initially was Minister of Energy and Mining under Correa, claims that the reform and renegotiations of 2010 lacked transparency and democratic deliberation, and that previous environmental damage by the companies was ignored. Acosta was also the president of the elected National Constitutional Assembly that wrote Ecuador's new Constitution. This constitution (approved by 64 per cent in a 2009 referendum) is remarkably progressive as it aims at an alternative idea of development, known as *sumak kawsay* (in Kichwa) or *buen vivir* (good living), and stresses both the rights of indigenous peoples and the rights of nature. While these are even international novelties, in practice limited progress has been made and President Correa has clashed repeatedly with indigenous and environmental organizations. These clashes predominantly concern concessions for oil extraction and mining. Several new areas have been opened for oil extraction, most of which are located in biodiverse areas in the Amazon. In 2013, Correa also decided to allow oil drilling in the Yasuní-ITT national park, thereby pulling back an innovative policy to protect this extremely vulnerable area, which his government had launched only a few years before. While large-scale mining is only starting up in Ecuador, mining projects such as El Mirador and Intaq have already seen major contestations. 'More than any other issue, the conflicts over mining illustrated the wide, growing, and seemingly unbridgeable gap between Correa and the social movements' (Becker 2011, 58). Correa has used a top-down attitude towards civil society groups mobilizing against projects that are likely to harm the environment and indigenous territories, and on several occasions anti-terrorism legislation and other criminalization tactics were used (Becker 2011; Santamaria 2013). Simultaneously, while Correa's government has used legal processes against environmental organizations such as Acción Ecológica and Pachamama, it has strategically adopted the terminology of *buen vivir*, which has become the key slogan of the National Development Plan. In effect, indigenous, environmental and other civil society groups feel that their ideas for a transformation towards sustainability have been abused, and *buen vivir* stands the risk of becoming an empty signifier (Van Teijlingen and Hogenboom 2014).

## Brazil

In contrast to the abovementioned presidents Chávez, Morales and Correa, in Brazil president Lula da Silva (2003–10) and president Dilma Rousseff (since 2011; and already Minister of Mines and Energy in Lula's first administration) of the leftist Workers' Party (PT) have opted for continuing most of their predecessor's economic policies, including those on mining and oil. Lula did not change the tax rules in these sectors, nor the status of the very large Brazilian companies Petrobras and Vale. Petrobras is a mixed (public/private) oil company and the region's largest company. Although it is still state-controlled, it was partly privatized in the 1990s and nowadays private investors hold around 60 per cent of the shares. In that same decade, Brazil's mining company Vale was completely privatized. Currently it is not only the largest mining company of Latin America (number 4 in the ranking of *AméricaEconomía*, following right after the oil giants Petrobras, PDVSA and Mexican Petroleums (PEMEX)) but also the second largest mining company in the world, with operations in about 30 countries. While numerous Brazilians, especially from the PT's electorate, would have liked to see Vale and Petrobras renationalized, Lula and Dilma have not done so. Arguably, this is the result of both inability and unwillingness. With regard to this first dimension, they lacked the majority in congress (and possibly society) that would have been politically necessary for legitimizing and realizing a more radical reform. With regard to the latter, as we will see, the neo-developmentalist debate stressing that the state needs to resume a central role in economic development in fact has informed some interesting reforms since Lula's second presidential period (Schutte 2013), but as existing legislation already was rather supportive of national industry, these policy changes have not been as radical as some of those mentioned above.[4]

Gradually, the oil and mining policies of Brazil have also become the subject of reform. In 2008, after the discovery of huge deep-sea oil reserves off Brazil's coast,

President Lula announced a reform of oil policies. While Petrobras is to be the operator of these offshore fields, the public sector's control over these oil reserves and revenues should be protected by a new (non-mixed) state company, Petrosal. In the words of Lula, this would allow for putting the revenues from future deep-sea oil drilling 'in hands of the Brazilian people'. In order to pay off 'the debt with the poor since 500 years', he also proposed the creation of a development fund, using the resources for education, health care and technological development. In addition, president Dilma started a process for a reform that would raise royalties in the mining sector (e.g. an increase for iron from 2 to 4 per cent, and for gold from 1 to 2 per cent), but the approval in Congress proved very slow. Despite the lack of radical economic policy changes, Lula's and Dilma's presidencies resemble those of other presidents of the new left in the sense that social spending has increased substantially, through programmes such as Bolsa Familia, a conditional cash transfer programme for poor families. Together with the effects of the growing economy, Lula's presidency also resulted in less poverty.

## New political elites and resource politics

Overall, the arrival of leftist presidents and governments have implied some interesting changes in the elites that influence oil, gas and mining policies. With the post-neoliberal legislation the balance between public and private gains and control has altered substantially, especially in Venezuela, Bolivia and Ecuador. In these particular sectors with their high-tech and large-scale operations that require particular expertise and massive investments, such a rebalancing act basically implies more control and gains for the national public sector, primarily at the expense of control and gains of MNCs. Evidently, history has proven that these multinationals can be very powerful and hard to confront. However, high global demand and prices softened the circumstances and many MNCs agreed to enter into negotiations (in which they had considerable leverage, as we will see in the following section) and settled for receiving a lower share of the highly increased revenues. In addition, in the case of oil and gas, state control and ownership is not uncommon, and companies are used to operating in countries where foreign direct investment is highly regulated and sometimes even extraction itself is forbidden (up-stream activities, e.g. in Mexico and Saudi Arabia). These characteristics mark a clear difference from the agricultural sector, with its more varied economic and political make-up, where reforms by progressive governments usually involve major clashes with oligarchic or modern rural elites (as witnessed in various chapters in this volume). As we have seen, in the cases of Venezuela and Bolivia there was also a set of national political elites that lost out and tried to resist the profound oil and gas reforms. However, they were unable to completely block them and gradually saw their influence decrease. The fact that the state's expanding control and revenues have allowed for effective redistribution via social programmes, which reach both the urban and the rural poor, provided presidents Chávez, Morales and Correa with the necessary electoral support and mobilization potential to resist opposing elites and lock in their reforms of the mineral sectors (this again differs from the political and social dynamics around agricultural policies).

With these parallel developments, the core of the political and bureaucratic players and institutions in charge of these mineral and social reforms has formed a new elite. In general, the new elite has successfully aimed at greater state control over the strategic sectors of oil, gas and mining as well as using the revenues for a model of more equitative development. Simultaneously, they have become dependent (or arguably 'addicted') to high rates of mineral extraction, not only to pay for their economic and social policies but also for their political survival (Hogenboom 2012). This may explain why on several occasions the new elites have tried to ignore local and national organizations and mobilizations that demand greater care of the environment. Furthermore, whereas increasing volumes of material are extracted and the extractive activities continue to expand into new areas, there are no indications of extra public spending on environmental expertise, controls and protection to at least keep up with the pace of the sector's growth.[5]

## Shifts in international elites

The processes discussed above have to be understood and analysed in an international political and economic context. Especially, resource-rich countries with leftist governments have been able to take greater distance from the 'guidance' of the Washington-based international financial institutions the World Bank (WB), the InterAmerican Development Bank (IDB) and the International Monetary Fund (IMF), as well as from the US influence through these institutions and its own government agencies. Helped by the extra revenues under booming market conditions, South American countries could pace up the payments to these international institutions (e.g. the Lula and Kirchner governments paid the remaining IMF debts before the deadlines) and thereby be liberated from their policy conditions and interventions.[6] Another important sign was the end of the plan for a Free Trade Agreement of the Americas (FTAA), which had been initiated by the US and discussed for ten years with Latin American governments, but was by 2005 effectively resisted by the latter, especially Venezuela, Brazil and Argentina (Philip and Panizza 2011).

In this section, we will look into the shifts among international economic elites. Next to a limited change in the role of Western MNCs (who lost some privileges and liberties but remained influential), we will look into the expansion and growing influence of *multilatinas* (both private companies and state companies). In more detail we will assess the arrival and influence of various Chinese actors, including (mainly state-owned) companies and banks. We will see that some interesting new regional organizations have been created, while the Economic Commission of Latin America and the Caribbean has continued to be an influential regional agenda-setting institution, favouring resource extraction for development.

## Multinationals and multilatinas

As key investors, MNCs continue to be important elites in South America's mineral sectors. This is even true in the case of oil and gas, which were less lib-eralized than the mining sector in the 1980s and 1990s, and in countries where the political elite shift has been more radically post-neoliberal. For instance, in Bolivia the renewed control of the state has come partly at the expense of for-eign investors, but simultaneously Morales has had to deal with the reality that multinationals remain indispensable for the development of extractive sectors. After his decree for nationalization of 1 May 2006, the companies operating in Bolivia's gas sector had to negotiate new contracts. In contrast with the 82 per cent rates for new investments, the negotiations resulted in overall tax rates (including royalties) of more than 50 per cent of profits for these com-panies. This is a substantial increase from the previous 18 per cent, and could be considered a success for the public sector of a small and very poor country. Critical views see the outcome as a sign of a lack of willingness of the new political elite to really confront MNCs, but it seems that the government really pushed the limits, and under the new regime it has in fact been hard to attract sufficient foreign investment. Meanwhile, in the mining sector Morales has sought alternative models of extraction, which has turned out to be also rather complicated as the events around new concessions for iron mining in El Mutún and lithium mining in Uyuni have shown. Considering the country's level of development, Morales's policies to stimulate up-graded production activities such as refining in order to expand local employment and national revenues and technological development, have been both understandable and bold. Despite booming iron prices and the promising market potential for lithium (for batteries, electric cars, etc.), in practice it has turned out to be extremely difficult to find multinationals willing to make large investments under the conditions set by Morales's government.

Interestingly, the main foreign investor affected by Morales's nationalization of gas and oil was not a Western but a Latin American multinational: Brazil's state-controlled giant Petrobras. This *multilatina* (Latin American multinational) was the largest investor in Bolivia, representing about one fifth of that country's GDP and foreign investment. Petrobras and the Brazilian government were not amused by Morales's new gas policy and the show of military occupation of one of Petrobras's gas installations on Labour Day 2006. After difficult months of conflicts and negotiations, Petrobras came to an agreement with the Bolivian government and accepted that it would only receive 18 per cent of the profits. In 2007, the Bolivian government also nationalized two oil refineries of Petrobras. Since these events, Petrobras has scaled down its investments.

This particular event illustrates the wider new trend of a few *multilatinas* becoming important actors in the region's oil, gas and mining sectors. The general growth of *multilatinas* took place in the 1980s and 1990s as a result of privatization and liberalization policies, resulting primarily in the expansion of private sector conglomerates and in greater autonomy of those companies that remained state-controlled (Fernández Jilberto and Hogenboom 2004). In the oil and gas sector *multilatinas* are generally state-owned, and have been so for several decades, but as we have seen there is considerable variation in how they are managed. While Petrobras operates basically as an autonomous entity, PDVSA became more state controlled and politicized under Chávez, and has also been used as a diplomatic instrument in cross-border relations (see the next section). Many other South American oil and gas companies are not *multilatinas* as they mainly or only operate on national territory. In the mining sector, the most noticeable *multilatina* has been the private company Vale, which is the world's largest iron producer, but there are some other ones. While Chile's state-owned but autonomously operated copper company CODELCO (created under Allende and never privatized under Pinochet) is the world's largest producer of this metal, until very recently all their mines were in Chile. In 2012, however, it made its first step outside by investing in Ecuador's Junín copper mine. Taken together, while these large oil, gas and mining companies are elites within their country of origin, there are only a few that are part of the international corporate elite operating in resource-rich countries in the region.

### Influences from China

An important new trend is the growing influence of various Chinese actors in the region. The recent arrival of Chinese capital (investments and credits) is related to wider trends of China's economic growth, increased Chinese demand for commodities (the country has replaced the US as the world's largest energy consumer and is the main importer of important commodities such as iron ore), and global effects on prices and extracted volumes. The value of exports from Latin America and the Caribbean to China increased no less than 25 times between 2000 and 2012. For resource-rich countries China has become a major export destination, and for countries such as Brazil, Chile and Peru it is even number one. Yet these massive flows of goods are hardly diversified: countries export mainly one or just a few primary products to China, such as metal ores, soy and oil (Rosales and Kuwayama 2012).

These exports to China as well as the growing investments of Chinese companies into Latin America's natural resource sectors have been encouraged and supported by the Chinese state and banks. Major government efforts have been directed at China's full insertion into the global economy and turning large Chinese companies into successful multinationals. Most of these companies, like the banks, are state-owned yet formally operate independently. Since the 1990s, the Chinese government has intensified its relations with all Latin American countries (Fernández Jilberto and Hogenboom 2010), some of which have culminated in strategic partnerships (Brazil, Venezuela) or Free Trade Agreements (Chile, Peru and Costa Rica). Since the latest international financial crisis, Chinese multinationals have started to seriously invest in the region. For instance, in 2010 Chinese companies invested $9.6 billion in Brazil and $5.5 billion in Argentina. While the US, Canadian and European MNCs are still the key foreign investors in Latin American oil and mining, companies from China are gradually increasing their involvement in extraction in the region.

Meanwhile, the China Development Bank (CDB) and China's Export–Import Bank have become a new source of foreign loans to South America. In the case of Ecuador, China has even become the main source of loans, with a total of $9 billion from the CDB, PetroChina and China's Export–Import Bank. Like Chinese direct investments, most of these credits to South America are natural-resource related, especially to oil. While South American countries seek to secure and diversify their oil exports, China aims to maximize its energy security and diversify its oil imports (Sun 2012). The CDB has provided a few large loans-for-oil to Brazil, Venezuela and Ecuador. In 2009, when North American and European investments were low, the CDB and Petrobras agreed on a $10 billion loan. This credit is part of a Sino-Brazilian loans-for-oil deal in which Petrobras will supply 200,000 barrels of oil per day to a subsidiary of Sinopec for ten years. In the case of Venezuela, total energy-backed loans from 2007 to 2011 valued over $28 billion; this makes Venezuela the largest foreign borrower of the CDB (Downs 2011, 46–53). Moreover, Venezuela and China have established an extensive model of energy cooperation, including a series of joint ventures between China National Petroleum Corporation (CNPC) and PDVSA, joint institutions such as the China–Venezuelan Joint Fund which finances large projects in Venezuela (co-funded by the CDB and Venezuela's Development Bank), and the China–Venezuela High Level mixed Joint Committee that coordinates decision making (Sun 2012, 234).

This brief account points at the centrality of commodities (metals, soy and especially oil) in the new but rapidly developing involvement of Chinese companies, banks and government in South American countries. The somewhat different relations and arrangements, compared to those with North American and European actors, are likely to have immediate as well as long-term implications for the governance of South America's natural resources. Since it is impossible to present here a detailed account on the still nascent, heavily debated and nationally diverging experiences with Chinese actors in extractive sectors, we will identify only a few special characteristics that deserve attention, and further inquiry. Chinese oil and mining companies are looking for resources to make profits, like any other company, but they sometimes take on projects that Western multinationals would not, as the latter may find the physical, economic or political and social conditions too risky or demanding.[7] While less internationally experienced, they partly invest in what we could label 'difficult' countries (e.g. Ecuador), areas (e.g. requiring additional infrastructure investments) and projects (e.g. with a conflictive history or also requiring extra expenditures). Indeed, compared to Western countries they can more easily invest in projects that require infrastructural development, they are less restrained by short-term shareholder value maximization, and they are less exposed to a series of (home-country) risks, such as financial, reputational and legal risks (Gonzalez-Vicente 2012). They thus sometimes function as 'investor of last resort', which arguably adds to their 'leeway' when making deals with South American governments.

Similarly, since 2005 Chinese banks have started to make such large (often oil-related) credits to Latin America that their loan commitments for 2010 even temporarily surpassed those of the World Bank, IDB and US Export–Import Bank together (Gallagher *et al.* 2012). The oil-based credits are to be repaid by long-term (10–30 years) oil deliveries to Chinese companies.

It is somewhat early to determine whether these Chinese actors are part of the international elites in South American countries. Considering its multi-billion-dollar loans connected to long-term oil contracts with Venezuela, Brazil and Ecuador, the CDB arguably has acquired that status. Similarly, at least in the case of Venezuela, the Chinese government has come to function as an international elite. Positive accounts stress the Chinese formal policy to not interfere in internal affairs of other countries and portray these banks as partners of (South–South) development that do not link macroeconomic policy conditions to their credits as the Washington-based institutions did; but it is clear that long-term oil contracts are nevertheless locking in policies, which may limit future room for change. A new government will for instance not have the liberty to sell the oil to other companies (and pay the CDB with the revenues), let alone decide to slow down oil extraction (and pay back the loans in cash). Still, the increasing economic importance of China has brought South American countries much-needed diversification of markets and relations, but it may also make them more susceptible to governmental Chinese influence. While China is also a developing country, the asymmetries with countries in the region are evident. And while the Chinese state no longer centrally controls the 'small kingdoms' of state-owned companies and banks, it still guides them (e.g. through the five-year development plans and the Communist Party apparatus) beyond ways seen in Europe and the US (Brødsgaard 2012).

## New regionalization around strategic sectors

Since the 2000s a few regionalization initiatives have taken shape that are worth mentioning in this overview of shifts in actors that stand in a privileged position to influence the use and management of mineral resources. First, from the start of his presidency, Hugo Chávez used part of Venezuela's large oil revenues and reserves to strengthen bilateral and regional relations, and to build a progressive model for regional cooperation and integration. This support included loans and projects for Bolivia after Evo Morales came into office, and a $2.3 billion credit to Argentina in 2005, when President Néstor Kirchner wanted to quickly pay off its remaining $9.8 billion debt to the IMF. In addition, he started the Bolivarian Alliance for the Peoples of Our America (ALBA) to allow for a more solidarity-based regional integration with countries such as Cuba, Bolivia and Ecuador. Other expressions of such oil diplomacy were initiatives such as Petrosur (with Brazil, Argentina and Uruguay) and Petrocaribe for energy cooperation.

Second, the creation of the Union of South American Nations (UNASUR) in 2008 and the Community of Latin American and Caribbean States (CELAC) in 2010 mark a further strengthening and institutionalization of ambitions for regional integration without the United States. The South American Union was formed after the US-guided idea for a Free Trade Area of the Americas had evaporated. Also the Banco del Sur was launched as a South American alternative for loans from WB and IDB, but this hardly materialized. Next, with CELAC, a community has come into being that next to South America also includes Mexico and the Central American and Caribbean countries. UNASUR and CELAC have so far functioned primarily as (non-ideological) platforms for regional dialogue and cooperation, but they aim at regional economic and political integration. Furthermore, CELAC has already turned into the organization for regional encounters with large international entities, such as the European Union and China (e.g. the EU–CELAC summit in 2013, and the China–CELAC ministerial-level forum created in 2014).

Third, the Economic Commission of Latin America and the Caribbean (ECLAC) plays a pivotal role in feeding and supporting regional policy-making processes. Since its creation in 1948, it has been gathering and analysing data on economic and social development in the region, pointing at risks, and formulating policy recommendations. Through its reports and activities, ECLAC has so far been the single most important agenda-setting agency from the region itself, and both UNASUR and CELAC have established strong relations with ECLAC. Its recent reports pay ample attention to natural resource sectors. The report *Natural Resources within the Union of South American Nations: Status and Trends for a Regional Development Agenda* (ECLAC 2013), prepared on invitation of the UNASUR, stresses the need to increase the public sector capture of mineral rents, and to improve the governance of mining, oil, hydroelectricity and water. Whereas the prologue and conclusions make brief mention of the need for a better public management of socio-environmental conflicts, the report itself does not elaborate on this. It needs mentioning that numerous ECLAC publications since the mid-2000s also deal with the relevance of China for the region, especially pointing at the benefits and potential of China as new destination for exports, a source of investments, credits, imports and technology, and a partner for mutual development.

Interestingly, these three regionalization trends affecting mineral politics express the different dimensions of the use of resources by elites (see Bull's definition in Chapter 2). Venezuela's oil diplomacy and the ALBA initiative are clear examples of how the availability of valuable natural resources can allow a government to influence political processes beyond its national borders. Next, UNASUR and CELAC seem to provide the organizational resources to the governments of South and Latin America, in their ambition to deepen regionalization without the involvement or 'guidance' of the US government. In the case of ECLAC, it is symbolic resources, that is knowledge and expertise, but also its regional and international networks, that explain its privileged position. Together with the growing role of a few giant mineral *multilatinas*, mentioned in the previous section, these trends point at a current of regionalization of elites in South America.

## Discussion and concluding thoughts

While we have seen a series of changes in the constellation of national and inter-national elites and other actors around oil, gas and mining in South America, the question remains, what are their implications for environmental governance in these sectors. This discussion requires us to go beyond early expectations and pre-conceptions. Initially, for instance, many believed that the new left-elites were more inclined to focus on the environment than old political elites, because of their critical attitude towards economic liberalization and their stronger rela-tions with indigenous groups and their views on living in harmony with nature. And Chinese companies were seen as less inclined to take local environmental concerns and community interests into account in their operations, because they are not as experienced (in their home country or globally) with new technolo-gies and civic demands as Western multinationals are. Over the past few years, however, experience has been gained, allowing us to make some more matured estimation of the extent to which elite shifts affect environmental governance.

The coming into power of new left-governments has probably involved the most relevant elite shift for the governance of South America's mineral resources. While our review has focussed on countries with the deepest politi-cal and policy changes (Venezuela, Bolivia and Ecuador), the more moderated experience of Brazil also pointed at changing views and attitudes. Generally speaking, leftist presidents from resource-rich countries distanced themselves from the Washington Consensus and took some (smaller or greater) steps to strengthen state control over mineral resources. These presidents have pictured their policies as anti-neoliberal initiatives to achieve equitable development and sovereignty. And indeed, next to the booming markets, the policies helped to further spur social and economic development as well as state-building (as stressed by Weber; see Chapter 2 of this volume). The strengthening of the position of state-owned companies and of the control by central state insti-tutions have not brought an end to the need for foreign investment and technology, which implies that what we have witnessed is a gradual shift of the public–private mix. However, expanding concession territories and increasing the volumes extracted indicate that the economic and political dependence on these resources has further deepened. While this may be democratically decided for good causes, it usually implies that nature and the interests of local communities (and future generations) are sacrificed.

Within this context, there are a few signs that environmental and indigenous organizations, whether governmental or non-governmental, have been granted the resources and influence necessary to bring a real change to the extensive local ecological damage of oil, gas and mining projects. In the past two decades, indigenous groups in countries such as Ecuador or Bolivia have been, or at least were for some time, quite influential. Notions of Pachamama (Bolivia), *buen vivir* and rights of nature (Ecuador) are still prominent in government discourses. However, while these (semi-)elites have had some social and political support, they have not achieved a privileged position in the governance of minerals. With the recentralization of mineral policies, the state's increased power has also come at the expense of groups from civil society. Some of the numerous conflicts that have emerged have been solved (or silenced) through dialogue and compensation, but leftist governments have also proven prone to making strong verbal attacks against local groups and indigenous and environmental organizations that are opposing an extractive project, in some cases even criminalizing them.

There are some interesting shifts in the international and regional elites around strategic resources in South America, ranging from companies such as Petrobras, Vale and PDVSA turning into *multilatinas*, the rapid arrival of many Chinese oil and mining companies, and the regionalization of discourses and policies. For environmental governance these shifts have not brought much of a change. The new investors operate as economic agents, and primarily try to make profits and become accepted global players. In political circles, social progress is stressed much more than environmental protection, despite extensive environmental discourses. All in all, the international and regional relations are mainly supportive of more extraction, for both economic and social reasons.

Finally, as much as these various elite shifts contribute to countering some social injustices, in the sense that poverty and to some extent (national and international) inequality are diminishing, their recent decisions and practices have increased the environmental injustices around mineral resource extraction in South America. Qualitatively, the increased profitability of oil, gas and mining activities and their centrality to socio-economic development has not contributed to a more sustainable use of mineral reserves. Moreover, for economic, political and social reasons, extraction is expanding into ever more areas, thereby negatively affecting more local communities and natural environments.

## Notes

1 This study builds on academic literature and discussions, and on information from primary documents, interviews and conversations, gathered during several visits to the region (Brazil, Ecuador, Argentina, Chile) between 2011 and 2013. The EU has been of support through the project on Environmental Governance in Latin America and the Caribbean – ENGOV (FP7-SSH-CT-2010-266710).
2 The national systems for the government's collection of resource rents differ greatly. They include a mix of royalties, taxes, public sector participation and other contributions (ECLAC 2013, 18–19).
3 Rafael Correa in an interview for Telesur, 30 July 2013, available at: www.presidencia. gob.ec/la-revolucion-en-america-se-profundizara-con-eficiencia-para-atender-a-la-ciudadania/ (accessed on 21 April 2014).
4 In the 1980s and 1990s Brazil combined liberalization strategies with industrial policies that stimulate productive linkages between multinational and domestic firms, such as a minimum local content requirement for offshore and onshore oil projects of 30 per cent and 70 per cent, respectively.
5 Some (academic and NGO) environmental experts from Venezuela, Ecuador and Bolivia even claim that the funding, quality of technical personnel and institutional independence of environmental ministries and agencies have gone down. Another point of concern is the capacity and willingness to control the operations of the state-owned companies.

6 For instance, in 2005 Ecuador's then Minister of Economy, (current President) Rafael Correa, was replaced after pressure and threats from international financial institutions that opposed his plans for more public social spending through limits on foreign debt payments, and higher taxes on oil extraction.
7 Explanations for this difference range from the fact that they are state-owned (and thus guided more by policy aims for national resource security, while coming together with bank credits and special bilateral cooperation schemes, or counting on some leeway in case projects falter or take longer to become profitable), that they are newcomers to contemporary globalization (and thus cannot be too picky about where and how to start up an operation), and that they surf on a high economic and financial wave when compared to the conditions of North American and European MNCs.

## References

Acosta, A. (2011) Ecuador: Unas reformas petroleras con muy poca reforma. *Ecuador Debate*, 82, 45–60.

Becker, M. (2011) Correa, indigenous movements, and the writing of a new constitution in Ecuador. *Latin American Perspectives*, 176, 47–62.

Brødsgaard, K. E. (2012) Politics and business group formation in China: The party in control? *The China Quarterly*, 211, 624–648.

CEPAL (2008) *Balance Preliminar de las Economías de América Latina y el Caribe*. CEPAL, Santiago.

Conaghan, C. M. (2008) Ecuador: Correa's plebiscitary presidency. *Journal of Democracy*, 19(2), 46–60.

Corrales, J. and Penfold, M. (2011) *Dragon in the Tropics: Hugo Chávez and the Political Economy of Revolution in Venezuela*. The Brookings Institution, Washington DC.

Downs, E. S. (2011) *Inside China, Inc.: China Developments Bank's Cross-Border Energy Deals*. The Brookings Institution, Washington DC.

ECLAC (2013) *Natural Resources within the Union of South American Nations: Status and Trends for a Regional Development Agenda*. ECLAC, Santiago.

Fernández Jilberto, A. E. and Hogenboom, B. (2004) Conglomerates and economic groups in neoliberal Latin America. *Journal of Developing Societies*, 20(3/4), 149–171.

Fernández Jilberto, A. E. and Hogenboom, B. (2010) Latin America and China: South–South Relations in a New Era, in A. E. Fernández Jilberto and B. Hogenboom (eds), *Latin America Facing China: South–South Relations beyond the Washington Consensus*. Berghahn Books, Oxford and New York, 1–32.

Gallagher, K. P., Irwin, A. and Koleski, K. (2012) *The New Banks In Town: Chinese Finance in Latin America*. Inter-American Dialogue, Washington DC.

Gonzalez-Vicente, R. (2012) Mapping Chinese mining investment in Latin America: Politics or market? *The China Quarterly*, 209, March, 35–58.

Hinojosa, L. (2009) Riqueza mineral y pobreza en los Andes, Preparado para LASA2009.

Hogenboom, B. (2012) Depoliticized and repoliticized minerals in Latin America. *Journal of Developing Societies*, 28(2), 133–158.

Philip, G. and Panizza, F. (2011) *The Triumph of Politics: The Return of the Left in Venezuela, Bolivia and Ecuador*. Polity, Cambridge.

Rosales, O. and Kuwayama, M. (2012) *China and Latin America and the Caribbean: Building a Strategic Economic and Trade Relationship*. ECLAC, Santiago.

Santamaria, P. (2013) Commentary: Ecuador and the rights of Indigenous peoples. *AlterNative: An International Journal of Indigenous Peoples*, 9(3), 262–266.

130   *Barbara Hogenboom*

Schutte, G. R. (2013) Brazil: new developmentalism and the management of offshore oil wealth. *European Review of Latin American and Caribbean Studies*, 95, 49–70.

Sun, H. (2012) Energy cooperation between China and Latin America: The case of Venezuela, in M. Parvizi Amineh and Y. Guang (eds), *Secure Oil and Alternative Energy: The Geopolitics of Energy Paths of China and the European*. Brill, Leiden, pp. 213–244.

Van Teijlingen, K. and Hogenboom, B. (2014) Debating *Buen Vivir* at the mining frontier: The conflict around El Mirador Mine in Ecuador, ENGOV Working paper No. 15.

Weisbrot, M. and Sandoval, L. (2008) *Update: The Venezuelan Economy in the Chávez Years*. Center for Economic and Policy Research, Washington DC.

# 8 Staying the same

## Transnational elites, mining and environmental governance in Guatemala

*Mariel Aguilar-Støen*

## Introduction

Mining related conflicts have multiplied in Guatemala during the last ten years as the number of mining exploration and exploitation licenses that have been granted in the country increased, particularly those related to gold and silver mining projects. Most scholarly literature has focused on one conflict in the Maya western highlands, the Marlin mine (Cuffe, 2005; Hurtado and Lungo, 2007; Fulmer *et al.*, 2008; Holden and Jacobson, 2009; Yagenova and Garcia, 2009; Nolin and Stephens, 2010; Sieder, 2011; Urkidi, 2011; Rasch, 2012). Since 2011 other mining conflicts have developed in places that have been commonly imagined as "ladinas"[1] (Metz, 2001), in the east and south-east.

In this chapter I present an analysis of the dynamics of mining conflicts focusing on south-eastern Guatemala, drawing from extended fieldwork (between 2009 and 2013) in the area. The aim is to highlight asymmetrical power relations and competing claims about the environment and about rural areas in Guatemala that are revealed through mining conflicts. Particular attention will be paid to the dynamics between elites and social movements in the country. Elites here refer to two groups. On the one hand, Guatemala's traditional business elites organized within the business peak association, the Coordinating Committee of Agricultural, Commercial, Industrial and Financial Associations (CACIF), a powerful political force in the country (Schneider, 2012). On the other hand, transnational mining companies that control metallic mineral extraction and its associated resources such as technology and commercial networks.

Guatemalan and transnational mining companies are organized in the Extractive Industries Business Association (*Gremial de Industrias Extractivas*) that belongs to the Industrial Chamber of Guatemala which is part of CACIF. Guatemalan business elites are dominated by a limited number of family networks that have absorbed rising sectors while maintaining control of agro-exports, industry, services and the financial sector as well as the media (Palencia-Prado, 2012; Schneider, 2012). Guatemalan business elites have been successful in keeping transnational elites in a subordinate position, because the former control important political resources, networks and information without which the latter could not operate (Schneider, 2012; Bull *et al.*, 2014) and also because of the different types of partnerships local elites have established with transnational mining companies.

The argument in this chapter is that mining conflicts are located within the politics of place. This means that given that places can have different and often conflicting meanings to different actors, ongoing struggles against mining in rural Guatemala are connected to broader political struggles in the country but manifest in the way in which different actors try to build and contest the identity of particular places and of the people connected to such places. By studying mining conflicts, in this chapter I shall illustrate the ways in which place meanings are connected to conflicting ideas about property to land, environmental governance, participation and development. The elites' ideas and values on this respect are often opposed to local movements' ideas and values.

Guatemala has taken a series of legal, discursive and policy initiatives to produce a mineral extraction space within its territory. The government and the elites have been involved in the production of such space. The production of the mineral extraction space in Guatemala has also been influenced by global processes such as the shifting geography of mineral demand, changes in prices and the re-positioning of Guatemala in the globalized market through free-trade agreements. However, the production of space does not occur without resistance from those whose lives will be affected. Although there are several on-going mining conflicts in Guatemala, contestations against mining are place-based and are not organized as a national movement against mining. Thus, mining protests constitute in practice a defense of the place. In that sense, I am referring to place both as material sites where people live, work and move, where they form attachments and practice their relations with each other and relate to the rest of the world (Massey, 1991) and to "networks of social relations" that are dynamic over time (Massey, 1994). Places are also sites where struggles over memory and identity occur in the sense that identities and difference are socially produced in the present, involving a negotiation with the past and possibilities for the future. Places are continually changing. Through trade, migration and cultural exchanges, a place changes as these connections transform its economic, institutional and cultural character (Massey, 1994). A place's specificity, its local uniqueness and the sense of place that people living in it attach to it, is the result of the combination of influences that have reached the place. In other words, places are not isolated but in contact with other places that constantly transform them (Massey, 1994).

This chapter is organized as follows. The first section discusses the position of Guatemala within the changing global geography of mineral extraction. That section is followed by a description of the processes involved in creating the space of mineral extraction in Guatemala. The subsequent section analyses contestations against mining and the dynamics these create vis-à-vis the Guatemalan elites, before the concluding section.

## Guatemala and the changing geography of mineral extraction

Mineral exploration in Guatemala grew by 1,000 per cent between 1998 and 2010, as a result of a combination of macroeconomic and sector reforms, influenced by global processes including changing patterns of mineral demand, technological innovations, the emergence of new global players, the rise of junior mining firms and the intensification of competition between these junior companies (Bridge, 2004; Bebbington *et al.*, 2008; Gordon and Webber, 2008; Dougherty, 2011). Junior firms are small exploration firms with no or very few production sites (Dougherty, 2011). Demand for minerals shifted towards Asia, with China as the largest buyer. Technological innovations in exploration, production and environmental management are pushing the mineral frontier forward by making it possible to access previously inaccessible deposits (Bridge, 2004; Bebbington *et al.*, 2008; Dougherty, 2011).

In 2009 there were 75 mining companies operating in Guatemala financed by a mix of local and foreign capital (Lee and Bonilla de Anzueto, 2009). Metallic mineral exploitation is dominated by Canadian groups: Goldcorp,[2] Tahoe Resources Inc.,[3] Argonaut Gold Inc.,[4] and one company with Russian capital: Solway Investment Group Limited Inc.,[5] which acquired the mining rights from the Canadian company HudBay Minerals in 2011 (Anderson, 2012). It is worth noting that Guatemalan elites have entered into partnerships with transnational mining companies through different forms of arrangements (Palencia-Prado, 2012). The largest nonmetallic mining company is the Guatemalan company Cementos Progreso, which makes the second largest contribution to mining investments in Guatemala (Lee and Bonilla de Anzueto, 2009).

The Central America and Dominican Republic Free Trade Agreement (CAFTA-DR) with the United States, signed by Guatemala in 2004 includes investor rights, by way of which mining companies registered in the USA can sue[6] the country for non-compliance with the agreement (Urkidi, 2011). Mining regulations in Guatemalan are in practice tied to international trade and commercial agreements.

In addition to the groups mentioned above, which are the largest, there are several other networks of junior and large firms involved in exploration. For example, the Canadian company Nichromet Extractions and its subsidiary Nichromet Guatemala operate eight exploration licenses, the Australian firm BHP/Billiton with its associated subsidiaries Maya Niquel and Jaguar Niquel operates 18 exploration licenses. The networks of mining companies change as junior exploration firms sell their discoveries and exploration rights to larger firms and new constellations of companies are formed.

Although mining contributed less than 1 percent to gross domestic product (GDP) in 2009, it contributed with 2 percent to GDP in 2013 and it is estimated that with the development of planned exploitation, mining could contribute with approximate 4 percent to GDP in the future (Lee and Bonilla de Anzueto, 2009). This growth, however, is expected to occur in a context where 51 percent of the population of the country (15 million) lives in rural areas and relies on agriculture for their livelihoods.

The mining history of the country is marked by resistance and opposition to mining, especially notorious during the civil war (see the cases of EXMIBAL and San Idelfonso Ixtahuacan ODHA, 1998; CEH, 1999; Solano, 2005). The fall in the global prices of minerals and political instability during the civil war were probably the most important factors explaining the loss of importance of mining activities in the country between 1980 and 1997. The signing of the peace accords inaugurated a new phase for mineral exploration and exploitation in Guatemala.

## Making the space of mineral extraction, setting the ground for contestation and opposition

In *The Production of Space* Henri Lefèbvre (1991) suggests that every society produces its specific space. Modes of production and social regimes are spatialized in a unique way. The production of space occurs through a series of mental, material and social practices (West, 2006). Through different mental, material and social practices (cf. Lefèbvre, 1991) that are historical, discursive, ideological, legislative and imaginative, spaces become constituted and produced (West, 2006). Space is not a flat, depoliticized and immobilized surface, it is fully implicated in both history and politics (Massey, 1994). Space is a way of thinking in terms of the ever-shifting geometry of social and power relations (Massey, 1994). The spatial can be seen as assembled by the multiplicity of social relations across all scales from the global reach of [mineral] demand and supply, through the geography of the national political power, to the social relations within the town, the settlement and the household. The mineral extraction space starts from an idea, a location and a social relation between people. Once brought into the world, space is always in the process of becoming something else and contributing to the production of other spaces, objects and subjects (West, 2006). To take stock of the increase in global demand of minerals, higher prices of gold and silver, and the mobility of capital requires that states re-shape the geographical configuration of places around new transport and communication systems and physical infrastructures, new centers and styles of production and consumption, new agglomerations of labor power and modified social infrastructures (i.e. systems of governance and regulation; Harvey, 1996).

### The legal environment, public policy and institutional arrangements

Since 1927, the political constitution gave the state sovereign rights over all resources in the subsoil. In 1945 changes in the constitution stipulated that mining and hydrocarbon exploitation could only be conducted by the state or by Guatemalan companies with a major share of Guatemalan capital with the authorization of the congress. Subsequent changes to the constitution removed the principle of privileging national companies and the state, and eliminated the role of the congress in approving mineral exploitation. From the 1945 to the 1954 political constitution there is a transition from a nationalist developmental ideology where natural resources were going to be exploited by Guatemalans for the development of the country, to an ideology in which, while the state retains sovereign rights to mineral resources, the state will create the conditions necessary for the promotion of national and foreign capital investments. This idea has remained dominant ever since.

Mining activities are currently regulated by a mining bill (Decree 48-97) that was passed by the congress in 1997. The rules for environmental evaluation, control and monitoring (Acuerdo Gubernativo 23-2003) regulate Environmental and Social Impact Assessments (ESIA). The ESIA is a technical instrument used to evaluate possible negative environmental and social impacts of projects and to suggest strategies to remediate those impacts. The ESIAs are conducted before the start of mining exploitation activities.

The mining bill was written with input from Guatemala's mining industry and foreign investors (Dougherty, 2011) during the government of Alvaro Arzú (1996–2000) which also pursued a series of other structural reforms towards privatization and liberalization. The spirit of the mining bill aims to promote extractive activities to attract foreign direct investment and privileging the mining sector as a "motor of development" for the economy. The most contested issue of the 1997 law is the reduction of royalties to the state from 6 to 1 percent of net profits (Dougherty, 2011; Yagenova, 2012). Another source of conflict is that the new mining bill does not require consent from landowners where mining activities will take place for companies' license applications (Yagenova, 2012). The new bill introduces three types of licenses, the size of concessions increases, and environmental studies are required (Dougherty, 2011; Yagenova, 2012). In 2007 the government of Oscar Berger (2004–08) declared the strengthening of the mining and energy sectors as of national interest for the promotion of economic and social development of the country (Acuerdo Gubernativo 499-2007). Mining is declared central for the economic development of local communities in the Mining and Energy Policy 2008–15. The centrality of mining as a "motor for development" has since remained unchanged in the official discourse and in the discourse of the elites. Both Arzú and Berger are representatives of the main Guatemalan business elites and family networks. Arzú and Berger established a political party in the 1980s and were able to unify different factions of the business elite around a program to deepen the market orientation and limit the state in Guatemala (Bull *et al.*, 2014).

According to an interviewee from the Ministry of Energy and Mines, the state has now become a promoter of the "corporate project," a mere broker between companies and local communities. According to this interviewee, the role of the government would be to assist communities in closing good deals with companies in that which concerns investments made by the companies in the communities, so that these communities can achieve economic development. A quote[7] from this interviewee is illustrative:

> Our role as a state is to create the conditions to establish a dialogue to avoid clashes between the corporate project and peasants' demands … but first we

have to recognize what the law says. The law says that they [private companies] can do what they please ... this place [the ministry] is only a contact point for mining procedures[8] ... so what we [the ministry] should do is to understand what the communities need ... once we have understood what they need then we can talk with the companies and tell them that they cannot simply develop their [corporate] social responsibility plans as they want ... give gifts like football shirts, or build a football pitch ... that might be applauded by the people for two years ... but then protests will come ... it is better if the company understands that they have to invest more so that later nobody protests, there would not be blockades or demonstrations ... that [to dialogue] is something that has not been done in this country before ... imagine an "indito"[9] talking with an empresario.

The main relationship between the Guatemalan state and mining companies happens through two institutions, the Ministry of Energy and Mines (MEM) and the Ministry of the Environment and Natural Resources (MARN). The MEM grants licenses (reconnaissance, exploration and exploitation) to private or public companies. Environmental and social concerns related to mining exploitation are addressed through the ESIAs that have to be authorized by the MARN. The MARN is a relatively new and weak institution, with less power than the MEM, as reflected by for example the budget allocated to each institution (e.g. for the 2009–10 budget the allocations to the MEM grew by 123 percent whereas the allocations to the MARN increased only by 40 percent[10]) and their competences. The MEM is the only institution that can grant or cancel mining licenses; the MARN is not involved until the moment in which a company applies for an exploitation license.

The political constitution recognizes some of the rights of indigenous peoples, but the state has failed to create legislation for the implementation of the International Labor Organization (ILO) 169 convention, particularly in regards to mechanisms to conduct "Free, Prior and Informed Consultation" (FPIC). However, three laws guarantee public participation in decision-making (Communitarian Councils for Development (COCODES) law, Codigo Municipal, Ley de participación ciudadana). These laws reflect a re-scaling of governance by way of which decision-making power was decentralized, transferring some responsibilities to the departments, municipalities and communities. The three laws were possible thanks to the active involvement of civil society in Guatemala. Lack of financial transfers is an important obstacle to realize the rescaling of decision-making power and in practice the role of municipalities and local community's development councils remains limited in regards to real participation in development planning (McNeish, 2012).

### Mining licenses: practices and geography

With the increase in the number of licenses in Guatemala, mining royalties increased from US\$1,389,229 in 2008 to US\$3,151,940 in 2012.[11] As of October

2013, there were about 946 licenses in different stages in the country (Table 8.1).[12] The space of mineral extraction is concentrated in the eastern and central regions of Guatemala (Table 8.1).

Owing to how the global mining industry is currently organized, junior firms are usually the first ones that come in contact with public institutions and communities. According to the law these companies do not have any obligation to inform local communities about their activities (see Table 8.2). These companies buy the land once valuable discoveries are made, and when land rights and mineral discoveries are secured, junior firms sell or merge with larger companies.

*Table 8.1* Mining licenses (approved and pending) by department and region

| Region | Department | Licenses (silver and gold) | Total per region | Regions combined |
|---|---|---|---|---|
| Metropolitan | Guatemala | 82 (4) | 82 (4) | Central + Metropolitan 108 (5) |
| Central | Sacatepequez | 7 (0) | 26 (1) | |
| | Chimaltenango | 5 (1) | | |
| | Escuintla | 14 (0) | | |
| South-western | Quetzaltenango | 11 (3) | 22 (20) | Western 78 (28) |
| | Retalhuleu | 1 (0) | | |
| | Totonicapan | 4 (1) | | |
| | Suchitepequez | 6 (0) | | |
| | Solola | 0 | | |
| | San Marcos | 21 (16) | | |
| North-western | Quiche | 20 (4) | 56 (8) | |
| | Huehuetenango | 36 (4) | | |
| North | Alta Verapaz | 38 (4) | 67 (14) | North 70 (14) |
| | Baja Verapaz | 29 (10) | | |
| El Peten | El Peten | 3 (0) | 3 (0) | |
| North-eastern | Izabal | 32 (11) | 138 (25) | Eastern 182 (41) |
| | Chiquimula | 22 (7) | | |
| | El Progreso | 57 (1) | | |
| | Zacapa | 27 (6) | | |
| South-eastern | Santa Rosa | 16 (3) | 44 (16) | |
| | Jalapa | 15 (7) | | |
| | Jutiapa | 13 (6) | | |

Source: Catastro Minero Ministry of Energy and Mines, 2013 data.

*Table 8.2* Procedures for license application and environmental studies

|  | Reconnaissance | Exploration | Exploitation |
|---|---|---|---|
| Environmental issues | Mitigation study | Mitigation study | ESIA |
| Social issues | – | – | ESIA |
| Information to the owner of the land/contact with community | Not required | Not required | Company should provide evidence that the population was "informed/consulted" about in the ESIA |
| Information about the process of license | MEM 30 days to approve Complaints 10 days | MEM 30 days to approve Complaints 10 days | MARN 30 days to approve ESIA Complaints 30 days MEM 30 days to approve license after MARN approves ESIA Complaints 30 days |
| Information channel about license | Official newspaper | Official newspaper | Official newspaper |
| Types of companies involved | Junior and large | Junior and large | Large |
| Where does the process takes place | Guatemala city | Guatemala city | Guatemala city |

The MEM handles the licenses for reconnaissance and exploration. Environmental issues are addressed through an environmental mitigation study. This mitigation study is a technical report describing the reconnaissance and exploration activities to be undertaken and the consequences that such activities would have on the environment. The MARN is not involved in evaluating these mitigation studies. There are no requirements to inform or involve local communities at the reconnaissance or exploration stage (Table 8.2). If the exploration activities lead to mineral discoveries, the company applies for an exploitation license to the MEM. Prior to approval of the license the company presents an ESIA to the MARN. Even when both the MARN and the MEM have regional offices, all the information about mining is maintained in the central offices, in Guatemala City.

The rules for environmental evaluation, control and monitoring stipulate that the MARN would stimulate public participation during the preparation of the ESIAs and in later monitoring of the project. However, according to said rules, it is the owner of the project who is responsible for involving the population in the ESIAs. The owner of the project should present evidence that the population has been "involved and/or consulted," and the owner of the project should suggest communication and consultation mechanisms with the population during the preparation of the ESIAs. Private actors use their "Corporate Social Responsibility (CSR)" plans to address environmental and social issues. The CSRs move the power to sanction away from the state to international standards, agreed and negotiated by private companies alone. Since the CSR standards are decided and implemented by companies and sanctioned by bodies without democratic mechanisms for participation and decision making, there is little room for local inhabitants to complain or denounce misconduct.

There is a very high rate of approved ESIAs. In 2006, 90 percent of the ESIAs were approved, 92 percent in 2007, 86 percent in 2008 and 92 percent in 2009 (Yagenova, 2012). According to an interviewee from the MARN who asked to remain anonymous, a few consultant firms, some of which have links to public servants in the MARN, conduct the ESIAs and there is high pressure within the Ministry to quickly approve mining ESIAs, but the ministry does not have the resources to monitor whether the studies are conducted in an adequate manner (see also Yagenova, 2012).

## Place-based contestations to the extractive space of mining and reactions from the state and the industry

The anti-mining campaign in south-eastern Guatemala involves different forms of organization and organizations from more than 30 communities, ten municipalities and three departments. These organizations include church-based organizations (Diocese Commission for the Defence of Nature (CODIDENA)), local development community councils (COCODEs), an indigenous organization: the Parliament of the Xinka People of Guatemala (PAPXIGUA), a local resistance committee (CDP) and the mayors of three municipalities.

The anti-mining campaign opposes the silver mine project "El Escobal" managed by the Canadian company "Tahoe Resources Inc."[13] The infrastructure of the mine and the first exploitation license is located in the municipality of San Rafael las Flores, Santa Rosa. However, the company has 23 other licenses in different stages. These other licenses are located in three departments, Jalapa, Jutiapa and Santa Rosa.

The claims of the movement are demands for recognition, representation, participation and memory. The movement argues that the effects of mining will be experienced in particular places, including human bodies, in south-eastern Guatemala. The resistance demands the implementation of decentralized environmental governance initiated, but never fully implemented, after the signing of the peace accords, by way of which municipalities and communities would have a larger role in environmental decision making. With this, also come claims for a different form of representation and democratic participation in the political life of the country. There are also claims for recognition of and respect for collective land rights. The Xinka communities are organized around the use, access, administration and defense of their lands and territories (Letona Zuleta et al., 2003). Opposition to the mine goes beyond ownership of the land; opposition articulates around collective control and administration of the Xinka territory by the Xinka people.[14] This involves claims for the recognition of the Xinka people as political actors and their legitimacy as environmental decision makers.

The claims of the Xinka also include claims for the recognition of their sufferings during the civil war[15] and claims for participating in the reconstruction of the memory of the war and that their voices would count in the history of the war.[16] Memory plays an important role in place making. As Harvey (1996, 306) suggests, "the construction of a sense of place is an active moment in the passage from memory to hope, from past to future ... places can reveal hidden memories that hold out prospects for different futures"—by struggling for the recognition of the past, many men in south-eastern Guatemala are also claiming their possibilities for the future.

Female participants in the anti-mining campaign are using their bodies as barriers against aggression from the police and the military. Female activists also bring, during discussions and meetings, the body as a place that should be considered when discussing the effects of mining. It is after all in their bodies that they would experience the effects of pollutants and of the transformation of agricultural activities. Women in the movement have, however, fewer resources than other groups and organizations and their claims remain subordinated to the priorities of other organizations.

## Struggles in defense of the place

With the introduction of the neoliberal reforms in Guatemala in the 1990s, the state, international financial institutions and other supporters of free-market globalization promote a world of "immense, unstructured, free, unbounded space" (cf. Massey, 1994) in which countries such as Guatemala are embedded. Places in this world should be open to flows of people, capital and commodities (Castree, 2004). By prioritizing mineral extraction as a strategy to create income revenues, the Guatemalan government disregards local interests and recasts places into "extractive spaces" (cf. Barton et al., 2012). Underlying mining conflicts are tensions between the current model of mineral extraction promoted by the central government and local claims for social and environmental justice, in other words conflicts between the commodification of spaces versus local aspirations for the development of places (Barton et al., 2012).

Power struggles between those creating a space and those defending the place can be understood spatially. Michel de Certeau (1984) suggests that certain popular practices manipulate the mechanisms of discipline imposed by a particular space. In this context his definition of strategy and tactics is useful. By strategy I mean the calculation and manipulation of power relationships to secure the position of powerful actors. Strategies define legitimate modes of action and establish the boundaries of acceptable practice but demand locations of power (a "proper," e.g. Ministries, trade chambers, universities, mining infrastructure).

Institutional processes setting norms and conventions are part of a strategy. A strategy may also entail controlling certain knowledge and discourses (see de Certeau, 1984). Tactics on the other hand is a course of action to achieve an immediate or short-term aim. Tactics are calculated actions that take advantage of certain opportunities, using cracks opened by particular conjunctions. Tactics lack a specific location, survive through improvisation and use the advantages of the weak against the strong. Tactics are action in constant state of reassessment and correction. Strategy is located in the service and site of power; tactics operate against these localities without relying on a spatial or institutional localization. Strategy and tactics operate in the same space: "what distinguish them are the types of operations and the role of spaces: strategies are able to produce, tabulate and impose the spaces where these operations take place, whereas tactics can only use, manipulate and divert these spaces" (de Certeau, 1984, 29). Below I discuss the tactics used by the resistance movement and the responses from the government and the elite.

### Disrupting time-space routines

The anti-mining movement in south-eastern Guatemala tried to disrupt the quotidian time–space routines of the mine by placing a blockade in the proximity of the mine's infrastructure. Lunch routines and the mobility of the mine's employees were disturbed by the demonstration. With the blockade the resistance campaign gained considerable visibility and support from other social movements in the country, as well as from international activists.

The private security of the mine used an approach to the protest that includes infiltrating the movement, gathering intelligence, intimidating participants in the protest, preparing reports to be used for filing arrest orders,[17] and so on. In April 2013 the private security of the mine shot and wounded six men who stood in the blockade. In May 2013 the government of Guatemala declared a state of siege[18] in Jalapa and Santa Rosa after a series of violent episodes. The approach to social protest deployed by the private security of the mine is anchored in the government and the elites' understanding of and discourse about the causes and consequences of social protest.[19] The president of Guatemala, Otto Pérez Molina claimed that the state of siege was directed against "organized crime."[20] A military post has been established in Santa Maria Xalapán, a Xinka community in Jalapa, to hold under surveillance the movement of people and the activities in the community.

Mainstream media, controlled by the economic elite[21] feeds the thesis presented in various documents circulating in academic circles close to the industry,[22] that resistance to mining is organized by foreign and national non-governmental organizations and the Catholic Church seeking to occupy an ideological niche left empty after the signing of the peace accords. According to this thesis, former guerrilla members and foreigners lost their income opportunities with the signing of the peace accords. Environmental and social protest constitutes a new niche where leftists[23] now work and earn an income.

Several actors, including some intellectuals from the right postulate the idea that resistance to mining is a sort of conspiracy against the economy of the country while at the same time that mining has the potential to become one of the most important motors for rural development. There are insinuations that organized crime has infiltrated indigenous organizations, particularly PAPXIGUA.[24] The media describes social protest as terrorism. Furthermore, the government's and elites' discourse justifies counter-insurgency practices by linking environmental and social protest to former guerrilla leaders.

### Contesting the representation of space

The anti-mining campaign challenges the visibility/invisibility resulting from the practices of granting/applying for licenses and the ESIAs and the space that results from those practices (cf. Harvey, 1990). Environmental and mining regulations in Guatemala allow for fragmenting a large project such as "El Escobal" in small "sub-projects" (i.e. reconnaissance/exploration/exploitation licenses). The separation of the ESIAs fragment and render invisible all the ecological interconnections including humans among the different sites for which licenses have been granted, while making visible only some portions of certain places.

Central to the dispute in south-eastern Guatemala is the geographical distribution of mining exploration and exploitation licenses. When discussing the mine, the government and the company refer exclusively to the area where the infrastructure of the mine is visible and to the 29 square kilometers for which the exploitation license has been granted. Opponents to the mine refer to the whole area involved in different types of licenses. That is why the anti-mining campaign gathers people from 30 communities from ten municipalities and three departments. The mineral extraction space created in south-eastern Guatemala is a tool of thought and action, a means of control, domination and exploitation (Lefèbvre, 1991; Quijano, 2000) that the anti-mining campaign is contesting. By only referring to the area where the mining infrastructure is located, where mining infrastructure is visible, the media, industrial actors and the government try to de-legitimize the involvement of people from other places in the movement. Opponents to the mine are using a map, produced by the mining company, to make visible the territory and all the places involved in mineral exploration and exploitation. The government and industrial actors' actions and arguments against the participation of citizens from various municipalities in the protest are efforts to define place as "bounded." With this I mean that the government and industrial actors attempt to enclose a particular space (the space that is visible in the exploitation license), endow it with fixed identities and claim such a space for mining.

### Claiming the place as the space for decision making

In south-eastern Guatemala, the discourse around community referendums does not make exclusive reference to the ILO 169, as in the western highlands, but to the Municipal Code and the rural and urban development councils' law.[25] The referendums become then a powerful tool in the campaign, allowing people who do not identify themselves as indigenous to support the referendums. The referendums are seen as means to show the communities' rejection to the project, to reclaim the right of participation by using spaces created by the legislation as political spaces demanding the democratization of the decision-making processes. Those in charge of organizing the referendums do not believe that the consultations *alone* could stop the operations of the mine; consultations were not seen only as legal but also as political means. Eventually, they think, the results from these referendums would force the government into a dialogue with them. A quote from a COCODE leader:

> The consultations do not have the necessary legal impact to close the San Rafael mine ... what would become evident is that we strongly reject them [the mine] ... we are fighting legal battles [in courts] against the licenses to close the mine ... the consultations ... are a political issue, 95 percent of the people reject the mine, we have to come to the point where the government has to dialogue with us.
>
> The largest shareholder of Tahoe has said internationally that the political system in San Rafael las Flores is different from the indigenous systems [in the highlands] ... he says that when foreign investors come here we all take off our hats for them, but he is wrong, neither we would take off our hats for him ... never ... and we will show him that with the consultations ...

Local referendums have been appealed in the constitutional court (CC) by the Industrial Chamber of Guatemala, the mining company[26] and CACIF. Different and multiple tactics (protest, litigation, prior consultation, alternative environmental impact assessments etc.) used by activists to confront the extractive industries seek to advance the scope and possibilities of negotiations. The elites are using the legal system to erode the anti-mining movement. There is an enormous disparity in the resources available to the resistance movement and the elite to fight all the legal battles in which they are involved.

### Manipulating royalties

The anti-mining movement has criticized the amount of royalties to be paid to the state for being too low. In 2012 the government of Guatemala and the president of the Chamber of Industry signed a voluntary agreement on mining royalties. Royalties from non-metallic mining increased from 1 to 3 percent whereas royalties from gold and silver increased from 1 to 4 percent. However, the voluntary agreement would not apply in case the price of minerals falls below a certain roof.[27] This agreement came as an initiative by way of which the government in alliance with the private sector seeks to palliate the opposition that mining is provoking in the country.

The government has taken initiatives to launch agreements between the mayors of communities where mining is taking place and the mining company. In 2013 the government acted as an intermediary to seal a deal between ten municipalities in Jalapa and Santa Rosa and Tahoe Resources Inc. Four of the ten mayors invited did not sign the deal. The mayors who did not sign the deal are from the municipalities that have arranged municipal consultations on mining, where the population has rejected mining projects in their territories. Municipal consultations have had an effect on how the municipality relates to initiatives from the central government. However, the pressure from local inhabitants influences the decisions from mayors and municipal councils as long as it does not conflict with party political commitments at the national level.[28]

## Conclusion

Mining activities re-emerged in Guatemala after the signing of the peace accords due to a series of domestic and external changes. Transnational mining companies entered the country and dominate gold and silver extraction activities. The business elite in Guatemala have successfully managed to maintain transnational mining companies in a subordinate position. One of the explanations for this situation is that governance in Guatemala is so little transparent that foreign companies need the support, networks and political resources controlled by the local elites to establish their operations in the country (Bull *et al.*, 2014). In this way, even with the arrival of new elites in the country, the traditional elites continue to be the most powerful actor in Guatemala, as well as in that which concerns environmental governance.

Mining has resulted in strong opposition from local inhabitants. Protests against mining are articulated as defense of the place. The claims of the anti-mining movement are claims for recognition, participation, representation and memory. To achieve their goals the movement against mining in south-eastern Guatemala has disrupted time–space routines of the mine, is contesting the representation of the space created by licensing practices and is claiming the place as the space for decision making about environmental governance. The government and industrial actors have responded with violence justified by an approach and discourse that delegitimize social protest. Another strategy of the government and industrial actors has been to manipulate royalties and in this way the state acts as an intermediary between the private companies' project and municipalities.

Among other things, mining conflicts reveal two opposed views about rural areas, natural resources and environmental governance. On the one hand, the elite's view of land and resources as commodities and an emphasis on private property. Environmental governance in this view would be a mere institutionalization of procedures that ensure the maximization of profits; social and environmental issues are addressed through the companies' CSR agendas. On the other hand, the anti-mining movement's view of land is as a collective territory that ensures the continuation of their lives and that is more than a mere material resource.

Environmental governance in this view is seen as privileging rural inhabitants' desires and aspirations.

## Notes

1  With this I want to stress the emphasis that has been given in the official discourse to ethnic markers (i.e. clothing, language) in defining the "indigenous" in Guatemala. Various state practices (e.g. census, naming, and military drafting) contribute to constructing the south-eastern part of Guatemala as "ladina" as opposed to the "indigenous" western. Ladino is a rather ambiguous term used in Guatemala to refer to those who do not identify themselves as indigenous. According to Dary (2010) the idea of [ethnic] authenticity and legitimacy as related to speaking a language or using particular clothing has prevailed in the official ethnic imaginaries of south-eastern Guatemala. The National Bureau of Statistics (INE) uses the criteria of language and clothing in the population census to register the ethnic identity of people. Dary (2010, 190–191) argues further that the INE together with other actors including some anthropologists have since 1940 contributed to constructing south-eastern Guatemala as a ladino territory. However, since the colony and, up until the early twentieth century, the government's practices have recognized this part of Guatemala as indigenous.
2  With its subsidiaries Montana Exploradora de Guatemala and Entre Mares de Guatemala.
3  Goldcorp owns 40 percent of Tahoe Resources.
4  Argonaut Gold Inc. operates the El Sastre mine in association with Guatemalan capital and companies.
5  With its subsidiary *Compañía Guatemalteca de Níquel* (CGN), also with Guatemalan capital.
6  For instance, in 2010 the Canadian mining company Pacific Rim sued the government of El Salvador for US$315 million. The mining company claims that by not awarding the company an exploitation permit for its proposed gold mine, El Salvador is in breach of the CAFTA-DR. Pacific Rim is using a World Bank trade tribunal to circumvent community consent and state regulations. El Salvador denied the mining license to protect water sources in the country. See www.biv.com/article/20130402/BIV0108/130409974/vancouver-mining-company-sues-el-salvador-for-us-315m.
7  Interview with a high level advisor of the MEM in April 2013. The interviewee asked to remain anonymous.
8  *Ventanilla de trámite.*
9  "Indito" is a derogatory term used to refer to indigenous people in Guatemala.
10  See www.kas.de/wf/doc/kas_18202-544-4-30.pdf.
11  See www.mem.gob.gt/wp-content/uploads/2012/05/ANUARIO-ESTAD%C3%8DSTICO-MINERO-2012.pdf.
12  See www.mem.gob.gt/viceministerio-de-mineria-e-hidrocarburos-2/estadisticas-mineras.
13  The El Escobal project has the potential to become one of the largest silver producers of the world. Tahoe Resources Inc. plans to invest a total of US$406 million in this mine. Available at: www.industrialinfo.com/news/abstract.jsp?newsitemID=220200; see also www.tahoeresourcesinc.com.
14  The majority of the indigenous population in Guatemala belongs to the Maya people constituted of 20 socio-cultural groups. During the peace process, the Agreement on identity and rights of indigenous peoples, signed in 1995 recognizes the existence of four distinct peoples in Guatemala: the Maya, the Xinka, the Garifuna and the Ladino. The inclusion of the Xinka people in the agreement was possible due to the active involvement of the Xinka leaders in the peace process.
15  In 1973 a massacre occurred in Sansirisay where 15 Xinka from the community of Santa María Xalapán were assassinated in connection with a land conflict. General

Efraín Rios Montt allegedly ordered and led the massacre. The massacre in Xinka territory was presumably the first one ordered by Ríos Montt, who is now accused of genocide during the civil war. Further, many Xinka men were forcefully recruited to military service during the civil war. Several other activists involved in the anti-mining campaign made frequent reference to their experiences during the civil war when talking about the responses from the government to the campaign. For example, the forced military service triggered the migration of hundreds of young men from southeastern Guatemala to the USA in the 1980s (see Aguilar-Støen, 2012). Some of the men who migrated during the civil war are back in Guatemala now and are involved in the anti-mining campaign.

16  The interpretation of the events that happened during the armed conflict is still a source of debate and confrontation in Guatemala. The Xinka claim their right to tell their history, a history that according to them has been silenced for centuries by the powerful. By referring to their experiences during the armed conflict the Xinka want to give significance and meaning to the events they lived individually or collectively in the past as a way to negotiate the present and the future. Such experiences include violence in the form of massacres but also prominent for my interviewees is the military service they were forced into, and the activities and consequences such forceful involvement in the war has had for them. Xinka former military claim that they were also victims, and not perpetrators, during the civil war. The conflict with the mine has been used as an arena where these men are voicing these feelings.

17  The private security of the El Escobal mine, prepared an "internal inform" identifying six individuals as being behind the protests, the document was delivered to the Public Prosecutor office and was used as part of the evidence backing detentions and arrest orders during the state of siege. The internal inform also included recommended actions to be taken to destroy the reputation of the catholic priests of the region.

18  More than 3,000 armed troops and police backed by tanks and armored cars mounted with anti-craft guns were sent to two municipalities in Santa Rosa (San Rafael las Flores and Casillas) and two in Jalapa (Jalapa and Mataquescuintla); the mayors of Nueva Santa Rosa, Casillas, Jalapa and Mataquescuintla refused to sign a voluntary agreement on royalties with the mining company two days before the state of siege was declared. The troops occupied towns and set up road blockades. The state of siege suspended basic constitutional rights, barring public assembly and allowing the military to indefinitely detain anyone without charge or trial. It also lifted restrictions on searches and seizures. The state of siege was, however, never authorized by the Guatemalan congress.

19  For example an anonymous document: *Informe preparado para el presidente de la república y autoridades gubernamentales en materia de seguridad, justicia y desarrollo energético*, "Organizaciones que promueven la conflictividad social en Guatemala. Redes de organizaciones locales e internacionales que promueven la conflictividad social, atentan contra el estado de derecho y desestimulan la inversión privada en Guatemala," March 2012, was allegedly prepared by a professor at *Universidad Francisco Marroquín* (UFM) and submitted to the presidency of the republic and to different media. See also a lecture at UFM by Mary O'Grady, member of the board of the *Wall Street Journal*. See http://newmedia.ufm.edu/gsm/index.php/Debate_sobre_la_miner%C3%ADa_en_Guatemala.

20  Some months later the president and the Ministers of Energy and Mines and of the Interior publicly recognized that the state of siege was imposed to control the resistance against the El Escobal mine.

21  The family of the Minister of Energy and Mines Erick Archila has shares in different media (radio and TV channels). The family of Archila is also involved in the oil industry.

22 For instance, Pedro Trujillo, director of the Institute for Political Studies and International Relations at *Universidad Francisco Marroquin*. Trujillo is also the president of the Chamber of Journalism in Guatemala, writes regularly in Guatemala's newspapers and leads together with Silvia Gereda a TV program. Silvia Gereda is married to one of the owners of Cementos Progreso.

23 Kevin McArthur, CEO of Tahoe Resources Inc. said that "the country wants mines, and the oil and gas industry to invest in the country. They want the jobs, the foreign exchange and the tax base ... it [Guatemala] is a noisy place, there's a very strong left contingent and we had some violent events around our project. But the president stepped in and established law and order" [referring to the state of siege], see www.bnamericas. com/news/mining/tahoe-resources-seeking-second-mine-in-guatemala-ceo-says.

24 *El Periodico*, May 3, 2013 "Estado de sitio se decretó por hechos delictivos." Marta Yolanda Diaz-Duran published an opinion article in *Siglo Veintiuno* on May 13 2013 where she blames "eco-terrorism" and drug traffickers for social instability in rural areas, particularly in south-eastern Guatemala.

25 As for December 2013, five local consultations based on the municipal code were conducted in Jalapa and Santa Rosa with the participation of over 50,000 people; over 95 percent of the population rejected the operation of mining companies in their territories. Seven community consultations were organized based on the COCODEs law in the municipality of San Rafael las Flores. These consultations were organized using the COCODEs law because the municipality did not agree to organizing consultations for the whole municipality.

26 The mining company is a member of the Industrial Chamber of Guatemala, and the chamber is part of CACIF.

27 See www.mem.gob.gt/2012/04.

28 During an open meeting between one of the mayors (San Rafael las Flores) and local inhabitants the mayor explained that his hands were tied by the decisions already made by the president. The mayor belongs to the ruling party (*Partido Patriota* (PP)) and has refused to organize municipal consultations.

# References

Aguilar-Støen, M. (2012) Con nuestro propio esfuerzo: Understanding the relationship between international migration and the environment in Guatemala. *European Review of Latin American and Caribbean Studies*, 93, 25–40.

Anderson, S. T. (2012) The mineral industry of Guatemala, *2010 Minerals Yearbook*. US Department of the Interior and US Geological Survey, Washington DC.

Barton, J., Román, A. and Fløysand, A. (2012) Resource extraction and local justice in Chile: Conflicts over commodification of spaces and the sustainable development of places, in H. Haarstad (ed.) *New Political Spaces in Latin American Natural Resource Governance*. Palgrave Macmillan, New York, 107–128.

Bebbington, A., Humphreys, Bebbington, D. Bury, J. Lingan, J. Muñoz, J. P. and Scurrah, M. (2008) Mining and social movements: Struggles over livelihood and rural territorial development in the Andes. *World Development*, 36, 2888–2905.

Bridge, G. (2004) Mapping the bonanza: Geographies of mining investment in an era of neoliberal reform. *The Professional Geographer*, 56, 406–421.

Bull, B., Castellacci, F. and Kasahara, Y. (2014) *Business Groups and Transnational Capitalism in Central America: Economic and Political Strategies*. Palgrave Macmillan, London.

Castree, N. (2004) Differential geographies: Place indigenous rights and "local" resources. *Political Geography*, 23, 133–167.

CEH (1999) *Guatemala: Memoria del Silencio*. Comision para El Esclarecimiento Histórico, Guatemala.

Cuffe, S. (2005) A *Backwards Upside-Down Kind of Development: Global Actors, Mining and Community-Based Resistance in Honduras and Guatemala*. Rights Action, Washington DC.

Dary, C. (2010) *Unidos por nuestro territorio: Identidad y organizacion social en Santa María Xalapán Editorial Universitaria*. Universidad de San Carlos de Guatemala, Guatemala City.

de Certeau, M. (1984) *The Practice of Everyday Life*. University of California Press, Berkeley, CA.

Dougherty, M. L. (2011) The global gold mining industry: Junior firms and civil society resistance in Guatemala. *Bulletin of Latin American Research*, 30, 403–418.

Fulmer, A. M., Godoy, A. S. and Neff, P. (2008) Indigenous rights resistance and the law: Lessons from a Guatemalan mine. *Latin American Politics and Society*, 50, 91–121.

Gordon, T. and Webber, J. R. (2008) Imperialism and resistance: Canadian mining companies in Latin America. *Third World Quarterly*, 29, 63–87.

Harvey, D. (1990) *The Condition of Postmodernity: An Enquiry into the Conditions of Cultural Change*. Blackwell, Oxford.

Harvey, D. (1996) *Justice Nature and the Geography of Difference*. Blackwell Publishing, Oxford.

Holden, W. N. and Jacobson, R. D. (2009) Ecclesial opposition to nonferrous mining in Guatemala: Neoliberalism meets the church of the poor in a shattered society. *Canadian Geographer/Le Géographe canadien*, 53, 145–164.

Hurtado, M. and Lungo, I. (2007) *Aproximaciones al movimiento ambiental en Centroamérica*. Facultad Latinoamericana de Ciencias Sociales, Guatemala.

Lee, S. L. and Bonilla de Anzueto, M. A. (2009) *Contribución de la industria minera al desarrollo de Guatemala*. Centro de Investigaciones Económicas Nacionales, Guatemala.

Lefèbvre, H. (1991) *The Production of Space*. Blackwell Publishing, Oxford.

Letona Zuleta, J. V., Camacho Nassar, C. and Fernández Gamarro, J. A. (2003) Las tierras comunales Xincas de Guatemala, in FLACSO (ed.), *Tierra identidad y conflicto en Guatemala*. Facultad Latinoamericana de Ciencias Sociales, Guatemala, 71–142.

Massey, D. (1991) A global sense of place. *Marxism Today*, 35, 24–29.

Massey, D. (1994) *Space Place and Gender*. University of Minnesota Press, Minneapolis, MN.

McNeish, J. A. (2012) More than beads and feathers: resource extraction and the indigenous challenge in Latin America, in H. Haarstad (ed.), *New Political Spaces in Latin American Natural Resource Governance*. Palgrave Macmillan: New York, 39–60.

Metz, B. (2001) Investigación y colaboración en el movimiento maya ch' orti, in P. Pitarach and J. López-Garcia (eds), *Los derechos humanos en tierras mayas Política representaciones y moralidad* Madrid: Sociedad Española de Estudios Mayas, 311–340.

Nolin, C. and Stephens, J. (2010) "We have to protect the investors": "Development" and Canadian mining companies in Guatemala. *Journal of Rural and Community Development*, 5, 37–70.

ODHA (1998) *Guatemala: Nunca más Informe del Proyecto Recuperación de la Memoria Histórica* (REMHI).Volumen III El entorno histórico Oficina de Derechos Humanos del Arzobispado de Guatemala, Guatemala.

Palencia-Prado, M. (2012) Elites y lógicas de acumulación en la modernización económica guatemalteca, available at: www.american.edu/clals/upload/Palencia_Elites_Ejes_Acumulación_Guate.pdf (accessed 25 March 2014).

Quijano, A. (2000) Colonialiadad del poder y clasificación social. *Journal of World-Systems Research*, 2, 342–386.

Rasch, E. D. (2012) Transformations in citizenship: Local resistance against mining projects in Huehuetenango (Guatemala). *Journal of Developing Societies*, 28, 159–184.

Schneider, A. (2012) *State-building and Tax Regimes in Central America*. Cambridge University Press, New York.

Sieder, R. (2011) "Emancipation" or "regulation"? Law globalization and indigenous peoples' rights in post-war Guatemala. *Economy and Society*, 40, 239–265.

Solano, L. (2005) *Guatemala petróleo y minería en las entrañas del poder*. Ciudad de Guatemala Infopress, Guatemala.

Urkidi, L. (2011) The defence of community in the anti-mining movement of Guatemala. *Journal of Agrarian Change*, 11, 556–580.

West, P. (2006) *Conservation Is Our Government Now: The Politics of Ecology in Papua New Guinea*. Duke University Press Books, Durham.

Yagenova, S. V. (2012) *La industria extractiva en Guatemala: Politicas publicas derechos humanos y procesos de resistencia popular en el periodo 2003–2011*. FLACSO, Guatemala.

Yagenova, S. V. and Garcia, R. (2009) Indigenous people's struggles against transnational mining companies in Guatemala: The Sipakapa people vs GoldCorp mining company. *Socialism and Democracy*, 23, 157–166.

# 9 Elite views about water and energy consumption in mining in Argentina, Chile, Colombia and Ecuador

*Cristián Parker G.*

## Introduction

Elites in extractive industries play a fundamental role in defining public and private policies in the context of capitalist development models oriented towards the global market. In the mining sector, there has been a significant increase in investment in developing countries (see also Chapter 3 in this book). This is not least true for South America, where the increase in mining projects has resulted in a burgeoning of socio-environmental conflicts involving a diversity of sectors (Weiss and Bustamante, 2008; Bebbington, 2012; see also Chapters 3 and 11 in this volume).

In the search to answer the main question of this book—what the role of elites constitutes in the prospect of change towards a more inclusive and sustainable model of development—this chapter will explore how elites in the energy and mining sectors specifically take into account issues of sustainability. The mining sector is chosen as a focus due to its high consumption of energy and water (Bebbington, 2012; Whitmore, 2006), and thus the implications this has for the environment and sustainability. This study will analyze the discourse of elites in the mining sectors in four South American countries—Argentina, Chile, Colombia and Ecuador—in an attempt to discern the meaning ascribed by them to sustainable consumption of energy and water in mining.[1]

The social discourses of elites regarding sustainable consumption of water and energy in mining will be analyzed through the lens of a "socio-technical complex"[2] in order to improve our understanding of the worldview of different elite groups towards environmental protection, as well as their perspective on transitioning towards sustainable development.

In other words, we aim to shed light on whether these actors are beginning to assume (or not) a shift towards sustainable consumption and production patterns in the context of structural (global, local and strategic) constraints and dynamics. As such, this study sets out to study whether we see the contours of an "elite re-orientation" (see Chapter 2) based on comparative empirical research.[3]

Our initial hypothesis was that regardless of worldview, the elites' main goal is economic growth, so they will promote large investments in mining, irrespective of its implication for the environment. However, this line of reasoning was only partially supported, specifically for the subset of the elites that we label "governing elites." We also found a discrepancy within another subset, the "technocratic elite," who at times held alternative and more sustainable visions. Rather than promoting orthodox, technocratic views on development, the technocratic elite has been able to mediate between technical approaches and socio-economic, political and environmental issues. Moreover, their interaction with other elite factions, from the ruling elite (in government and business) to leaders of civil society groups, has also led to a movement towards a more sustainable vision.

In terms of methods, we have analyzed a number of institutional documents and sources and conducted interviews with 65 actors considered to be members of the elite related to the mining sector.[4] They were involved, furthermore, in the following mining mega-projects: in Argentina, Cerro Vanguardia, a public–private consortium of Anglo Gold and FormiCruz; in Chile, Anglo American, with its mines in Mantos Blancos, Manto Verde, Soldado, Chagres y Los Bronces, as well as the state-owned mining company CODELCO; in Colombia, Anglo Gold Ashanti's La Colosa mine; and in Ecuador, Anglo Gold Ashanti's Fruta del Norte mine and Ecuacorrientes's El Mirador mine.

After conducting the interviews, we analyzed the discourses based on the assumption that it is fundamental to comprehend the social meaning of environmental issues in order to understand social and institutional practices towards sustainable consumption (Alvarez-Rivero *et al.*, 1999; Brown and Cameron, 2000; Gonzales, 2006).

The cases were chosen from countries with very different governments, all playing different roles in the global mining industry. The four countries included, furthermore, received jointly in 2012 more than 10 percent of the global investments in mining exploration.[5] Chile is the leading mining country in Latin America and the third largest producer of metals in the world (after China and Australia), with 7.3 percent of global production. The main mining product of Chile is copper, while it also produces molybdenum and silver. In South America, Chile is followed by Brazil and Peru, Colombia, Argentina and Ecuador in terms of actual production and projections for future production between 2011 and 2020. The wide array of different political situations in each case country at the time research was undertaken, furthermore, serves to represent the influence of different political ideologies on the mining sector. Argentina and Ecuador had leftist governments (of Cristina Fernández de Kirchner and Rafael Correa, respectively), while Colombia and Chile had conservative governments (governed by Juan Manuel Santos and Sebastián Piñera, respectively).

## Main results: elites, thematic experts and discursive models

### Mapping of the actors and interactions of the elite

This section presents the web of relations between different elites that influence mining projects within the case countries of this chapter. Figure 9.1 illustrates

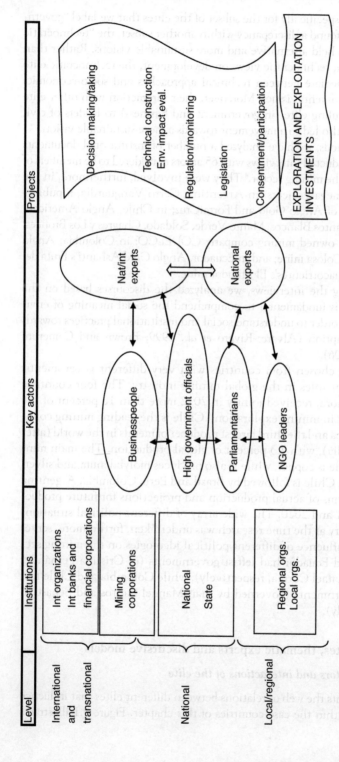

*Figure 9.1* Diagram of strategic actors of various elites and their involvement in megaprojects in the mining sector

Source: ENGOV study in Argentina, Chile, Colombia and Ecuador; author's elaboration, 2013.

how these strategic actors from various groups of elites are related, in turn providing the frame of analysis for this chapter.

This schematic map was developed from the perspective of environmental governance, specifically through the lens of mega-projects and their economic evolution. As such, the interactions and multiple dynamics between actors, as well as their political relations, are emphasized. Although banking and financial institutions undoubtedly play a part in these projects, for the purposes of our study, we focus mainly on the issue of sustainable consumption of water and energy.

Within Figure 9.1, four main classes of elites are identified. First, "business managers" are identified. They are part of the business elites, but of the modernizing segment, not the classical segment with oligarchic roots. They interact mainly with their national and international equivalents, as well as with government elites.

Second, "high-level government officials" constitute part of the state bureaucratic elite and occasionally the high-level political elite. They interact with parliamentarian elites, business elites and technocratic elites, but to a lesser degree with social elites (in NGOs) in the case of decision making in the extractive industry sector.

"Parliamentarians" derive from political parliamentarian elites, generally members of the leadership of reigning or opposing political parties. They mainly interact with government elites and, subsequently, with technocratic elites and occasionally social organization elites, including from relevant leaders of environmental, local or indigenous organizations. To a lesser degree they engage directly with business elites, although they do maintain relations via lobbyists.

Next, "NGOs" or leaders/directors of these—especially on the national level—come from the pool of elite civic leaders. In the case of mining, they include organizations with environment and ecology as their primary focus, and to a lesser, but still important extent, indigenous issues. These actors interact with expert and parliamentarian elites principally, and to a much lesser extent with governmental elites.

Lastly, "experts" form part of the technocratic elite,[6] of which there are classic pragmatic technocrats—expert engineering and economic elites in this study—and the "technopol" expert elite, or political technocrats—principally lawyers, economists and various other professions. The classic technocrats interact principally with governmental elites, international organizations and business elites (Haas, 1992; Ford, 2004). The "technopols" mainly interact with parliamentarian elites and elites from civil society organizations. Quite often, these actors have formed part of international organizations or maintain links with them and also interact to some degree with governmental elites.

It is important to mention the fact that the boundaries between these groups of elites are fuzzy and in this study, at times, certain experts we might associate with the technocratic elite are also high-level public officials. By the same token, elite directors of NGOs can be classified as technocratic elites, or at least "technopol" elites. For example, various environmental movement leaders that were interviewed for this study have higher technical education or have even been international consultants, ministers or high-level political officials. In turn, various high-level public servants, ministers and deputy ministers have advanced technical skills that greatly influence their disposition, causing a prevalence of technocratic criteria over techno-political ones—all of which qualifies them as "technopol" elites.

### The consumption of water and energy in mining: depoliticization of an "expert" issue

Analysis of the sources for this study reveals that the consumption of water and energy in mining is treated as an expert issue whose techno-scientific connotations imply that it is reserved for expert knowledge and removed from its social and political connotations. Moreover, the contrast between institutional discourses—contained in official documents of international, transnational and governmental corporations—and the discourse of local agents—contained in interviews from the field—reveals disagreement between the technical and political character of the factors at play regarding consumption of water and energy in mining. Clearly, the institutional discourses and those of the elites that create them—internationally and nationally—are of technocratic and universalist character and they tend to deny the socio-political nature of local socio-environmental impacts (which otherwise are emphasized by the discourses of elite community leaders, environmentalists and local indigenous groups).

It is possible to understand the discourse on water and energy consumption in mining through the lens of "bounded rationality" (Jeroen et al., 2006). In contrast to rational and optimal behavior from neoclassical theory, evolutionary economics posit that the economic agent is neither fully informed nor considers all possibilities at the moment of economic decision making.

In this case, institutional discourse—primarily international, but also at the national level—develops a "hard core" of knowledge and highly technical practical proposals on the water–energy–mining complex. However, this "hard core," due to bounded rationality, is not considered by national-level elites and even becomes marginal in the process of environmental regulations. In fact, to substantiate the above statement, it is first necessary to define what "hard core" means and see how it appears in institutional discourses and in the discourse of the interviewees.

We can conceptualize the water–energy–mining complex from a systems perspective, rather than considering each element alone, in order to better understand the sustainable consumption of water and energy in mining. In fact, water, energy and mining can be addressed as a complex system of interrelated parts. Energy is as necessary for water consumption as water is for the production of energy as both are indispensable for any mining operation to function. At present, one of the main challenges facing sustainable consumption of water and energy in mining is what is termed "resource intensity," which for copper mining (Northey et al., 2013), as for gold mining (Mudd, 2007), has been increasing recently (Mudd, 2010) due to decreasing ore grades (Mudd, 2008;

Norgate and Haque, 2010). Large multinational corporations included in the World Council for Sustainable Development (WCSD) are concerned about this problem and are attempting to approach the issue in an integrated manner, while the set of principles known as BellagioSTAMP (Fonseca *et al.*, 2012) address the issue in a holistic manner.[7]

Studies on energy consumption and water in the mining process (Northey *et al.*, 2013), based on the sustainability reports of mining companies, show that they are realizing now more in detail issues that were not previously reported

This "hard core" has a technocratizing connotation that not only depoliticizes the issues, but concedes authority and power to the traditional technocratic elite. Thus, this study verifies what other authors have described about the growing dominance of managerial and technocratic discourse within environmental governance (Wesselink *et al.*, 2013). Consequently the analysis of a body of documents and relevant information indicates that within institutional discourse there are declarations and initiatives that tend to address the consumption of water and energy in mining resulting from large meetings, seminars, conferences that bring together experts of international organizations, parliamentarians and on occasion high-level business executives in South America. ECLAC, since the 1990s, and inter-parliamentary conferences in recent years have addressed the issues of energy and hydrologic efficiency and sustainability,[8] but they have not been linked to the mining sector.

In general, the water and energy consumption issue is represented as "specialized" and "high level." In the most recent international meetings on water and energy in mining[9] organized in South America, issues such as energy supply for mining, the general status of the electricity sector and renewable energy, water scarcity and utilization of salt water are addressed in a reserved and exclusive manner. Energy and water efficiency are also addressed.

Institutional discourses allow us to affirm that the concept of efficiency as applied to water and energy resources is the most developed, extensive and mentioned (Rábago *et al.*, 2001; CEPAL, 2009; SGE2, 2011; COCHILCO, 2012). Regarding the incorporation of renewable sources of energy in mining, there is, in general, little information produced within institutional discourses.

The concepts of eco-efficiency and natural capital (Hawken *et al.*, 2000; Berkel, 2007; WBCSD, 2013) have also been applied to consumption of water and energy in mining, but they are virtually non-existent in the mining sector discourse of the four cases studied. In contrast, the "hard core" in relation to the consumption of water and energy in mining was not mentioned explicitly in the majority of our interviews, with few exceptions—mainly experts, but only a very few business elites, high-level officials and environmentalist leaders. But what is certain is that the social and environmental repercussions of decisions on water and energy in the mines—in other words the political connotations of these practices—were only highlighted by environmentalist discourses and some politicians.

For the majority of the interviewees, the problem of water and energy consumption focuses on considerations such as efficiency, recycling, management, regulation and control of emissions. Consideration of the actual social and environmental implications are viewed in general in the texts as an external factor to the consumption of water and energy.

The cross-sectional analysis developed here suggests that although sustainable water and energy consumption in mining are present in the discourse of the elite, and that the environment is presented as a factor to take into account, the relevance, depth and complexity of the problem is considered to widely varying degrees.

## Discursive models: the elites and their different visions

In a more profound analysis of the discourses of the interviewees in the four case countries, it appears that they respond according to different modalities that can be classified into types of discourse. Semantic analysis has allowed us to reconstruct significant structures that frame visions related to the use of water and energy, and it has allowed us to understand their general orientations.

1    The first model is based on an idea of minimizing consumption of water and energy, or at least maximizing efficiency in consumption, for which reason it privileges rational use and the recycling of such resources.

The starting point for this model is the general support for mining as an economic activity that is crucial to national development. One considers that there is an abundance of water resources and that they can be recycled with the use of efficient technologies. Energy is viewed as a resource on which mining is completely dependent, and energy consumption is essentially viewed as problematic because insufficient access to it affects international competitiveness.

This discursive model proposes responsible mining that achieves a balanced relation between the search for profitability on the one hand, and social needs and the environment on the other. It is a kind of mining activity in which everybody has confidence. Thus, it conceives of the consumption of water and energy as indispensable inputs to a very important economic activity, national development, in a business that seeks to be competitive and profitable in an international metal market. Minimizing energy costs and optimizing energetic efficiency is key.

In sum, this discursive model prioritizes a market-environmentalism that favors private initiative, and views it through an economic optic and has an optimistic view of technology. However, it is conscious that one has to take responsibility for certain social and environmental externalities. That is why it proposes responsible consumption in mining. Such responsible mining should be developed in the framework of national legislation and policies that should not hinder private investment, nor the functioning of the markets (of water and energy), observing international good practice standards in mining. This first discursive model is found principally in the discourse of business managers, and among some governmental officials; it is not apparent in the interviews with politicians, experts nor environmental activists (see Table 9.1).

*Table 9.1* Discursive models by occupation category (relative frequencies)

| | Discursive model | | | | |
|---|---|---|---|---|---|
| | One | Two | Three | Four | Total |
| Business manager | 89 | 5 | 5 | 0 | 100 |
| Public servant | 36 | 36 | 18 | 9 | 100 |
| Politician | 8 | 17 | 42 | 33 | 100 |
| Expert | 8 | 42 | 42 | 8 | 100 |
| Environmentalist | 0 | 0 | 18 | 82 | 100 |

Note: Percentages are rounded, so their sum is not necessarily equal to 100.

2   The core of the second type of discourse is efficiency and adequate management of resources.

It is based on a general acceptance of mining as an important development instrument, but it includes critiques against its negative environmental impacts, which can nevertheless be repaired with adequate rules and regulation. The responsible consumption of water and energy in mining implies avoiding the negative consequences of mineral extraction. This responsibility should rest primarily with private economic actors, but in their absence, the subsidiary state should determine the conditions of this responsibility, and should therefore set standards and regulations.

The semantic, rhetorical emphasis of this discourse is conveyed in the idea of an integral and regulated management with the clear understanding that the state should intervene to correct market imperfections and deficiencies of business practices based exclusively on private interests.

In sum, this discursive model generates a clear sense of water and energy consumption in mining with such central concepts as efficiency, recycling, integrated management and responsible consumption. It adds to the overall positive assessment of mining, without denying the irresponsible and destructive practices of certain companies interested only in their own well-being and growth at the expense of the environment and communities.

For this reason, the model places secondary emphasis on establishing the best institutional and regulatory conditions that enable better regulation and establishment of regulatory certainty to assure private investment and framing of responsible consumption of water and energy in mining. This model is supported first by experts and second by high-level officials, but is absent in both business and environmentalist texts.

3   The third type of discourse proposes consumption of water and energy in mining that should strive for sustainability in the context of integrated policies and the pursuit of sustainable development.

This discursive model establishes principles on the consumption of water and energy in mining, placing central meaning around the more political concept of sustainable development.

Assuming that large-scale mining has undeniable environmental impacts, and that the negative environmental and health effects are considerable, this discursive model gives rise to various degrees of criticism of extractivism, but it agrees that under certain conditions mining is necessary.

The recurring idea is that consumption of water and energy in mining is problematic so efficiency and recycling should always be pursued. The problem, furthermore, is associated with heavy metal contamination, which affects the food chain and human health. This type of discourse emphasizes political factors of control and regulation of mining activities. Moreover, it reveals a sort of anti-business political orientation that distrusts purely technocratic criteria, and values responsibility against the threat of corruption. It is against the depoliticization of environmental issues and proposes citizen participation.

In relation to energy consumption, it chooses an energy matrix including more decisively renewable energy sources (conventional or not), aiming to reduce emissions of greenhouse gas (GHG) emissions in the atmosphere.

In sum, this model, regarding the basis for a sustainable development policy proposal—which includes mining as an element of development, but subjects it to controls, rules and regulations—looks to move toward sustainable consumption of water and energy, promoting efficiency, recycling and the transition toward renewable energy, and identifying this transition as something from within the mining sector itself as well as with citizen participation. This model is affirmed by politicians and experts, but is slightly more significant in the case of politicians because the majority of them exemplify this model. It is clearly less prevalent among business elites, and only somewhat touted by environmentalists and officials.

4   Finally, the last discursive model presents an alternative political stance.

It triggers criticism of water and energy consumption due to the environmental consequences that accompany mining activities: pollution and environmental destruction. In general, this discursive model goes beyond reference to specific issues such as water management or energy efficiency in terms of industrial mining consumption. Its meaning shifts toward a more comprehensive understanding based on ecosystems and concern about over-consumption (of water and energy sources) that may affect the carrying capacity of these systems or the planet.

This model refers to the relationship between energy consumption in mining and the potential increase in GHG emissions resulting from the increase in demand of fossil fuels. This reveals an intergenerational perception of environmental impacts and their long-term nature.

In sum, this discursive model formulates social and political representations of water and energy consumption in the mining sector originating from ideas proposing socioecological change with reference to communities and especially indigenous groups. Some texts that employ this discursive model place alternative, sustainable development approaches as their centerpiece, including the change of the modus of capitalist production, encouraging citizen participation and decentralized, self-managed forms of production, and a clear choice of clean modes of production and unconventional renewable energies.

This is the only model that demands a review of the viability of the socio-technical forms of prevailing hydrologic and energetic systems, and proposes integral, transformative alternatives aimed at the protection of ecosystems and energy cycles. This model is prominent among environmental leaders and some politicians, but not experts or parliamentarians.

### Elites and visions: the role of experts

The different discursive models outlined above correspond with different visions held by the elites on science, technology and the environment. Figure 9.2 shows the opinions of different representatives from the elite in relation to science and technology and their impacts on the environment. Not surprisingly, the environmentalist elite opinion is that scientific and technological advancement threatens biodiversity, followed by experts, public servants and politicians. Although there are differences between these categories, the most striking difference is between environmentalists, experts and politicians on the one hand and elite business managers on the other hand.

Business professionals express more optimism in regard to the advance of science and technology and the risks it involves for the environment. This opinion, which we characterize as "technocratic" is to some degree shared by public servants. It is interesting to highlight that the positive opinion towards science and

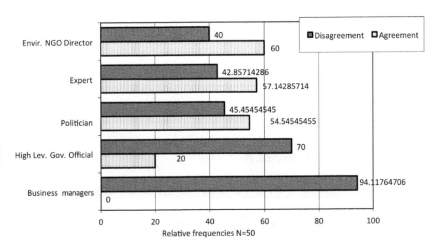

*Figure 9.2* Elite opinions about technology and biodiversity

Note: Chi.Square Test 16,62 (df 4), Sig. .0,002 in Kruskal-Wallis test.

Source: Author's elaboration.

technology is not shared by those who in theory are the members of the technocratic elite, but namely the experts. We suggest, then, that it would be wrong
to classify all experts as technocrats and at the same time that it is important to
recognize that there exist some technocratic tendencies among the bureaucratic
elite. This illuminates us to the fact that among experts we find various technocratic tendencies: pragmatists, politicians, "technopols" and experts.

The very positive opinion among business elites towards science and technology (apparently not negative toward biodiversity) is perhaps anchored in a
worldview that is less favorable to the environment than to their role as technocrats. This raises the question of to what extent business elites are serious when
they talk about sustainable development.

The differences between elites and their environmental visions become clearer
when considering their position in regards to the environmental future of their
countries (Figure 9.3). Whereas for environmentalists, experts and politicians, the
environmental future of the country does not seem so positive (they think the
country will be polluted), public servants and business professionals think more
positively about the environmental future of the country (they think the country
will be "clean"). It is clear that the bureaucratic elite are the most optimistic—as
long as when they evaluate the future of the country, they do so in relation with
their assessment of public environmental policies. Bureaucrats tend to believe in
the success of such policies insofar as they would contribute to a cleaner environmental future. On the other extreme, environmentalists are the most pessimistic,
although experts' and politicians' opinions are closer to those of the environmentalists than to those of the business elites. The future's vision of each elite category
seems to influence also their appraisal of the environmental measures implemented
in the present. The most optimistic views are expressed by those who benefit from

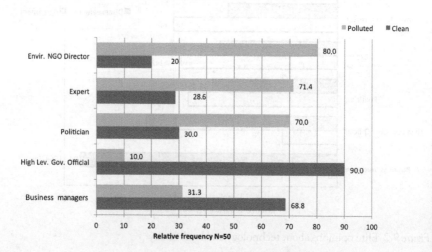

*Figure 9.3* Elite visions about the environmental future of their countries

the extractive economy (business elites) and from the public mining policy (public servants). A negative vision is expressed by environmentalists who probably are in closer contact with the communities that are suffering the negative impacts of mining. Probably because the future of their voters concerns politicians, they tend to express a less optimistic vision. Experts, who belong to what we have defined as a technocratic elite, also express a rather pessimistic vision, contrary to what could be expected from a technocratic elite that is optimistic in relation to the advance of science and technology, and thus optimistic towards the possibility of solving environmental problems with science and technology.

The analysis of deep semantic codes reveals that behind the visions of different categories of elites lay contrasting and at some point contradictory ideas about the environment, the responsibility of different actors in regard to resources (water and energy), on the role of the government and authorities, all of which are grounded in different worldviews on the relationship between society and nature. The mentioned variety of visions of different segments of the elites permit us to better understand their role and orientations. Dodging those differences would be an analytical error.

## Technocratic elites and the environment

Technocratic elites emerged with the double transition process of the 1990s: the democratization and the transition towards neoliberalism in the aftermath of the fall of the Soviet Union and the end to the military dictatorships in Latin America (Centeno, 1993; E. Silva, 1996; Estrada and Puello-Socarras, 2005; Mansilla, 2006).

The rise of technocracies were by some considered a useful element in the new democracies as their anti-ideological views reduced conflicts and enabled democratic practices (Burnham, 1967). Others, however, considered technocratic elites a democratic problem since their instrumental rationality increased the dominance of the "objective necessities" generating authoritarian practices, as for example argued by Adorno, Horkheimer and Marcuse, as well as Habermas from a different perspective (see Centeno 1993 and Feenberg, 1993). To a significant extent, this negative view of technocrats was based on their association with economists, and particularly with the neoliberal economists, that was found to significantly influence the economic reorientation (E. Silva, 1996; Estrada, 2005; Ossandón, 2011). Their neoclassic orientation has generally been found to be unfavorable to ecological perspectives (Gligo, 1995; Daly, 1996 ; Martinez Allier and Roca, 2013). The focus on maintaining macroeconomic equilibriums and increasing economic growth have also marked decisions about energy and mining megaprojects made at the expense of ecological concerns. We have seen this in countries governed both by right-wing and left-wing governments included in the study. In Colombia, the neoliberals in the government even confronted the General Prosecutor's office over these issues, while both Cristina Kirchner and Rafael Correa justified mega investments in mining to boost growth, and socialist president Michelle Bachelet in Chile (2006–10) introduced highly questionable energy projects as a means to confront the 2008–09 crisis (Reyes, 2012).

However, the more recent analysis of technocratic elites introduces new aspects and allows us also to consider "environmental technocrats" and experts as a driving force for more sustainable policies. In the more recent analysis of technocratic elites, the concept of "technopols" has been used in order to understand new relations between political and technical knowledge in democratic processes.[10] Joignant (2011) distinguishes between three main types of technocrats: (a) pragmatic technocrats; (b) political technocrats, including first those who are independent and recruited in a meritocratic way to governments of whatever color, and second those who are members of a political party; and (c) the technopols (or technopoliticians) that control two types of "capital": technical capacity and political power. However, to these categories, you have to add a fourth one: (d) the "expert elites" (Aguilera and Fuentes, 2011): groups of advisors that influence the formulation of policy but that do not have privileged positions in the political system.

The role of experts and knowledge in environmental conflicts have been studied in different contexts (Pellizzoni, 2011), and so has the science–political interface in environmental governance (Wesselink et al., 2013; see also Chapter 4 in this book). However, the role of technocratic elites in relation to the environment and sustainability has not been studied to any great extent in South America. This study has shown that this is an important area to study if we are to understand the possibility of moving towards greater sustainability.

In the countries studied here it is possible to trace the trajectory of technocratic elites that have been placed in influential positions in the ministries of mining, energy and the environment and that have introduced new norms and rules for environmental protection and evaluation of environmental impact. In general, these are public policies that are introduced by technocratic–bureaucratic elites, and they lack institutional robustness and efficient mechanisms for monitoring. They are also created without major citizens' participation, and for that reason some have considered them a democratic problem (Dávila, 2011). However, in terms of environmental sustainability they do represent an improvement, and as we have shown above, we find technocrats associated with not only the government but also, for example, environmental movements.

## Conclusion

This study elucidates the environmental perceptions and attitudes of the elite and of the different subgroups linked to the mining and energy sector within the four case countries of Colombia, Ecuador, Chile and Argentina. The analysis presented also sheds light onto elites' roles, interaction and links to technical knowledge and their inclination towards a transition to sustainable development. From the point of view of environmental governance, the importance of the role of experts—as identified in the field—shows that any case or mechanism for resolving environmental conflicts should not take only the main parties in conflict into account, in this case business managers, local communities and environmental groups. However, the analysis of how technical issues are dealt with—water and energy consumption in this case—indicates that the tendency to ignore their socio-political dimensions can over-technify the issues, and thereby paralyze dialogue. Particularly regarding mega mining projects, the search for solutions guaranteeing adequate respect for diverse interests should first, respect the environment and guarantee the rights of the most vulnerable, and second, consider technical aspects and knowledge, which in this case includes the water–energy–mining complex, and their social–environmental aspects (in other words, their political connotations).

We have observed that experts are involved in the construction of discursive models, such as models that have a technocratic tendency but are open to political considerations (model two, above) and a model that is more political but has technical considerations (model three, above).

Based on the analysis, there is potential to encourage negotiations around the process of decision making by creating spaces for experts from each side to meet—as we have observed in various spaces for negotiation of expertise, power and decisions on the level of parliamentary organizations, or that of negotiation over mega mining projects' approval and environmental evaluation.

Water and energy consumption is not only bound by physical availability of these resources, nor by technologies, but by the combination of decisions that the actors—members of the elite—make, within the framework of their representative discursive model. So, water and energy resources are transformed since they are charged with social and political connotations.

Ideally, NGO advisors can help the citizenry to understand socio-technical issues and their complexity, empowering their cause for environmental justice, just as business consultants can help business elites who make economic and environmental decisions understand social issues. As such, a technocracy that is linked to governments and politicians can help better understand the socio-technical articulation of problems. But these processes are neither obvious nor automatic, and they require, on the one hand, will for political change and management, and on the other hand, avoidance of technocratic dominance or political manipulation that would again stall democratic and sustainable processes.

Although technocracy is usually considered problematic because it disempowers the citizenry (Laird, 1990), this study has revealed that we must distinguish between different currents of the technocratic elite: although there are pragmatic traditionalists, there are also the techno-political type ("technopol") or "expert elites" with technical and political orientations; we have also observed technocratic character within some business professionals, and above all high-office public officials.

The power relations between different groups of elites is not the only issue of importance here, but also the trade of scientific–technical information and knowledge, which can transform possibilities; and we know that that knowledge is fundamental for action (Gibbons, 2001). Within power relations, during the process of decision making, there is room for exchanges that are direct and institutional, but also interstitial (Reed, 2012) and informal.

This analysis forces us to revise our approach toward these technocratic elites and their diverse manifestations: not all of them structure power relations and knowledge inevitably oriented toward authoritarian, anti-environmental, and unsustainable practices and policies.

Feenberg (1993) rightly argues that the thesis of the Frankfurt School (particularly of Adorno and Marcuse) on the mono-dimensionality of technocracy, devoid of space for social conflict, must be revised. Elites and their power can be challenged by emergent groups, albeit with difficulty. But what Feenberg fails to see is that new public spaces in which knowledge and socio-technical practices are played out not only provide the possibility of seeing that pragmatic and traditional technocracies are not invincible forces, but that factions of technocratic elites playing different roles are real, with some of them having counter-hegemonic functions, as we observe in this study.

Pellizzoni (2011, 779) concludes his study on the role of experts in environmental conflicts arguing that the confrontation between democratic and technocratic alternatives for policy makers should be replaced with a more nuanced analysis. The politics of facts is subtly intertwined with the politics of values and interests. This study shows evidence in the same direction.

Analysis of elites, from business professionals to civic elites, should consider technocratic tendencies and elites—experts, consultants and advisers—and how they can be mobilized toward governance practices aimed towards participatory and inclusive sustainability. This aspect should be further researched. This study has only provided us a few clues to understand this phenomenon. Further studies should be conducted for each case so that our general theoretical foci do not create an obstacle, but a heuristic tool to advance the transition toward sustainable consumption and production in the extractive economy and in society as a whole.

## Notes

1  This chapter is based on two research projects, the first, ENGOV (work packages 3 and 4), funded by the EU FP7 (see www.enogov.ce), and the second, FONDECYT No. 1120662 from Chile. The author acknowledges several researchers for their support toward the completion of this work, especially Gloria Baigorrotegui, Fernando Estenssoro, Benedicte Bull, Mariel Aguilar-Støen and Juan Muñoz.

2  A socio-technical complex is a specific form of production that not only utilizes technology, but also social relations of production, property, scale, territory, socio-political arrangements, norms and institutions. An example of a socio-technical system is a large surface mine, such as an open pit mine, or a small-scale artisanal mining operation.

3  See Parker *et al.* (2013) and Proyecto Fondecyt No. 1120662.

4  Applying qualitative criteria by sector and country, a theoretical sample of 52 cases was constructed, resulting in 65 interviews of 19 business people from mining corporations, 11 high-level government officials, 12 parliamentarians, 12 experts, and 11 national NGO directors, of which 13 were from Argentina, 19 from Chile, 14 from Colombia, 17 from Ecuador, and two experts from international organizations from the region.

5  The portfolio of anticipated mining projects in Latin America and the Caribbean requires an expected investment of more than US$300 billion from now until 2020, according to the estimates of *Sociedad Nacional de Minería* (SONAMI) and *Centro de Estudios del Cobre y la Minería* (CESCO). The region remains the main target of investment for mining exploration, according to Metals Economics Group (2013, 1).

6  See Lemke (1990), Haas (1992), Montecinos (1997), Ford (2004), Tong (2007), Joignant (2009) and Estenssoro and Déves (2013).

7  Institutions such as the International Council on Mining and Metals (ICMM)—the most important organization of its kind in mining—has developed a set of sustainable development principles for mining, but of the 46 sub-principles announced, only one relates to the responsible consumption of water and energy in mining. Analysis of institutional discourse shows that the role of principles is relevant, just as much as best practices initiated by companies and transnational organizations. In this respect it is necessary to mention here the norms of the International Finance Corporation (IFC) and the principles of environmental evaluation and reporting established internationally (such as the Global Reporting Initiative and the principles known as BellagioSTAMP).

8  See Ruiz (2001), Parlamento Latinoamericano (2010); Comisión energía y minas del Parlamento Latinoamericano (2012).

9  CESCO Week 2013 and 2014, Mining, Energy and Water Summit, available at: www.cescoweek.com/program-2014-.html

10  See Joignant (2009), and Joignant, Delamaza, Ossandon, Aguilera, and Fuentes and P. Silva in Joignant and Guell (2011).

# References

Aguilera, C. and Fuentes, C. (2011) Elites y asesoría experta en Chile: comisiones y políticas públicas en el gobierno de Bachelet, in A. Joignant and P. Guell (eds), *Notables Tecnócratas y Mandarines Elementos de sociología de las elites en Chile 1990–2010*. Ediciones Universidad Diego Portales, Santiago de Chile, 127–151.

Alvarez-Rivero, T., Chipman, R. and Bryld, E. (1999) *Promoting Sustainable Production and Consumption: Five Policy Studies*. ST/ESA/1998/DP 7 DESA Discussion Paper No. 7. United Nations, New York.

Bebbington, A. J. (ed.) (2012) *Social Conflict Economic Development and Extractive Industry: Evidence from South America*. Routledge, London.

Berkel, R. (2007) Eco-efficiency in the Australian minerals processing sector. *Journal of Cleaner Production*, 15, 772–781.

Brown, P. M. and Cameron, L. (2000) What can be done to reduce overconsumption? *Ecological Economics* XXXII(1), 27–41.

Burnham, J. (1967) *La revolución de los directores*. Sudamericana, Buenos Aires.

Centeno, M. A. (1993) The new Leviathan: The dynamics and limits of technocracy. *Theory and Society*, 22(3), 307–335.

CEPAL (2009) *Situación y perspectivas de la Eficiencia Energética en América latina y el Caribe*. CEPAL, Santiago de Chile.

COCHILCO (2012) *Consumo de agua en la minería del cobre (2011)*, DE/09/2012. Dirección de Estudios y Políticas Públicas Comisión Chilena del Cobre, Santiago.

Comisión energía y minas del Parlamento Latinoamericano (2012) Resolución Comisión energía y minas del Parlamento Latinoamericano Panamá, November 16. In Parlamento Latinoamericano, available at: www.parlatino.org/es/organos-principales/la-junta-directiva/resoluciones-de-junta/resoluciones/1915.html (accessed January 3, 2014).

Daly, H. (1996) *Beyond Growth: The Economics of Sustainable Development.* Beacon Press, Boston, MA.

Dávila, M. (2011) Tecnocracia y política en el Chile postautoritario 1990–2010, in A. Joignant and P. Guell (eds) *Notables Tecnócratas y Mandarines Elementos de sociología de las elites en Chile 1990–2010.* Ediciones Universidad Diego Portales, Santiago de Chile, 23–47.

Delamaza, G. (2011) Elitismo democrático líderes civiles y tecnopolítica en la reconfiguración de las elites políticas, in A. Joignant and P. Guell (eds), *Notables Tecnócratas y Mandarines Elementos de sociología de las elites en Chile 1990–2010.* Ediciones Universidad Diego Portales, Santiago de Chile, 77–108.

Estenssoro, F. and Déves, E. (2013) Institutions and intellectuals that configure the concept of the environment and development in Latin America and its global impact. *Journal of Environmental Protection,* 4(9), 1002–1010.

Estrada, A. J. (2005) Elites intelectuales y producción de política económica en Colombia, in Estrada A. J. (ed.), *Intelectuales tecnócratas y reformas neoliberales en América Latina.* Universidad Nacional de Colombia, Bogotá, 259–320.

Estrada A. J. and Puello-Socarras, J. F. (2005) Elites intelectuales y tecnocracia Calidoscopio contemporáneo y fenómeno latinoamericano actual. *Colombia Internacional.* July–December, 100–119, available at: http://colombiainternacional.uniandes.edu.co/view.php/473/view.php (accessed March 29, 2014).

Feenberg, A. (1993) The technocracy thesis revisited: On the critique of power. *Inquiry,* 87, 85–102.

Fonseca, A., McAllister, M. L. and Fitzpatrick, P. (2012) Sustainability reporting among mining corporations: A constructive critique of the GRI approach. *Journal of Cleaner Production,* online available at: http://dx.doi.org/10.1016/j.jclepro.2012.11.050 (accessed March 24, 2014).

Ford, L. H. (2004) The power of technocracy: A critical analysis of global environmental governance', in A. K. Haugestad and J. D. Wulfhorst (eds), Future as Fairness: Ecological Justice and Global Citizenship. Rodopi, Amsterdam and New York, 105–120.

Gibbons, J. (2001) Knowledge in action. *Philosophy and Phenomenological Research,* LXII(3), May, 569–600.

Gligo, N. (1995) El debate espistemológico en la integración de la dimension ambiental, in N. Gligo (ed.), *Hacia una mayor integración de la dimensión ambiental en el quehacer de la CEPAL.* CEPAL, Santiago de Chile.

Gonzalez, M. T. (2006) La perspectiva de los agentes sociales ante cuestiones ambientales: Elementos para su comprensión, in Luis Camarero (coord), *Medio Ambiente y Sociedad Elementos de Explicación Sociológica.* Thompson, Madrid, 215–241.

Haas, P. M. (1992) Introduction: Epistemic communities and international policy coordination. *International Organization,* 46(1), 1–35.

Hawken, P., Lovins, A. B. and Lovins, L. H. (2000) *Natural Capitalism: The Next Industrial Revolution.* Earthscan, London.

Jeroen, C. J. M., van den Bergh, A., Faber, A., Idenburg, M. and Oosterhuis, F. H. (2006) Survival of the greenest: Evolutionary economics and policies for energy innovation. *Environmental Sciences,* 3(1), 57–71.

Joignant, A. (2009) *El estudio de las élites: Un estado del arte.* Santiago de Chile, Serie de Políticas Públicas, UDP Documentos de Trabajo No. 1, available at: www.expansivaudp.cl/publicaciones/wpapers (accessed March 29, 2014).

Joignant, A. (2011) Tecnócratas technopols y dirigentes de partido: tipos de agentes y especies de capital en las elites gubernamentales de la Concertación 1990–2010, in

A. Joignant and P. Guell (eds), *Notables Tecnócratas y Mandarines Elementos de sociología de las elites en Chile 1990–2010*. Ediciones Universidad Diego Portales, Santiago de Chile, 49–76.

Joignant, A. and Guell, P. (eds) (2011) *Notables TecnÓcratas y Mandarines Elementos de sociología de las elites en Chile 1990–2010*. Ediciones Universidad Diego Portales, Santiago de Chile.

Laird, F. N. (1990) Technocracy revisited: Knowledge, power and the crisis in energy decision making. *Organization Environment*, 4(1), March, 49–61.

Lemke, J. L. (1990) Technical discourse and technocratic ideology, in *Learning, Keeping and Using Language: Selected Papers from the 8th World Congress of Applied Linguistics Sydney 16–21 August 1987*, edited by M. A. K. Halliday, J. Gibbons, H. N. Amsterdam. John Benjamins Publishing Company, 435–460.

Mansilla, H. C. F. (2006) Las transformaciones de las élites políticas en América Latina: Una visión inusual de la temática. *Revista de Ciencias Sociales*, 12(1), 9–20.

Martinez-Aller, J. and Roca, J. J. (2013) *Economía Ecológica y Política Ambiental*. FCE Tercera Ed, México DF.

Metals Economics Group (2013) *Worldwide Explorations Trends 2013*, available at: www.metalseconomics.com/sites/default/files/uploads/PDFs/meg_wetbrochure2013.pdf (accessed July 30, 2013).

Montecinos, V. (1997) Los economistas y las élites políticas en América Latina. *Estudios Internacionales*, 30, 119–120.

Mudd, G. M. (2007) Global trends in gold mining: Towards quantifying environmental and resource sustainability? *Resources Policy*, 32, 42–56.

Mudd, G. M. (2008) Sustainability reporting and water resources: A preliminary assessment of embodied water and sustainable mining. *Mine Water and the Environment*, 27(3), 136–144.

Mudd, G. (2010) The environmental sustainability of mining in Australia: Key mega-trends and looming constraints. *Resource Policy*, 35, 98–115.

Norgate, T. and Haque, N. (2010) Energy and greenhouse gas impacts of mining and mineral processing operations. *Journal of Cleaner Production*, 18, 266–274.

Northey, S., Haque, N. and Mudd, G. (2013) Using sustainability reporting to assess the environmental footprint of copper mining. *Journal of Cleaner Production*, 40, 118–128, available at: http://dx.doi.org/10.1016/j.jclepro.2012.09.027 (accessed November 4, 2013).

Ossandón, J. (2011) Economistas en la elite: Entre tecnopolítica y tecnociencia, in A. Joignant and P. Guell (eds), *Notables Tecnócratas y Mandarines Elementos de sociología de las elites en Chile 1990–2010*. Ediciones Universidad Diego Portales, Santiago de Chile, 109–126.

Parker, C., Baigorrotegui, G. and Estenssoro, F. (2013) Actores estratégicos y consumo sustentable representaciones sociales e institucionales de consumo de agua y energía en el sector minero de países selectos en Sudamérica. Informe Final de Investigación WP4 3 Proyecto ENGOV IDEA-USACH, available at: en.www.engov.eu.

Parlamento Latinoamericano (2010) Declaración Adhesión a las Conclusiones de la III Conferencia Interparlamentaria de Energía del Parlamento Latinoamericano y El Instituto para el Desarrollo Energético y Minero de América Latina Declaración: AO/2010/05 Veracruz México, August 2010, available at: www.parlatino.org/es/organos-principales/la-asamblea/declaraciones-y-resoluciones-de-la-asamblea/declaraciones-aprobadas-xxvi/declaraciones-xxvi/1716 html (accessed May 5, 2013).

Pellizzoni, L. (2011) The politics of facts: Local environmental conflicts and expertise. *Environmental Politics*, 20(6), 765–785.

Rábago, K. R., Lovins, A. B. and Feiler, T. E. (2001) Energy and sustainable development in the mining and minerals industries. *Mining Minerals and Sustainable Development MMSD*, 41. London: International Institute for Environment and Development, available at: http://pubs.iied.org/G00540 html (accessed May 5, 2013).

Reed, M. I. (2012) Masters of the universe: Power and elites in organization studies. *Organization Studies*, 33(2), 203–221

Reyes, C. (2012) Las Elites y los Nadies: Caso de estudio sobre la influencia de la elite chilena en un conflicto ambiental. Master's thesis in Latin American Studies. Faculty of Humanities, University of Oslo, Oslo.

Ruiz, C. A. R. (2001) V Conferencia Interparlamentaria de Minería y Energía para América Latina. *CIME 2001 CEPAL Santiago de Chile 18 al 20 de julio de 2001*. Santiago: CEPAL.

SGE2 (2011) *Revisión de políticas vigentes de eficiencia energética. Informe Final Estudio para la Subsecretaría de Energía Coord División de Eficiencia Energética.* Santiago: Ministerio de Energía Gobierno de Chile.

Silva, P. (2011) La elite tecnocrática en la era de la Concertación, in A. Joignant and P. Guell (eds), *Notables Tecnócratas y Mandarines Elementos de sociología de las elites en Chile 1990–2010.* Ediciones Universidad Diego Portales, Santiago de Chile, 241–269.

Silva, E. (1996) *The State and Capital in Chile: Business Elites Technocrats and Market Economics.* Westview Press, Boulder, CO.

Tong, Y. (2007) Bureaucracy meets the environment: Elite perceptions in six Chinese cities. *The China Quarterly*, 189 (March), 100–121.

WBCSD (2013) Eco-efficiency learning module. World Business Council for Sustainable Development, available at: www.wbcsd.org/Pages/EDocument/EDocumentDetails.asp x?ID=13593&NoSearchContextKey=true (accessed March 29, 2013).

Weiss, J. and Bustamente, T. (eds) (2008) *Ajedrez ambiental Manejo de recursos naturales comunidades conflictos y cooperación.* FLACSO–Ecuador, Ministerio de Cultura, Quito.

Wesselink, A., Buchman, K., Georgiadou, Y. and Turnhout, E. (2013) Technical knowledge discursive spaces and politics at the science-policy interface. *Environmental Science and Policy*, 30(1), 1–9.

Whitmore, A. (2006) The emperors new clothes: Sustainable mining? *Journal of Cleaner Production*, 14, 309–314, available at: www sciencedirect.com (accessed May 5, 2013).

# Part 3

# Forestry

# 10 REDD+ and forest governance in Latin America

## The role of science–policy networks

*Mariel Aguilar-Støen and Cecilie Hirsch*

## Introduction

"Reducing Emissions from Deforestation and forest Degradation (REDD)" was originally presented as a technological fix (cf. Li, 2007) to confront the global problem of deforestation and to reduce global carbon emissions, but the focus of REDD quickly moved from strictly carbon storage and uptake to multiple objectives (Angelsen and McNeill, 2012). The *plus* was added to REDD to signalize a stronger commitment, that the so-called "co-benefits" of forest conservation (e.g. protecting biodiversity and livelihoods) are included on an equal footing with carbon functions.[1] The inclusion of additional objectives into the REDD project reflects the diversity of actors involved in REDD arenas and their ability and power to advance their agendas (Brockhaus and Angelsen, 2012). REDD is based on the idea that it is possible to reduce deforestation and forest degradation by offering economic compensation to various actors (for not) changing the use of forest lands.

Global interest and attention on forests has grown as concerns about global warming and climate change have taken a heightened position in international policy debates. Especially since the presentation of the Stern Review in 2006, forests have been repositioned in international arenas as repositories of global value for their contribution to carbon sequestration and climate mitigation (Fairhead and Leach, 2003; Stern, 2006; Peet *et al.*, 2011).

In Latin America, forests cover about 11.1 million km$^2$ and savannahs 3.3 million km$^2$ comprising several different types of vegetation (Pacheco *et al.*, 2010). The region as a whole has the world's highest rate of forest loss; deforestation and land use change account for nearly three-quarters of greenhouse gas (GHG) emissions in the Amazon region (Hall, 2012). Brazil accounts for 5 percent of global GHG emissions, fourth after China, the US and Russia (Hall, 2012). Consequently, the situation of the Amazonian forests is seen as an issue of global concern for climate change mitigation.

About 20 percent of the total rural population in Latin America uses forest resources to support their livelihoods. Ten million people in the Amazon basin make a living in tropical forests ranging from small-scale agriculture to large-scale cattle ranching; many are also involved in timber felling, processing, trade and provision of services around forest activities, or non-timber forest products. Economic activities taking place in or around forests constitute important sources of employment and income and can also make contributions to the broader economy through taxes. There are significant trade-offs between forest conservation and economic development. As the role of forests in climate change mitigation has gained global importance, the debate about the trade-offs has become more relevant (Pacheco *et al.*, 2010). REDD is seen as a win–win approach that would potentially address the trade-offs between forest conservation and economic development. Forests are economically, socially and symbolically valuable to different actors, including to indigenous peoples, local users, governments, corporations, illegal cartels, non-governmental organizations (NGOs), nations and the globe, albeit in different ways, and for different reasons (Fairhead and Leach, 2003). All these actors have different possibilities for exerting power and accessing arenas to influence REDD-related policy making.

In this chapter we argue that science–policy networks have emerged as new elites in the development of REDD preparations in the Amazon countries, and we examine their role in these processes. A further question we address in this paper is whether REDD science–policy networks affect the position and ideas of other elites, and how. The chapter builds on on-going fieldwork in the region as well as a literature review and review of secondary sources. It is organized as follows. After this introduction we explain how we can understand science–policy networks as elites; we then examine the development of REDD projects in the Amazon basin, discuss examples of the involvement of REDD science–policy networks in the process of REDD planning and the outcome of such involvement. The next section discusses REDD science–policy networks as elites. The section is followed by a discussion on the effect REDD science–policy networks may have on elite reorientation. Finally a section with conclusions is presented.

## Science–policy networks as elites

We argue that science–policy networks, defined as interactions between groups of people and organizations that are implicated in the co-production of knowledge and social order (Forsyth, 2003), can be conceptualized as elites insofar as they control key resources: the production and promotion of specific knowledge (or "frames") and access to policy-making forums (see Chapter 2). Networks refer here to coalitions of actors who share values, interests and practices, and can be defined as a social system in which actors develop durable patterns of interaction and communication aimed at a specific issue (Bressers and O'Toole, 1998). Ideas, values and resources circulate within networks, and by this the networks may set the limits or boundaries of how reality is to be understood or to set apart what constitutes expert and non-expert knowledge.

Certain actors can control the co-production of environmental science by fostering linkages between specific science and policy networks; this might happen for example by providing funds for certain types of research or research institutions, or by engaging certain actors in research or implementation projects. Various scholars have discussed the embedded nature of knowledge production (Harding, 1986; Haraway, 1988; Forsyth, 2003). Scientific knowledge is created by people within particular institutions with situated and partial perspectives and consequently the questions science aims to answer are biased and respond to partial interests. Science production is organized within both centers of power and subaltern regions, hence knowledge has a geo-historical origin and knowledge production is relevant to legitimize certain social orders (Mignolo, 2002). The notion of "science–policy networks" used in this chapter builds from discussions within political ecology (Fairhead and Leach, 2003; Forsyth, 2003; Goldman *et al.*, 2011), feminist critiques of science (e.g. Harding, 1986; Haraway, 1988), Science and Technology Studies (Latour, 1987; Jasanoff, 1990) and post-colonial critiques of knowledge production (Quijano, 2000; Mignolo, 2002). Science–policy refers to the joint enforcement rather than a neat division between science and policy (Jasanoff, 1990). With network(s) we want to highlight agency as resting not with individuals but in the dynamic interaction among different actors. Here networks are seen as in a dialectic relation with the institutional and structural context, with a conception of power and agency that acknowledges both the influence of actors on networks and the impact of the structural context in which networks operate (Goverde and van Tatenhove, 2000; Forsyth, 2003).

## REDD projects and the Amazon Basin

An important component of the planning phase of REDD is the so-called demonstration and readiness activities. These are REDD-like projects implemented at the local level to test the different options available for countries and communities. "REDD projects" are means to understand how REDD will unfold on the ground and to provide lessons for future implementation. Early implementation projects influence debates about REDD, the ways in which so-called co-benefits are being addressed, who is involved and benefits from REDD.

In principle, "REDD strategies" supported by UN-REDD, the World Bank FCPF or bilaterally, are the first step in the implementation of REDD national policies. These strategies will define the current situation in each country, and the direction in which the country is going to move in terms of reduced carbon emissions from deforestation, addressing co-benefits and defining who would benefit from economic payments. In practice however, a myriad of projects are taking place in parallel with the design of a country's official REDD strategy. Consequently, proponents of "REDD projects" stand in a better position than other actors who do not have the same resources and power to define such projects, and to influence REDD debates. Simply because not having the necessary knowledge is a barrier for being included in the debates.

We have identified the following strategies employed by actors involved in early projects and the consequences of such strategies. The first strategy is "knowledge production and dissemination." The second strategy is the "creation of technologies or standards to legitimize or validate projects." The third strategy is "enrolment in emerging or alternative networks." In what follows we analyze these three strategies, highlighting the actors involved, the resources mobilized for employing each strategy and the outcome.

## Knowledge production and dissemination

Several scholars have provided insights into the close ties between knowledge and power and between the co-production of knowledge and social order (Foucault, 1980; Latour, 1987; Jasanoff, 1990; Quijano, 2000; Mignolo, 2002; Fairhead and Leach, 2003; Forsyth, 2003; Goldman et al., 2011). Others have highlighted the various and conflicting interpretations of REDD as an idea and of the aspects that should be emphasized (Angelsen and McNeill, 2012). REDD debates are characterized by a very complex and technical language that is not readily accessible to those who do not have experience with REDD. Paradoxically, to get information about REDD it is necessary to participate in forums and networks where knowledge about REDD is being produced, often in the form of international conferences or national level forums. Accessing such forums requires previous knowledge about REDD, as our interviews with some local NGOs and leaders of indigenous organizations indicate.[2] In this way, controlling knowledge production and dissemination is an important factor in shaping who will participate in REDD debates and how, and consequently the direction REDD is going to take. Our research shows that dissemination to local communities has been fragmented and dependent on particular networks' access to these communities and their interest in presenting REDD in a certain manner.

The first outcome we identify is that, in lieu of a definition, any project defined as REDD by proponents supported by REDD science–policy networks can become a REDD project. Knowledge produced by or about such projects is circulating and being accepted as "REDD relevant" knowledge. However, to be able to define that a project is in effect a REDD project, its proponents must be able to access the networks where knowledge is validated. Barriers to access such networks include for example lack of funding or ideological discrepancies.

Our findings indicate that to a great degree, networks involving NGOs and international research institutions with support from development cooperation agencies and private actors are creating and disseminating knowledge about REDD at different levels. These networks systematize information about REDD in the Amazon basin and are having a great influence in defining what a REDD project is, who the legitimate implementers are, who will benefit from it and how.

To illustrate, research institutions such as the Center for International Forestry Research (CIFOR), "the REDD desk" by the NGO Global Canopy Programme,[3] the "voluntary REDD database"[4] created at the Oslo Climate and Forest Conference in 2010 and the "knowledge database"[5] of the initiative Governors' Climate and Forest Taskforce (GCFT)"[6] produce REDD-Project's[7] catalogs[8] and databases. The projects included in these catalogues comprise projects for avoided deforestation and carbon capture, and also projects designed to increase carbon sequestration through plantations[9] and other activities such as eco-tourism, fair-trade coffee and cacao production.

The first CIFOR study trying to systematize local REDD projects (Wertz-Kanounnikoff and Kongphan-Apirak, 2009) explicitly recognizes (p. 1) that "a limitation of [their] survey is the lack of any clear definition of what constitutes a REDD demonstration activity. Despite these shortcomings this survey offers insights on current trends to inform future REDD investments." The second CIFOR study (Madeira *et al.*, 2010, p. 1) defines REDD as "activities aimed at directly reducing emissions from deforestation and degradation in geographically distinct and contiguous areas, which are identified by their proponents as REDD and are operating under official agreements with some level of government."

The second outcome we observe is that pilot project proponents, most of whom are networks of private actors, act as de facto researchers testing REDD implementation modalities and producing information and knowledge about the projects. Most REDD projects in the Amazon basin are initiated or planned by private actors, including national and international private companies, and local and international NGOs such as World Wildlife Fund (WWF), Conservation International (CI), the Wildlife Conservation Society (WCS), The Nature Conservancy, International Union for Conservation of Nature (IUCN) and Rainforest Alliance) in private lands. In some cases pilot projects are executed with the participation of state governments in coalition with big international NGOs (BINGOs). Fair trade cooperatives, carbon certifiers and research institutions are also involved in pilot projects.

The third outcome we identify is that, because of their involvement in capacity building activities, networks of private actors are in a dominant position to spread their ideas and knowledge about REDD.

Aside of being direct proponents of REDD projects, these networks are involved in capacity building activities. Since navigating the REDD landscape requires highly specialized knowledge and the process of creating and legitimizing REDD projects is complex, a new form of expertise and consultancy has emerged. International and local NGOs, as well as consultant firms and individuals are being recast as "REDD experts" in the process. This gives them considerable leverage in defining what REDD would be, repackaging their own projects as REDD, and also opens the doors to policy-making arenas at national and international levels.

Knowledge production is highly selective when it comes to who defines problems and who participates in policy making, what the problem is and the solution for it (Beymer-Farris and Bassett, 2012; Goldman *et al.*, 2011). By producing, systematizing and spreading information about REDD projects the networks identified above contribute to define who decides what a REDD project in Latin America is, who participates in them and consequently how related questions are going to be addressed. Findings made by these networks are also published through international networks where they contribute to the production of learned lessons that influence future REDD projects. Creating and disseminating knowledge also contributes to enhancing the reputation of those actors involved in the network, ultimately reinforcing their power in discourse formation.

*Creating techniques to legitimize or validate projects*

Networks of NGOs, corporations and research institutions are involved in creating standards to certify carbon offsets that can be traded in the voluntary carbon market or in a future REDD carbon market. Organizations involved in pilot projects are also creating standards to demonstrate how they involve local populations in REDD projects. We conceptualize such standards as techniques. With technique we mean procedures designed to govern the conduct of those involved in REDD projects (cf. Foucault, 2002).

The fourth outcome we identify is that networks of private actors, NGOs and research institutions are involved in creating mechanisms to regulate and control the behavior of other actors. An illustrative example of this is the Rainforest Standard (RFS). This standard was developed by Columbia University in New York in collaboration with private environmental funds from Bolivia, Peru, Brazil, Ecuador and Colombia. According to its proponents, "this standard integrates carbon-accounting, socio-cultural/socio-economic impacts and biodiversity outcomes into one single REDD standard."[10] Projects certified with RFS can be registered in the Climate Community and Biodiversity Alliance (CCBA)[11] and in the Verified Carbon Standards (VCS)[12] to be traded in the voluntary carbon market. The alliances and associations built between NGOs, the private sector and research institutions contribute to the creation of facts, standards, knowledge and concepts seen as accepted "truths" (cf. Goldman and Turner, 2011). These accepted truths are shaping the direction of REDD in the Amazon basin before governments have managed to put in place a plan of action. For example, in Colombia where the readiness process is still incipient, BINGOs and local NGOs have managed to include the RFS as a standard to certify REDD projects by the government in the national REDD strategy. Projects that do not comply with the RFS will not be included in the national REDD register of Colombia, and their proponents are not invited to participate in the debate.

The fifth outcome we identified is that private actors are appropriating disputed concepts, such as Free Prior and Informed Consent/Consultation (FPIC), giving such concepts meanings that accommodate their interests with little involvement of states or affected actors. In addition to setting standards to validate and include projects in REDD, pilot project's proponents are creating techniques to include local populations in planning and implementation of "benefit sharing" arrangements of the project.

Our empirical material suggests that private companies are using concepts such as FPIC, emptying them of meaning, and wrongly presenting them as "Free Prior and Informed Consultation" instead of "Free Prior and Informed Consent."[13] How to implement this concept is unclear for most countries in the region. FPIC is among the claims of indigenous peoples' discourses on participation in natural resource governance in the region, but it is unclear how to implement it (Haarstad, 2012). International jurisprudence emitted by the Inter-American Court of Human Rights has stressed that implementing FPIC and consultations with indigenous peoples is the responsibility of states (Yrigoyen, 2011), and not NGOs or private actors as is often practiced.

In addition, the situation for other rural populations who are not indigenous is unclear, such as migrants or squatters. In the case of squatters, for example, in Brazil private companies are signing contracts and memorandums of understanding (MoUs) with local communities. These MoUs include provisions as to how to solve land disputes and how to share benefits arising from the sale of carbon. They are usually implemented without the involvement of the state. All the activities to be implemented by the project are decided by private companies who claim to have obtained FPIC from local (indigenous and non-indigenous) populations. In many instances, private companies have the sole power to decide the terms under which local communities are going to participate and benefit from a REDD project. Land conflicts between private companies and local communities are often solved through the conditions determined by the company, which do not necessarily secure a just solution for all parties. In cases where indigenous groups have been granted land titles for their territories, poor migrant peasants in the area with weaker legal ties to the land might be excluded in the processes. Indigenous organization may also have stronger international alliances to support their participation in international negotiations than other groups (such as those tied to COICA—see below).

### Enrolling in emerging and alternative networks

The sixth outcome we observed is that by enrolling in alternative networks, actors and networks of actors who do not share the mainstream approach to REDD are also bringing their concerns to international arenas. Participation in REDD networks is conditioned by overriding narratives about the role of economic incentives in tackling deforestation. Activists and other actors seeking to influence existing networks may have to decide between working within such dominant rules or establishing alternative and competing networks (Forsyth, 2003; Taylor, 2012).

Initially, many indigenous peoples' organizations were skeptical to REDD and rejected carbon markets for considering that they do not offer real solutions to climate change (see the Anchorage declaration adopted by the participants at the indigenous peoples' global summit on climate change in 2009[14]). Indigenous organizations in the global south criticized carbon markets and carbon sequestration projects for their oversimplified portrayal of ecosystems and forests and for ignoring the socio-economic, political and institutional implications of carbon sequestration for indigenous peoples (Schroeder, 2010).

Indigenous peoples' organizations in Latin America and particularly in the Amazon basin countries have since engaged in networks supporting REDD or in alternative networks that are skeptical about REDD and carbon markets. The different paths taken by different indigenous peoples' organizations are in part explained by previous engagements with pro-REDD NGOs and by their own experiences with REDD named projects, as well as experience with government policies and the organization's own visions and priorities.

The Coordinator of Indigenous Organizations of the Amazon Basin (COICA[15]) in alliance with its associated national organizations are defining and proposing a model of indigenous peoples' REDD. The position of COICA is that REDD should be defined based on the priorities of indigenous peoples to guarantee the territorial land rights of indigenous peoples, through holistic management plans that secure the livelihoods and rights of indigenous peoples and the titling and consolidation of indigenous territories. COICA's vision places greater emphasis on addressing the drivers of deforestation such as oil exploitation, mining, dams, large infrastructure and agribusiness, which are also seen as serious threats to indigenous peoples' rights and livelihoods. COICA's indigenous REDD plans also stress the multiple services/functions of ecosystems in addition to carbon sequestration and the implementation of pilot REDD projects led by communities and indigenous organizations. Internally, in COICA there has been disagreement about carbon markets, where parts of the organizations are skeptical while others are open for carbon markets under regulation and transparency, respecting indigenous rights. COICA has stated that they view carbon markets as threats and that signing contracts concerning carbon credits is risky, and advocates for an international carbon fund.[16] COICA has engaged with private actors (such as the Ford Foundation), a variety of NGOs and the World Bank, who support REDD market schemes.

The experience of some indigenous peoples' organizations with so-called "carbon cowboys," particularly in Brazil, Peru, Bolivia and Colombia have made them extra aware of some of the risks REDD projects might entail. Peruvian, Brazilian, Bolivian and Colombian indigenous organizations have denounced community leaders for signing disadvantageous contracts with private actors.[17] While the Peruvian, Bolivian and Brazilian governments took action against the "carbon cowboys," the Colombian government was more passive. The regional COICA offers a channel for collectively raising awareness about the threat of carbon cowboys at the international level. COICA has access to international forums where irregularities can be denounced. Such forums might offer better pathways to influence national governments in more effective ways. As has been the case with other indigenous peoples' demands, these actors are using international arenas (e.g. United Nations forums) to support the advance of their REDD agendas at national levels. Having access to information and knowledge about REDD is a critical condition for the effective participation of indigenous peoples and for their possibilities of benefiting from REDD in a fair way. However, information is not enough if it does not allow for addressing the concerns of indigenous peoples and strengthening their rights.

Finally, other actors are becoming increasingly engaged in opposing REDD for a variety of reasons. The seventh outcome we observe is that governments or alternative networks that resist or oppose the mainstream view of REDD are also bringing their concerns to the international arena, but so far have failed to gather support to re-open a discussion of the definition of REDD. This proves the power of the dominant version of REDD.

Opponents argue that REDD might entail threats to human rights, food security (e.g. by higher food prices, exclusions from cultivation areas or change in local livelihoods), rural poverty alleviation and biodiversity conservation. Notable among REDD opponents are certain governments from the Amazon basin. The Bolivarian Alliance for the Peoples of Our America (ALBA) bloc[18] supported Bolivia's proposal to reject the idea of seeing forests as simply carbon-offsets to be traded in the carbon market, and to opt for a new alternative mechanism. Scholars supporting their position point to the insecurities related to the pricing of carbon, effectiveness of offsets and the related unequal terms of trade, the opening up of the arena for a variety of private actors through the carbon market, and the control they can potentially get over certain areas and processes, threatens both national and local sovereignty (Bumpus, 2011). The Alba countries also supported the Bolivian idea for climate funding from an alternative tax. The Bolivian alternative mechanism was supported by a range of developing and like-minded countries in Doha,[19] and in 2013 Denmark, Switzerland and the EU granted a support of over US$43 million to the Bolivian mechanism. Bolivia further won support for their insistence on working for non-market based approaches for the funding of climate change initiatives in Doha. The Bolivian position on carbon markets, the Cochabamba declaration from 2010 and the proposed alternative mechanism have all been marginalized at the international level by both strong REDD countries and BINGOs.

## New elites: funding, science–policy networks and REDD

REDD is a broad and vague enough idea to allow different interpretations of it that can fit the goals of different actors (Angelsen and McNeill, 2012). This has permitted that different actors define differently the actions necessary to implement REDD at local levels. In the process, certain narratives, values and visions gain prominence and those promoting such ideas gain power to define what REDD should look like in specific contexts. Controlling the production of knowledge seems to be a prominent strategy of different actors to position themselves in the REDD debate in the Amazon countries.

A further mechanism involved in the production of science–policy is funding. Certain industrialized countries are financing REDD through development cooperation money. Through funding, these countries and agencies foster cooperation and alliances between science and policy networks. Take the example of how readiness preparations for REDD are financed. There are two main mechanisms for financing phase 1:[20] through the UN-REDD program or through the Forest Carbon Partnership Facility (FCPF) of the World Bank. Some countries such as Bolivia,[21] Peru and Ecuador have applied to both. On the other hand Brazil established its own Amazon fund in 2008 to finance reduced deforestation in the country. Guyana established the Guyana REDD Investment Fund (GRIF) in 2010 as part of a cooperation agreement with Norway in the framework of the Low Carbon Development Strategy (LCDS) of Guyana.[22] Venezuela and French Guyana do not participate in any REDD initiative.

Norway is the single major financial contributor to the UN-REDD, FCPF the Brazilian Amazon fund and the GRIF. Norway contributes with 82 percent of the total budget of the UN-REDD; with 44 percent of the total budget of FCPF; with

87 percent of the total budget of the Amazon fund and with 100 percent to the GRIF.[23] Norway is one of the major players in defining REDD at the global level but also influences the way in which REDD is advancing at national levels.

Initially, Norway supported only Brazil through bilateral assistance, and channeled most of the funds through the FCPF or the UN-REDD program. Later Norway decided to support Guyana by supporting the GRIF, but realized subsequently that conserving the forests in the Amazon basin required supporting all the countries in the region and new programs were underway as we conducted fieldwork. However, one country was excluded: Bolivia. The reasons for not supporting Bolivia relate to the country's opposing position to carbon markets and the perceived Bolivian "activism" and ambiguity in international negotiations, as well as resistance to financing the alternative mechanism Bolivia has presented at international climate negotiations and other forums.[24] Norwegian bureaucrats have referred to the Bolivian alternative as a "fragmentation of REDD" and as "unfinished," albeit Bolivia has agreed to measure and monitor carbon. The Bolivian alternative proposes a combination of mitigation and adaptation in forest efforts, as well as acknowledging the different functions of forests beyond carbon, starting with protected forest areas and indigenous territories. The initiative has received little REDD money per se (only a small share from UN-REDD). This shows that if a country or a group of countries (e.g. Bolivia and the ALBA bloc) presents a different position or wants to develop different mechanisms for REDD, this position stands little chance of receiving any economic support.

As for funding sources for demonstration projects, development cooperation aid money as well as private funds are the most important sources. Private funds include direct investments in particular projects from investors from the USA, Europe, China and India; direct investments from companies (e.g. from the largest Brazilian mining company Vale); investments that private companies do in BINGOs, or in some cases a national NGO "sells" a project to actors from the industry to become part of the industry's Corporate Social Responsibility (CSR) portfolio. National NGOs have in some cases such as in Colombia alliances and cooperation with local-level environmental authorities (CARs), national and international business partners (mining and energy-producing companies, plantation companies, forest companies and carbon marketing companies), international research organizations, development cooperation agencies and indigenous leaders.[25] These alliances influence the emphasis given to particular components in the projects, particularly in regard to carbon markets and market mechanisms for trading carbon offsets.

Our empirical material suggests that large international research centers and universities receive more economic support and are in a better position to engage in transnational networks than Latin American ones. For example while Columbia University in the United States receives ample support, our Colombian interviewees from the national university claim to have been excluded from the Colombian REDD table, a network of mostly NGOs that leads the REDD talks in the country. Colombian academics claim to have produced alternative procedures to measure forest carbon that are more appropriate for the tropical context. However, this knowledge is not enough to affect policy making. The knowledge required to participate in the REDD debates is not just any type of knowledge. It has to be maintained and strengthened through particular networks in which different concepts and arguments are socially constructed and legitimated through complex processes that have produced new dominant forms of expertise and consultancy (Fairhead and Leach, 2003; Bumpus and Liverman, 2011).

Science–policy networks or actors within such networks might take advantage of the opening of policy spaces to effect change and promote their interests. Prominent among them in the Amazon basin countries are BINGOs and national NGOs in coalition with private actors and research institutions. As we have seen, networks can bring about coalitions between actors with seemingly disparate interests such as NGOs, businesses, academics etc. to pursue specific goals at particular times. Networks are not place bounded and might include transnational links between actors who share common analytical perspectives, values, discourses and interests. Thus a pertinent question here is whether "science–policy networks," as related to REDD and climate change, might affect the dominant ideas of other elites. A related question is, if that is the case, how these science–policy networks are influencing other elites' orientation.

## REDD science–policy networks and elite reorientation?

At the global level, as has been the case with other issues related to climate negotiations (e.g. Forsyth, 2003, p. 143), science–policy networks can influence the position of different actors. In the case of REDD, although neither the only factor nor the most important, reports prepared by not-for-profit organizations that are part of REDD science–policy networks have been used in the discussions of the conference of the parties to the United Nations Framework Convention on Climate Change (UNFCCC). An important impact of such report making is, for example, the adoption of the "phased approach" to REDD, launched by a report (Angelsen *et al.*, 2009) hosted by the Meridian institute and commissioned by the government of Norway. The "phased approach" has now been adopted by most governments in the Latin American region for preparations to REDD; this is an example of the influence science–policy networks have on national processes and governments.

REDD science–policy networks are influencing, although not necessarily reorienting, the position of other elite actors. For example, various transnational and national companies, such as mining and energy producing companies, plantation companies, forestry companies and carbon market companies engage in REDD demonstration activities by funding specific projects. Since dominant REDD science–policy networks have ideological positions that do not conflict with the ideological position of corporations, it has been possible to establish alliances between them. Our findings concur with those of Meckling (2011), who shows how a transnational business coalition (energy firms and energy-intensive manufacturers) have actively promoted the global rise of carbon trading.

Angelsen and McNeill (2012, pp. 36–38) identify four broad ideological positions on REDD: market liberalism, institutionalism, bio-environmentalism and social greens. These positions differ in the way in which the role of forests in economic and social terms is perceived and thus in how REDD should be implemented. Market liberals emphasize the role of markets, commodification of environmental services and forests for economic growth and development, and privilege the involvement of the private sector in REDD; their position relies on a strong emphasis on carbon markets, and some private actors and governments in the region identify with this position. Institutionalists emphasize the design of institutions, governance models and legislation to protect the environment and guarantee human well-being. For them both state and markets and other mechanisms are necessary for the success of REDD; this position is prominent among donors. The position of bio-environmentalists is based on the idea of ecological limits demanding ambitious targets for reduction in emissions and deforestation rates; their vision does not conflict with that of market liberalists in relation to the role of carbon markets; this position is common among NGOs. Social greens draw on radical social and economic thought and argue that society and the environment are inseparable entities. They emphasize a "rights-based approach" for REDD. These are also often critical to carbon markets. Most of the actors involved in networks producing knowledge or designing techniques to govern REDD identify with the first three positions, whereas those involved in alternative networks identify themselves with the fourth position. Narratives behind these positions are powerful frames conditioning the position and the options seen as available by most bureaucrats in the environmental public administration of the Amazon countries. However, environment ministries and related offices stand in a less privileged position than, for example, parts of the public administration related to sectors that generate income through the exploitation of natural resources.

Resource extraction continues to be central for the economies of most Amazon countries (Bebbington and Bebbington, 2012), often at the expense of forests. Mining, gas and oil extraction are the most important activities to generate economic revenues for most of the countries in the Amazon basin. The development of infrastructure such as hydropower and road building are also priorities for these countries. All these activities are in most cases planned to occur in forest areas. In addition, the agricultural frontier is expanding in many of the Latin American countries. Therefore we cannot affirm that REDD elites have a strong influence in the Amazon countries' broader development policy making or in the visions of development. Guyana is an interesting exception.

A former president of Guyana, Bharrat Jagdeo, launched a campaign to attract funding for the country's Low Carbon Development Strategy (LCDS), of which REDD is an important part. Prior to the campaign lead by Jagdeo, a report was commissioned to McKinsey and company to estimate the value of Guyana's rainforest. McKinsey has since 2008 been the market leader in REDD advice. The advice provided by McKinsey & Co. is highly influenced by government and business interests (Bock, 2014).

With the report in his hands, Jagdeo visited Europe to seek alternatives for protecting the entirety of the Guyanese rainforest in exchange for economic incentives.[26] In 2009 Guyana and Norway signed a MoU for funding up to US$250 million over five years. We argue that president Jagdeo, an economist himself with a wide network of contacts in high level policy-making, business and NGO circles[27] managed "to speak" the right language with other like-minded politicians such as former prime Minister of Norway, Jens Stoltenberg and to get support from Norway for its LCDS. It is worth mentioning that, in addition to Guyana, McKinsey & Co. has produced REDD reports for the governments of Brazil, the Democratic Republic of Congo, Indonesia, Papua New Guinea and Mexico (Bock, 2014), all of which receive support from Norway.

Guyana's LCDS is perhaps the most ambitious strategy for climate change mitigation in the region. Guyana uses REDD as the primary framework of the LCDS. LCDS' goals include contributing to global carbon abatement through forest conservation, making the country's economy low in carbon emissions and more sustainable, and lifting Guyana's population out of poverty. The LCDS aims to incentivize Guyana to develop its economy and infrastructure in a manner that reduces carbon emissions,[28] which in turn will finance Guyana's LCDS. The development of the LCDS and its funding occurred in part thanks to the influence of science–policy networks in which former president Jagdeo was involved.

## Conclusion

This chapter is based on a relational definition of elites based on their control over resources, including financial, political and discursive, as well as natural resources, knowledge and expertise as discussed in Chapter 2. We have examined the role of science–policy networks in the development of REDD preparations in the Amazon countries, and argued that they can be conceptualized as elites, given that they control specific resources, in this case the production and promotion of certain framings of REDD and access to arenas for policy making by excluding and including certain knowledge, projects and actors. These networks are supported by specific discourses (such as market liberalism), or economic and legal structures, and can also be aligned with other elite interests. The networks include influential groups that control knowledge and framings, and thereby the definition of areas, projects, models, and actors that participate in REDD.

We have identified three strategies employed by different actors; knowledge production and dissemination, creation of technologies/standards to legitimize or validate projects and the enrolment in emerging networks.

We have shown that these networks to a large degree are dominated by NGOs, consultants, think tanks, international research institutions, with support from development cooperation agencies and private actors. These groups of REDD experts might further become new technocratic elites as discussed in Chapter 2. More importantly than the specific actors, is the kind of knowledge, projects and models that are accepted as REDD. Access to these networks, specific knowledge, arenas and technical language facilitates and makes it possible for the same actors to define REDD projects and validate them as REDD. Barriers to accessing these networks can be related to both funding and ideological discrepancies. The networks are not completely closed, as in the case of indigenous peoples, where we see the opening and closing of networks, depending on their openness to economic mechanisms, where indigenous allied with international NGOs can access important international arenas. Networks including private actors are giving stronger emphasis to carbon markets and carbon trading, and with their involvement in capacity building activities they are in a dominant position to spread their ideas and knowledge about REDD.

We have also shed light on the funding mechanisms for REDD, and the actors involved in funding, both industrialized countries through development cooperation, and private actor's involvement. Funding fosters cooperation and alliances between specific science and policy networks, in which certain concepts and arguments are constructed and legitimated. On the other hand, alternative ideas, such as those from indigenous organizations (e.g. COICA), the alternative climate justice movement and Bolivia, or domestic researchers (such as in Colombia), have been given little space to develop further alternatives to the dominant REDD regime upheld by science–policy networks, partly due to the belief in the technical superiority of the phased approach, economic and market mechanisms, specific standards for monitoring and verification, and exclusionary technical language.

Links have also been made between the science–policy REDD networks and other elite interests. We have seen how a range of different private actors and companies support REDD activities, forming alliances, and promoting certain models. REDD has offered a new regime of profit making possibilities through a possible carbon market, trading carbon offsets, but also in developing a new form of expertise, standards and consultancy. Cross-national alliances have also emerged between private actors and local authorities, facilitated by NGOs and research institutions. The private actors dominance in REDD in Latin America has further led to the appropriation of disputed concepts, such as FPIC, with consequences for the involvement of local communities and indigenous peoples.

In addition, we discuss whether these science–policy networks affect the position and ideas of other elites, and how. As we have seen, other elites, such as those based on economic resources (land and capital) can support with funding and find possibilities for control over areas and profits, and support the model for their own interests.

In conclusion, we see that as a result of REDD, a new network of elite actors is emerging, who generate and disseminate knowledge about REDD, forming a new form of expertise and consultancy. The actors involved in the dominant science–policy networks are recast as "REDD experts," defining the limits to how far actors and knowledge can participate in policy-making arenas at national and international levels. By producing, systematizing and spreading information about REDD, these networks contribute to defining who decides what a REDD project in Latin America is, and consequently how questions related to environmental and social justice are going to be addressed.

How sustainable are the models that these science–policy networks are promoting? There is a danger that alternative ideas, knowledge and more domestically suitable models of environmental governance and knowledge will be excluded from REDD processes in Latin America, which will have impacts for both people and nature.

## Notes

1   From here we will only use the term REDD, although it includes REDD+.
2   Interviews with representatives from Colombia, Bolivia and COICA.
3   The REDD desk is funded by the Gordon and Betty More Foundation, the Climate and Land Use Alliance, the Department of Climate Change and Energy Efficiency of the Australian Government, the German International Cooperation Agency (GIZ) and the US Agency for International Development (USAID).
4   See http://reddplusdatabase.org.
5   See www.gcftaskforce-database.org/Home.
6   See www.gcftaskforce.org. The GCFT brings together subnational level authorities from Brazil, Mexico, Peru and countries in Africa, Indonesia and the governors' offices of California and Illinois. In this project California and Illinois will potentially be able to purchase carbon offsets from projects in developing countries, as part of the cap-and-trade program of California and Illinois, which will use a market-based mechanism to lower GHG. The GCFT receives funding from Gordon and Betty Moore Foundation, ClimateWorks, Climate and Land Use Alliance, the Norwegian Agency for Development Cooperation (Norad) and the David and Lucile Packard Foundation. Collaborating partners include NGOs from Brazil IDESAM and IPAM, Indonesia Kemitraan, Mexico ProNatura, a transnational private company ClimateFocus, and the American based private research organizations Carnegie Institution for Science and Woods Hole Research Center.
7   CIFOR produces this catalogue as part of the project Global Comparative Study on REDD (GCS-REDD) funded by the Norwegian NIFCI with a total grant of NOK 80 million (2009–12).
8   See www.forestclimatechange.org/redd-map/about.html.
9   The database "included all forest carbon projects because of the difficulty in distinguishing REDD schemes from afforestation/reforestation projects across all countries"; see http://www.forestclimatechange.org/redd-map (accessed February 12, 2013).
10   See http://cees.columbia.edu/the-rainforest-standard; interview, FAN, Colombia.
11   The CCBA is a partnership among research institutions (Tropical Agricultural Research and Higher Education Center (CATIE), CIFOR and International Centre for Research in Agroforestry (ICRAF)), corporations (The Blue Moon Fund, The Kraft Fund, BP, Hyundai, Intel, SC Johnson, Sustainable Forestry Management and Weyerhaeuser), and NGOs (Cooperative for Assistance and Relief Everywhere (CARE), CI, The Nature Conservancy, Rainforest Alliance and WCS).
12   The VCS was established in 2005 by the Climate Group, the International Trading Association, and the World Business Council for Sustainable Development. The VCS is one of the world's most widely used carbon-accounting standards. Projects across the world have issued more than 100 million carbon credits using VCS standards. The VCS headquarters are in Washington, DC, with offices in China and South America.
13   Interviews in Colombia with the private company CI Consult. The ILO 169 convention on the rights of indigenous and tribal peoples living in independent countries establishes that states signatories of the convention are obliged to obtain "free prior and informed consent" to actions that affect their lands, territories and natural resources. UN-REDD has pledged to uphold the UN declaration on the Rights of

Indigenous Peoples and to extend the principle of FPIC to indigenous peoples and other forest dependent communities (Lawlor *et al.*, 2010).

14  See  www.unutki.org/downloads/File/Events/2009-04_Climate_Change_Summit/Anchorage _Declaration.pdf.

15  COICA (*Coordinadora de las Organizaciones Indigenas de la Cuenca Amazonica*) is an umbrella organizaton composed of organizations of indigenous peoples from Peru (AIDESEF), Guyana (Amerindian Peoples Association—APA), Bolivia (Confederation of Indigenous People of Bolivia—CIDOB), Brazil (Coordination of Indigenous Organisations of the Brazilian Amazon—COIAB), Ecuador (Confederation of Indigenous Nationalities of the Ecuadorian Amazon—CONFENIAE), Venezuela (Amazon Indigenous People's Regional Organization—ORPIA), French Guyana (*Fédération des Organisations Amérindiennes de Guyane*—FOAG), Suriname (Organization of Indigenous People in Suriname—OIS) and Colombia (Organization of Indigenous Peoples of the Colombian Amazon—OPIAC).

16  Interview with Edwin Vasquez, president of COICA and his presentation at the REDD workshop in Ås.

17  Interviews Colombia (CI, IRSA), Edwin Vasquez, AIDESEP-Peru, interviews Bolivia.

18  A Latin American alternative trade bloc consisting of Antigua and Barbuda, Bolivia, Cuba, Dominica, Ecuador, Nicaragua, Saint Vincent and the Grenadines and Venezuela.

19  Twenty countries including China, India, Iran, Iraq, Egypt, etc.

20  In 2010 during the conference of the parties to the UNFCCC, governments agreed to adopt a phased approach for REDD. The idea of a phased approach was adopted by the UNFCCC Cancun agreement (Agrawal *et al.*, 2011). The Cancun agreement stipulates that countries participating in REDD should implement activities by phases. These phases are: (1) development of a national REDD plan and capacity building; (2) implementation of national plan and demonstration activities; and (3) result-based actions with full reporting and verification. See http://unfccc.int/resource/docs/2010/cop16/eng/07a01.pdf; see also page 3 in Angelsen *et al.* (2009).

21  The final Readiness Plan Idea Notes (R-PIN) was never signed by the Bolivian authorities.

22  See www.lcds.gov.gy.

23  Other donors contributing to UN-REDD are in order of the size of their contribution the European Union, Denmark, Spain, Japan and Luxembourg. Germany provides 34 percent of the total budget of the FCPF. Other donors include Australia, UK, USA, Canada, European Commission, The Nature Conservancy and two private companies: BP Technology Ventures an alternative energy company with venture investments in projects on biofuels, wind and solar energy; and CDC Climat, a company that includes emissions trading and energy investments in its portfolio. The other contributors to the Amazon fund are Germany and the Brazilian oil company Petrobras. Sources: http://mptf.undp.org/factsheet/fund/CCF00; www.forestcarbonpartnership.org/sites/fcp/files/2013/FCPF%20Carbon%20Fund%20Contributions%20as%20of%20Dec%2031_2012.pdf; www.amazonfund.gov.br/FundoAmazonia/fam/site_en/Esquerdo/doacoes/; www.guyanareddfund.org/index.php?option=com_content&view=article&id=101&Itemid=116.

24  Interviews Bolivia and the Government of Norway's Climate and Forest project.

25  Interview FAN; interviews Colombia.

26  See http://news.bbc.co.uk/2/hi/science/nature/7603695.stm.

27  In 2008 Britain's Prince Charles urged business leaders to act to save the world's rainforest; he called Jagdeo's initiative one of the best for fighting against climate change. Jagdeo met informally with Stoltenberg during the meeting organized by

Prince Charles (see www.stabroeknews.com/2008/archives/09/15/prince-charles-applauds-jagdeo-climate-change-proposal). In 2013 Jagdeo and Prince Charles chaired a meeting of the commonwealth expert group on climate finance. In 2012 the international NGO IUCN appointed Jagdeo as IUCN high level envoy for sustainable development in forest countries and patron of Nature. See www.iucn.org/news_homepage/?9405/A-Presidential-drive-for-sustainable-development-in-forest-countries.

28  See www.uncsd2012.org/content/documents/Revised-LCDS-May-20-2010-draft-for-MSSC.pdf. The consultant firm McKinsey & Co. prepared the technical analysis for the LCDS. Then president of Guyana, Bharrat Jagdeo embarked in an international campaign to gather financial support for the strategy.

## References

Agrawal, A., Nepstadd, D. and Chhatre, A. (2011) Reducing emissions from deforestation and forest degradation. *Annual Review of Environment and Resources*, 36, 373–396.

Angelsen, A. and McNeill, D. (2012) The evolution of REDD+, in A. Angelsen, M. Brockhaus, W. D. Sunderlin and L. V. Verchot (eds), *Analysing REDD+: Challenges and choices*. CIFOR, Bogor, Indonesia, 31–49.

Angelsen, A., Brown, S., Loisel, C., Peskett, L., Streck, C. and Zarin, D. (2009) *Reducing Emissions from Deforestation and Forest Degradation (REDD): An Options Assessment Report Prepared for the Government of Norway*. Meridian Institute, Washington, DC.

Bebbington, A. and Bebbington, D. (2012) Extractive industries narratives of development and socio-environmental disputes across the (ostensible changing) Andean region, in H. Haarstad (ed.), *New Political Spaces in Latin American Natural Resource Governance*. Palgrave Macmillan, Basingstoke, 17–38.

Beymer-Farris, B. A. and Bassett, T. J. (2012) The REDD menace: Resurgent protectionism in Tanzania's mangrove forests. *Global Environmental Change*, 22, 332–341.

Bock, S. (2014) Politicized expertise: An analysis of the political dimensions of consultants' policy recommendations to developing countries with a case study of McKinsey's advice on REDD+ policies. *Innovation: The European Journal of Social Science Research*, 1–19.

Bressers, H.T.A. and O'Toole, L. J. (1998) The selection of policy instruments: a network-based perspective. *Journal of Public Policy*, 18 (3), 213–239.

Brockhaus, M. and Angelsen, A. (2012) Seeing REDD+ through 4Is: A political economy framework, in A. Angelsen, M. Brockhaus, W. D. Sunderlin and L. V. Verchot (eds), *Analysing REDD+: Challenges and choices*. CIFOR, Bogor, Indonesia, CIFOR, 15–31.

Bumpus, A. G. (2011) The matter of carbon: Understanding the materiality of tCO2e in carbon offsets. *Antipode*, 43, 612–638.

Bumpus, A. G. and Liverman, D. (2011) Carbon colonialism? Offsets greenhouse gas reduction and sustainable development, in R. Peet, P. Robbins and M. J. Watts (eds), *Global Political Ecology*. Routledge, New York, 203–224.

Fairhead, J. and Leach, M. (2003) *Science Society and Power: Environmental Knowledge and Policy in West Africa and the Caribbean*. Cambridge University Press, Cambridge.

Forsyth, T. (2003) *Critical Political Ecology: The Politics of Environmental Science*. Routledge, New York.

Foucault, M. (1980) Two lectures, in C. Gordon (ed.), *Power/Knowledge: Selected Interviews and Other Writings 1972–1977*. Pantheon, New York, 78–108.

Foucault, M. (2002) *Order of Things*. Routledge Classics, London.

Goldman, M. and Turner, M. D. (2011) Introduction, in M. Goldman, P. Nadasdy and M. D. Turner (eds), *Knowing Nature: Conversations at the Intersection of Political Ecology and Science Studies*. University of Chicago Press, Chicago, IL.

Goldman, M., Nadasdy, P. and Turner, M. D. (2011) *Knowing Nature: Conversations at the Intersection of Political Ecology and Science Studies*. University of Chicago Press, Chicago, IL.

Goverde, H. and Van Tatenhove, J. (2000) Power and policy networks, in H. Goverde, P. Cerny, M. Haugaard and H. Lentner (eds), *Power in Contemporary Politics: Theories, Practices, Globalizations*. SAGE Publications, London, 96–111.

Haarstad, H. (2012) Extracting justice? Critical themes and challenges in Latin American natural resource governance, in H. Haarstad (ed.), *New Political Spaces in Latin American Natural Resource Governance*. Palgrave Macmillan, Basingstoke, 1–16.

Hall, A. (2012) *Forests and Climate Change: The Social Dimensions of REDD in Latin America*. Edward Elgar Publishing, Cheltenham.

Haraway, D. (1988) Situated knowledges: The science question in feminism and the privilege of partial perspective. *Feminist Studies*, 14, 575–599.

Harding, S. (1986) *The Science Question in Feminism*. Cornell University Press, Ithaca, NY.

Jasanoff, S. (1990) *The Fifth Branch Science Advisers and Policymakers*. Harvard University Press, Cambridge, MA.

Latour, B. (1987) *Science in Action: How to Follow Scientists and Engineers through Society*. Harvard University Press, Cambridge, MA.

Lawlor, K., Weinthal, E. and Olander, L. (2010) Institutions and policies to protect rural livelihoods in REDD+ regimes. *Global Environmental Politics*, 10, 1–11.

Li, T. M. (2007) *The Will to Improve Governmentality Development and the Practice of Politics*. Duke University Press, Durham, NC.

Madeira, E. M., Sills, E., Brockhaus, M., Verchot, L. and Kanninen, M. (2010) What is a REDD+ pilot? A preliminary typology based on early actions in Indonesia. CIFOR *Infobrief* 8 pp.

Meckling, J. (2011) The globalization of carbon trading: Transnational business coalitions in climate politics. *Global Environmental Politics*, 11, 26–50.

Mignolo, W. (2002) The geopolitics of knowledge and the colonial difference. *The South Atlantic Quarterly*, 101, 57–96.

Pacheco, P., Aguilar-Støen, M. Börner, J., Etter, A., Putzel, L. L. and Diaz, M. D. C. V. (2010) Landscape transformation in tropical Latin America: Assessing trends and policy implications for REDD+. *Forests*, 2, 1–29.

Peet, R., Robbins, P. and Watts, M. (2011) Global nature, in R. Peet, P. Robbins and M. Watts (eds), *Global Political Ecology*. Routledge, Abingdon, 1–48.

Quijano, A. (2000) Colonialiadad del poder y clasificación social. *Journal of World-Systems Research*, 2, 342–386.

Schroeder, H. (2010) Agency in international climate negotiations: The case of indigenous peoples and avoided deforestation. *International Environmental Agreements: Politics Law and Economics*, 10, 317–332.

Stern, N. (2006) *The Economics of Climate Change: The Stern Review*. Cambridge University Press, Cambridge.

Taylor, P. J. (2012) Agency structuredness and the production of knowledge within intersecting processes, in M. Goldman, P. Nadasdy and M. D. Turner (eds), *Knowing Nature Conversations at the Intersection of Political Ecology and Science Studies*. University of Chicago Press, Chicago, IL, 81–98.

Wertz-Kanounnikoff, S. and Kongphan-Apirak, M. (2009) Emerging REDD+: A preliminary survey of demonstration and readiness activities. CIFOR *Working Paper*, ix + 44 pp.

Yrigoyen, R. (2011) El derecho a la libre determinacion del desarrollo la participacion la consulta y el consentimiento, in M. Aparicio (ed.), *Los derechos de los pueblos indigenas a los recursos naturales y al territorio: Conflictos y desafios en America Latina*. Icaria, 103–146.

# 11 State governments and forest policy

## A new elite in the Brazilian Amazon?

*Fabiano Toni, Larissa C. L. Villarroel*
*and Bruno Taitson Bueno*

## Introduction

A few years before the 2002 presidential election, Luiz Inácio Lula da Silva's wing in the Workers' Party (PT) made a sharp shift to the right. During the elections he attracted a conservative alliance to support him in order to avoid losing its third election in a row (Arretche, 2013). Yet there were hopes that a post-neoliberal era of environmental policies was coming. The choice of Marina Silva as environmental minister fed those hopes. Silva, born in the rubber-rich forests of Acre, was an iconic environmental militant who fought along with Chico Mendes against the deforestation of Amazonia. However, hopes faded away, as the conservative alliance that supported President Lula in Congress opposed any legislative innovation that could threaten their interests, particularly those of the rural caucus. Moreover, the Lula administration also represented the return of the national developmentalist state, whose project places a high value on increasing commodity exports.

During the PT's three terms in office, environmentalists have been facing a series of political setbacks. Congress approved the use of genetically modified organisms (GMOs), and revised the forest legislation to lift land-use restrictions; the Brazilian Institute of Environment and Renewable Natural Resources (IBAMA) licensed mega-dams in Amazonia in controversial processes, and the federal government sharply slowed down the creation of protected areas (PAs) and indigenous lands.

However, news from the environmental front was not all bad during this period. Thanks to the Brazilian federalist system, state governments have a fair degree of autonomy, which can be used to pass and implement innovative policies. Traditionally, the states that have advanced further in environmental policies are those that are rich, whose economies are less dependent on natural resources, and who have stronger social movements and knowledge networks (Toni, 2006).

States in Amazonia do not fall within this category. They are on the agricultural frontier and part of their political elite thrives on the free exploitation of natural resources. Traditional discourses in these states depict environmental policies as a burden that hinders economic growth and development at the state/local level. Nevertheless, since the late 1990s, some states in Amazonia have engaged in promoting biodiversity conservation and protecting the livelihoods of traditional populations that dwell in forests.

In this chapter we analyze the trajectory of environmental policies in two Amazonian states: Acre and Amazonas. In both cases we identify a set of innovative environmental policies that marked the state administration and have endured for almost 16 years in Acre and 12 years in Amazonas. We call those polices innovative because they did not come gradually. Rather, they represented a rupture—at least partial—with a conventional development model. Moreover, they were only possible after electoral changes. In the case of Acre, change meant a new elite coming to power, whereas in Amazonas elections brought a change within the ruling elite. Nevertheless, the outcomes of this change were no less impressive than in Acre.

Electoral and policy changes in Acre and Amazonas are discussed in parts two and three of this chapter. Before that, in the first part after this introduction, we briefly discuss the relation between the states and the federal government, and the role that each one can play in environmental policies. In the fourth part the chapter examines how the governors of Acre and Amazonas engaged in politics outside the state arena, specifically in negotiations to affect carbon policies in the federal and international arena and, after leaving office, as senators.

## Political and legal context

Brazil is a federation of 26 states and a federal district, divided into 5,561 municipalities. Each government level has its own executive and legislative branch. The legislators at all three levels, as well as the heads of their executive branches (president, governors and mayors), are directly elected by popular vote. Brazil's political history is marked by continual changes in the relationships between these three government levels (Nickson, 1995).

Brazil has a peculiar federal system that is marked by constant disputes between the states and the central government. Although the federal system drew on the US system, the two have significant differences. It has been argued that the US Federation was created for the existing states to "come together" in a union, whereas the Brazilian Federation was created to hold together administrative units that otherwise could easily fragment, as had occurred in Spanish America (Stepan, 1999).

In other words, in Brazil a central government preceded the states. Rather than surrendering power to a central state, the then provinces claimed power and further autonomy from the central state during the transition from an empire to a republic, in 1889 (Abrucio, 1994). This new arrangement ensured state elections and enabled local elites to form political parties, which could run in national elections, or simply be used as a bargaining tool in dealings with the federal government.

Although current legislation requires political parties to have national representation, governors still hold significant power over federal deputies and even senators elected in their states. That kind of power allows state elites to form veto coalition, which increases the costs of political bargaining (Abrucio and Samuels, 1997).

Brazil's 1988 Constitution places environmental issues in the sphere of common and convergent competencies between the federal, state and municipal governments. This means that none of the three has exclusive power to legislate or implement environmental policy. The Constitution specifically establishes that all three levels have a duty to preserve "an ecologically balanced environment," which explicitly includes forests. The most important pieces of legislation related to forests are the Forest Code and the laws that establish the National System of Protected Areas (SNUC). Forests and PAs are precisely the issue areas in which state governments have made the most impressive advances, as we discuss in part 2 and 3 of this chapter.

The 1965 Forest Code (Law No. 4771) is a set of laws regulating not only forestry but also land use in public and private areas. The code established the possibility of creating parks, reserves and public forests, and introduced the concepts of permanent conservation areas and legal reserves. The code thus established an obligation for owners to conserve part of the forest cover on their properties as legal reserves. This coverage varies from 20 percent in most of the country to 80 percent in Amazonia. In 2011, after long discussions, the code was revised and became less restrictive concerning land use in private properties.

Law No. 9985 of July 18, 2000, which created the SNUC, mentions the participation of states and municipalities in forest resource management. The SNUC covers all public PAs, be they federal, state or municipal. According to the law, the three different government levels may create both "strict use PAs," in which natural resource exploitation is totally prohibited, and "sustainable use PAs," which can be exploited in accordance with a management plan.

The most common strict use PAs are parks, mainly national parks. Many states have delimited state parks, which are usually smaller than the national ones; there are very few municipal parks in the Amazon. The most common sustainable use PAs are the extractive reserves (RESEX) and sustainable development reserves (RDS). As we will show, state governments, particularly in Amazonas, invested resources and political capital to dramatically extend the coverage on sustainable use PAs.

## New elites, new policies: Acre between 1998 and 2014

The state of Acre has a territorial surface of 164,221 km$^2$, which corresponds to less than 4 percent of the Brazilian Amazon area and less than 2 percent of the national territory (IBGE, 2010). About 14 percent of the area of original forest has been removed by human action, making the state one of the least deforested in the Brazilian Amazon. The population of Acre in 2010 was 733,559, of which 46 percent lived in the capital, Rio Branco (IBGE, 2010) .

Politics in the state of Acre experienced a turning point in 1998, when Jorge Viana, a young politician affiliated with the PT, was elected governor. Thus far, political power in Acre had been changing hands between the two largest and most traditional Brazilian parties—the Brazilian Democratic Movement Party (PMDB) and the Social Democratic Party (PDS).[1] Prior to the election of Viana, the conservative PDS held power for eight consecutive years. The 1998 election was held amidst serious denunciations of corruption and involvement of old elites with drug traffic and death squads. The Brazilian Congress created a Parliamentary Investigation Committee and the Federal Police engaged in investigating criminal activities in the State. As a result, the incumbent governor (1995–98) was charged with embezzlement, fiscal fraud, and nepotism. He was also accused of drug trafficking, keeping rural workers in semi-slavery in his ranch, and illegally felling trees in indigenous lands.

Amidst the political scandal, the governor decided not run for re-election in 1998. That represented an unprecedented opportunity for the PT to finally win the top executive post in the state. That was so not only because the top contestant was out of the race, but also because other political parties lost their natural ally and sought to make new political alliances to keep at least part of their power. More parties siding with the PT would mean more resources in the campaign, especially free on-air time on radio and TV. Jorge Viana was very pragmatic and built a coalition that housed 12 parties, including the Brazilian Social Democratic Party (PSDB), whose presidential candidate, Fernando Henrique Cardoso, defeated the PT's candidate, Lula da Silva in 1994. In 1998, Lula was running again against Cardoso, and the PT, who led a fierce opposition during Cardoso's first term, blocked any alliance between PT and PSDB. The only exception was Acre.

Besides his political skills within the party machine, Viana had proved to be a popular politician and good administrator. Although he had unsuccessfully run for governor in 1990, he won the election for mayor of the Capital city, Rio Branco, in 1992. During his term, he invested in establishing political connections and structuring the party beyond the capital (Bezerra, 2006). His good work as mayor consolidated his political power in a city that housed about half the state voters. During the 1998 campaign, Viana reached out to the rural communities across the state to broaden his support.

Rural issues were not new to either the PT or to Viana. In fact, the party grew steadily from a rural support. In 1975, the National Confederation of Rural Workers (CONTAG) opened its branch office in Acre, and announced support for the creation of rural labor organizations across the state. Some of the most influential public figures in Acre, such as Marina Silva, Wilson Pinheiro, and Chico Mendes emerged from the rural labor movement and helped found the PT in Acre in 1980. It was only in 1988, however, that the PT elected its first politician, when Marina Silva became City Councilor in Rio Branco. Nevertheless, the party grew along with the so-called socio-environmental movement that drew attention to the struggle of rubber tappers against deforestation in Amazonia.

In sum, Viana's election was a confluence of thee main factors: the electoral opportunity opened by the crumbling of an old elite; the strengthening of the socio-environmental movement; and the candidate's skills to tame the party machine and to bring together urban and rural supporters.

During his campaign, Viana promised to seek an alternative development model in which forests would be conserved and yet yield income to the rural population and to the state as a whole. This was not lip service to the rural dwellers whose votes he was after. Viana was a forester who had worked for the labor movement and for Acre's Technology Foundation, a state agency that does research on natural resource use, particularly on forest products.

Once in office, the new governor inaugurated what he called the Forest Government (Governo da Floresta). In order to keep up with his promises, he promoted a general administrative reform. Among other measures, he created three secretariats to foment the rural economy: (1) Secretariat for Extractivism and Family Agriculture, (2) Secretariat of Forests, and (3) Secretariat for Technical Assistance and Rural extension. Also, the government strengthened the Secretariat of Environment and Natural Resources and its operative branch, the Acre Environment Institute (IMAC). Together, these two agencies were responsible for environmental regulation and land use planning in the state.

As part of the effort to strengthen environmental policies and the sustainable use of the forest, the state signed a decentralization agreement with the federal government. According to the agreement, effective in 1999, the state gradually took responsibility for issuing land-clearing permits[2]—a prerogative of the national environmental agency (IBAMA). In 2004 the power to issue logging permits and to collect logging fees was also transferred to the state (Toni, 2006). The idea behind this decentralization agreement was to reduce the bureaucracy, the transaction costs, and the length of those processes, which usually pushed rural dweller into illegality. At the same time, controlling the permits could also facilitate law enforcement by the state agencies.

Another important accomplishment of the new government was the elaboration of the state Ecological–Economic Zoning (ZEE), at a 1:1,000,000 scale. The zoning required a series of studies and public hearings and produced thematic maps that helped determine areas where specific uses might be encouraged. Particularly important was the identification of priority spots for the establishment of PAs. The ZEE was possible thanks to collaboration among the state government, the German International Cooperation Agency (then GTZ, now GIZ) and the federal government, through the Brazilian Pilot Program to Conserve the Rainforest (PP-G7).[3] The PP-G7 also supported capacity building at the state level, particularly by training and equipping IMAC and the State Attorney's office in order to strengthen law enforcement (Toni, 2006).

In the non-timber sector, the main activities undertaken aimed at structuring the Brazil nut and rubber productive sector. The state invested in assembling nut-processing plants to avoid exports to Bolivia. Concerning rubber, the state government created a subsidy that increased prices at the farm gate by 33 percent (SEPLANDS, 2004). Rubber output jumped from 900 tons in 1999 to 1,600 tons after six months. In 2004 it reached 3,500 tons. Also, the state signed an agreement with the federal Ministry of Health to build a condom plant in the municipality of Xapuri, to increase local demand for rubber, and to promote the vertical integration of the value chain. Together, the state and the federal governments invested some US$8 million in the plant, which was inaugurated in 2008.

The state government sought to encourage private and community forestry management in the timber sector, as well as certification and the vertical integration of the industry. Community management was encouraged by the formation of cooperatives and technical assistance offered by government extensionists. Verticalization was mainly sought through implementation of a timber pole in Rio Branco, in partnership with the Brazilian Service for Support to Micro and Small Business (SEBRAE) and the National Service for Industrial Apprenticeship (SENAI) and with funding from the Manaus Free-port Zone Superintendency (SUFRAMA). A small furniture pole was also installed in Xapuri, where a high-standard furniture factory opened a plant with full certification. Small and artisanal furniture makers also entered business to meet the local demand.

The negotiated decentralization of forest policies, the collaboration with the PP-G7, and the joint venture with the federal government to build the condom factory are examples of Viana's pragmatism. Despite the wounds that fierce electoral campaigns[4] left between the PT and the PSDB, he was able to engage in a productive collaboration with the federal government that brought valuable resources to move forward with his agenda. This pragmatism and his popularity by the end of his second term in office[5] allowed Viana to elect his successor and to win the election for senator.

In 2006 the state of Acre elected Arnóbio (alias Binho) Marques as governor. He was one of the founders of the PT and a long-time close collaborator of Jorge Viana. He served as municipal secretary of education when Viana was the mayor of Rio Branco, and then as state secretary of education and vice-governor during Viana's first and second terms as governor. The fact that he won his first election shows how strong and popular the coalition led by the PT was after eight years in power.

Considering his close ties to the former governor, it comes as no surprise that his administration closely followed his predecessor's, although his career and militancy had been aimed at education rather than environment and forests. Among other policies, Marques finished the second phase of the ZEE (this time at a 1:250,000 scale), and put the condom factory to work. In 2008 he launched a certification program designed to prevent unsustainable agricultural practices, particularly the use of fire. The program involved conditional cash transfers as well as technical assistance and provision of access to credit and infrastructure for certified farmers.

In 2010 the government boosted the technical assistance and rural extension services and launched its most ambitious program—the Carbon Environmental Services Program. The program was aimed at including Acre in the global carbon market, specifically to reap the potential benefits of Reduction of Emissions from Deforestation and Forest Degradation (REDD) initiatives. This program exemplifies the affinity between Marques's and Viana's administrations; the latter became personally engaged in negotiations around REDD by the end of his second term in office.

Marques decided not to try for re-election. Instead, the PT chose as candidate Sebastião Viana, Jorge Viana's brother. This time the election was harder for the party. Even though the Viana brothers were elected Governor and Senator, it was only by a slim margin. Tião Viana soon made clear that the emphasis in his administration would no longer be the forest economy. Tião Viana, a medical doctor by training, has never been as close to the environmental movement as his brother and Binho Marques. On the contrary, grassroots organizations and environmental movements conflict with Tião Viana's old proposal to explore gas and oil in Acre.

Soon after taking office, Tião Viana abolished the iconic Secretary of Forests, a landmark of PT's first administration promotions. On a more symbolic ground, he also abandoned the slogan "government of the forest" to adopt a new one—"government of the people." Some analysts argue that besides his lack of enthusiasm for the forests, those changes came as a response to the poor performance of the PT in the 2010 election.

An old ally of the PT administrations[6] and critic of Tião Viana claimed that the governor indeed shifted priorities, but this fact should not be overrated. He argues that most of the top officials in the environmental agencies were kept in their posts. He has also pointed to changes outside Acre that help to explain the timid advances in environmental policies. For him, president Roussef has moved the country backward concerning the commitments made in Brazil after the Rio 92 conference. The lack of support from the federal government has had a significant impact on state policies.

Forester João Paulo Mastrangelo,[7] who has worked for five years in the Secretariat for Forests and became the state secretary for forests at the beginning of Tião Vianas's term, agrees that the changes were not so drastic. Rather than abandon environmental policies, the governor chose new tools to develop them. He chose to emphasize and stimulate the economic use by farmers of already deforested areas in order to decrease deforestation. He acknowledges that this shift may indeed have a political component. The forest policies implemented between 1999 and 2010 were taking too long to yield substantial results and the PT paid a toll in the 2010 election. Investing in agriculture may bring faster economic return, which will reflect on the governor's popularity.

## Amazonas: new wine in old bottles?

Amazonas is the largest state in Brazil. It covers 37 percent of the Brazilian Amazon, and 18 percent of the national territory. In 2010, the population of Amazonas was 3,493,985. In 2009, less than 3 percent of the territory had been deforested (Lemos and de Arimatea Silva, 2011).

Since the last year of the authoritarian regime (1964–84), when the military government re-established free elections for the governor (1988), the state of Amazonas has been ruled by a small and relatively closed political group. Its members shift positions from supporting to opposing each other, according to the political context and their personal interests. Former governor Gilberto

Mestrinho, a populist politician, has been leading this group for decades (Hoefler, 2003). He was mayor of Manaus, the state capital city, between 1956 and 1958, and state governor during 1959–63, 1983–87, and 1991–95.

Mestrinho had a very conventional and nationalistic view on development and use of natural resources. For him, the state should spur economic growth by directly investing in and encouraging investors to use the rich natural resource stock of Amazonas. In his view, concerns about the environment disguised the interests of international groups that want to hold back the region and the country (Herculano, 1992).

Despite this developmentalist view of the former governor, Amazonas still has the majority of its territory under native forests. In part, this is due to the fact that a vast tract of the state is not suitable for large-scale agriculture and ranching due to excessive rainfall or lack of roads. The exception is the Southern portion of the state, which is drier and is linked to Manaus and to the rest of the country by road. The state's gross domestic product (GDP) is concentrated in Manaus, where 52 percent of the population lives (IBGE, 2010). Moreover, the capital houses a free trade and export-processing zone: the Manaus Free Trade Zone.

The presence and importance of the Manaus Free Trade Zone makes the local political economy very peculiar. Although most of the GDP of the state is in the industrial sector, the elite who controls that sector lives outside the state, as most companies are transnational or Brazilian corporations whose head offices are located in the South or abroad. Political elites are composed of politicians who control large party machines and know how to deal with the federal government, which ultimately controls decisions over incentives and tax breaks offered to private enterprises to move businesses to the Free Trade Zone.

In a public rally in 1982, Mestrinho told his supporters that he and his supporters would stay in power for 20 years. He proved to be right, as two of his protégées—Amazonino Mendes and Eduardo Braga—successfully bid for the governor office in the following elections (Villarroel and Toni, 2012). Amazonino Mendes entered politics as a student in the late 1950s and soon met Mestrinho who became his political mentor. He was a key player in the 1982 gubernatorial election that put Mestrinho in office. As he had good connections with the economic elite of Amazonas, he gathered votes and valuable financial support for his mentor.

As a consequence of his good job in the campaign he was appointed Mayor of Manaus and took office in 1983.[8] Following Mestrinho's steps, Mendes was the party (PMDB) candidate for Governor in 1986, and won the election. He also had a developmentalist discourse, and during the campaign declared that he would promote the development of the state, at any cost, even if that required felling the whole forest. Despite this furor, he had to bend to the media pressure that built up during the late 1980s. As a result he created the first state PAs in Amazonas—six PAs that together covered some 30,000 km². This was still a very incipient policy, for the PAs were not fully funded.

In 1990 Mendes renounced his post to run for senator and supported Mestrinho in the gubernatorial race. Both were elected, but soon their alliance broke as both wanted exclusive credit for sponsoring the paving of a highway. Mendes left the PMDB and ran for mayor again in 1992. This time he chose a protégé of his—Eduardo Braga—to be the vice-mayor. At that point, Braga had already served as councilman in Manaus, state deputy, and federal deputy. He soon became the mayor, for Mendes renounced the post to successfully run again for governor, in 1993.

During his term as mayor, Braga invested public resources in infrastructure, health, and housing. Environmental protection and sustainable development were marginal in his political agenda. That started to change in 1998, when he broke with his old ally, Amazonino Mendes and faced him in the gubernatorial race. In order to compete with Mendes, Braga had to search for a new discourse and occupy a new political niche. He did that by moving to the left and embracing a social and environmental discourse. Although Braga had broad support in Manaus, Mendes won the election. Nevertheless, Braga realized that his strategy paid off and ran again for Mayor in 2000. This time he stressed the environmental component of his electoral program, and he was not alone. Two other candidates emphasized the environmental agenda during their campaigns and the issue became part of the local political discourse.

Braga lost again, by a very narrow margin (1 percent), but he established himself as a strong political leader in Manaus. Back to the federal legislative chamber, he worked hard to benefit his state during the legislature and to broaden his support in smaller urban and rural areas. In 2002 he was back to the gubernatorial race, advocating a strong environmental agenda. He promised to revamp the Manaus Free Trade Zone and to create a "Green Free Trade Zone."

The choice of words was not accidental. The Free Trade Zone is deeply embedded in the local political culture. It's a source of jobs, income, and revenues, highly prized by the local population and by the political elite. Governors, mayors, deputies, and senators have always promised their constituents to battle the federal government to extend the fiscal benefits given to the Free Trade Zone. In part, their faith in the polls has been linked to their ability to keep up with those promises. The idea of a Green Free Trade Zone therefore sounded like an ambitious plan to extend to remote areas the same benefits that Manaus had been enjoying for so many years.

Indeed, the plan was ambitious. Once in office, Braga created a set of new institutions to implement the Green Free Trade Zone (ZFV) program. They included: (1) a Secretary of Environment and Sustainable Development, responsible for policy design; (2) the Agency for Sustainable Development (ADS), in charge of forestry extension aimed at sustainable land use; and (3) the Amazonas Land Tenure Institute (ITEAM) to secure land rights to forest dwellers and riverine populations (Viana, 2010).

The ZFV was designed to boost the forest sector, and focused on fiscal breaks for non-timber forest products, credit for small-scale sustainable projects, technical assistance for small farmers, subsidies to native products, and the development of markets and value chains accessible to rural dwellers.

Arguably, the most impacting components of the ZFV was a payment for the environmental services program and the creation of PAs, two programs that are closely connected. The main component of the program, which became known as a Bolsa Floresta, is a monthly cash transfer—about US$50.00/month—to the indigenous and traditional populations living in PAs. Obviously it has a social component, for it reaches the poorest strata of the rural population. On the other hand, the transfers are contingent on substantial change in behavior, which includes a commitment to abolishing the clearing of primary forests.

In 2009 the Bolsa Floresta program reached 6,000 beneficiaries in 14 PAs that cover over 10 million hectares. The total budget in 2008 was about US$8.1 million per year (Viana, 2010). The *Bolsa Floresta* helped break the resistance against the creation of PAs, which are usually considered a barrier to economic development. Also, the conditionality of the payments was a strong incentive for residents of PAs to take care of the whole area, particularly because, in practice, those people live under a common property regime. Also, the program has a collective action component, for it channels some resources through grass-roots organizations.

The most visible component of the ZFV was the creation of PAs, though. Until 2002, the state had created only 12 PAs, which covered 7.3 million hectares. The Braga administration created 29 new PAs, so that the total area protected by the state government rose to 18.8 million hectares. Most of those new areas are sustainable use PAs, particularly RDS. This category was prioritized because it allows a wide range of economic activities, including timber extraction through community forest management. Although some environmentalists criticize this choice (Bentes, 2006) for being too permissive, the strategy has helped gather popular support to the creation of PAs (CEPAL, 2007).[9]

Although the causes of deforestation are multiple and complex, there is an association between the creation of new PAs and a decrease in deforestation rates. In 2003 Amazonas lost 1,558 km² of native forest. This number declined steadily and reached 405 km² in 2009 (INPE, 2014).

Many times the federal and state governments in Brazil create PAs by law only to leave them abandoned or what environmentalists and scholars usually call paper PAs. That was not the case in Amazonas. As of 2010, 29 PAs had a full-time manager, 30 out of the 41 had received over US$100,000 in investments on management implementation (Viana, 2010).

In 2010, few months before finishing his second term, Braga renounced his post to run for senator. His vice-governor—Omar Aziz—took office and was re-elected in that same year. Although they worked together for eight years, Aziz was not as enthusiastic about forest conservation as Braga. He did not do anything to jeopardize what had been done during Braga's two terms in office. However, he did not demonstrate the same kind of political entrepreneurship that his predecessor had concerning the state's environmental policies.

An important initiative during Braga's term may have played a key role in avoiding a roll back of the environmental policies. In 2007 the state government began to negotiate an agreement with one of the largest banks in Brasil—Bradesco—in order to create and fund a private organization to implement environmental policies. To make that possible, in 2007 legislation had been passed allowing the state to join not-for-profit organizations designed to develop projects related to climate change, environmental conservation, and sustainable development.

In 2008 the government and Bradesco came to an agreement and created the *Fundação Amazonas Sustentável* (FAS). Each partner made an initial contribution of about US$10 million to a trust fund that has been used, among other things, to pay the benefits of the Bolsa Verde Program. Braga's secretary of environment left the government to become the superintendent of FAS. This partnership therefor shielded the policies implemented between 2003 and 2010 from a potential political setback. Indeed, even though Braga's successor did not show the same enthusiasm for environmental policies, the beneficiaries of the Bolsa Verde grew in numbers, from 6,325 in 2009 to 8,856 in 2014 (FAS, 2014; Viana, 2010).

## Politics beyond state borders

Both Eduardo Braga and Jorge Viana joined the Governors' Climate and Forests Task Force (GCF), a subnational collaborative group comprising 14 states and provinces from the United States, Brazil, Indonesia, Nigeria, and Mexico. The GCF seeks to integrate REDD+ and other forest carbon activities into emerging greenhouse gas compliance regimes. One of its main goals is to develop institutions and programs for linking subnational REDD activities with ongoing national and international efforts. In their own words, "GCF members want to be early movers on the effort to bring REDD into climate policy" (GCF, 2010). Behind the initiative lies an attempt to avoid central governments, non-governmental organizations (NGOs), or market enterprises to capture and control the benefits of REDD.

In the domestic arena, in 2009 governors who were members of the task force took the lead in the discussion of a national REDD+ policy. After a meeting of the governors of all nine Amazonia states, they sent a letter to the president, pointing out that Brazil was lagging behind other developing countries in the carbon market. They argued that if Brazil was to receive more funds from carbon credits and to reduce its own carbon emissions, REDD+ mechanisms had to be included in the international carbon market, under the UN Framework Convention on Climate Change (UNFCCC).

In their letter, the governors sought the creation of: (1) a task force consisting of representatives from federal and state governments; (2) a federal office to coordinate the development, implementation, and management of a National Emission Reduction System that would coordinate and support federal, state, and municipal governments; and (3) an Amazonian Governors Committee to take part in COP 15 alongside the president. Their requests were partially met: The task force was formed and governors from Amazonian states went to COP 15, but as of mid 2010, no new federal office had been created to coordinate action. However, the Ministry of the Environment assumed responsibility for discussions on REDD+, under the leadership of a market and finance expert. This was no minor achievement for the governors because, until then, the Environment and

Foreign Relations Ministries had been opposing the use of market-based compensatory mechanisms to curb deforestation.

Viana and Braga left their office after two terms and were both elected senators in 2010. Although in different parties, PT and PMDB, they became members of the majority group supporting the incumbent president Dilma Roussef (2011–14). Braga served as government leader in the Senate between 2012 and 2014.

Roussef's administration was not marked by an impressive environmental record. On the contrary, she has been severely criticized for slowing down the creation of PAs and the recognition of indigenous lands; pressing IBAMA to expedite the environmental licensing of large dams in Amazonia; and supporting the revision of the restrictive Forest Code. Despite their discourse and environmental achievements, both Braga and Viana had to follow the lead of the federal administration in Congress. That was so not only because they were members of the majority, but also due to the peculiarities of the relation between states and the federal government.

Acre and Amazonas are small states in terms of population, so they have only eight representatives each in the Chamber of Deputies.[10] Their political power therefore, is very limited. On the other hand, the states also have small economies and their governments rely on resource transfers from the federal government. This dependency is particularly salient in the case of Amazonas, whose Free Trade Zone owes its existence to federal tax breaks. Indeed, Braga's main task as senator was to gather support for a Constitutional Amendment aimed at extending the fiscal benefits of the Free Trade Zone for 50 years. In his discourses supporting the amendment, he stated that the success of the conservation policies in Amazonas was due to the Free Trade Zone, a source of economic growth to which the fate of the forest is directly linked. In his words:

> The challenge that we are facing and willfully wining is to reconcile the economic and social growth, promoted by the Free Trade Zone, with forest conservation. So much so that, according to the specialized organizations, 98% of the forest in Amazonas are preserved, 45 year after the inauguration of the Manaus Free Trade Zone.
>
> (Braga, 2012, p. 38)

Braga directly affected the federal government's decision to elaborate a program similar to the Bolsa Floresta, named Bolsa Verde, which was officially launched in Manaus, in 2011. He was also the rapporteur of the legislation passed in 2012 that established the National REDD+ System. Viana was another outspoken supporter of this legislation, which was inspired and affected by the political lobbying promoted by the Governor's Task Force.

As supporters of the federal government, Braga and Viana had to defend the interests of the executive power in the discussions around the controversial revision of the Forest Code. Environmentalists and scholars considered that the new legislation, passed in 2011 was an unprecedented step backward in the Brazilian environmental legislation, aimed at lifting restrictions on land use and granting a general pardon for those who had violated the law (Silva *et al.*, 2012). Viana was rapporteur of the new legislation. In his defense, he declared that the new Code was not his Code; it was the possible outcome of a long bargain process. Moreover, he pointed out that the defense of the old Code was hypocritical, for the law was very good on paper, but proved impossible to be enforced. The new Code, on the other hand, established a rural environmental registry, which, in theory will allow law enforcement agencies to easily detect landowners liable for illegal deforestation.

## Conclusions

In Chapter 2, the authors identify three sources of change towards more inclusive and sustainable development oriented institutions: (1) the rise of new non-elite groups to power through democratic change; (2) the break down of old elites due to changes in the global economy and; (3) a "reorientation of elites," that is, when elites adopt new perspectives, ideas or even ideologies that lead them to change practices and policies pursued. In the introduction to this chapter we pointed out how the election of President Lula, in 2002, raised expectations about a democratic change. However, it ended up representing the opposite of an elite reorientation. A non-elite group came to power, was promptly co-opted, and started mimicking the previous elite.

Obviously, a democratic system with clear division of powers and a bicameral legislative makes it difficult for the executive power to shift policies at its will. As the PT's developmentalist project also sought to increase commodities exports, there was no point in challenging congress on environmental issues, particularly because the most pressing of those issues in Brazil are linked to land use and forest conversion.

In spite of those difficulties, significant policy shift occurred at the state level. The states of Acre and Amazonas experienced a sharp turn in their environmental policies. Newly elected governors invested scarce resources to build institutions and human capacity. They implemented several programs to deal with rural licensing, carbon emissions, forest management, and biodiversity conservation.

Those changes came after elections that have different meanings. In Acre, the PT won a gubernatorial election for the first time. Political change was thorough and reached the whole administration. The coalition backing the governor included NGOs, unions, students, researchers, and scholars, and a plethora of grass-roots organizations, mainly rural. There is no doubt it represented the rise of a new elite and new opportunities for political participation.

Contrastingly, Amazonas is a clear instance of elite reorientation. The governor who sponsored environmental policy changes was a member of a powerful group that had been controlling state power for decades. He had played distinct roles in this group before his election, in 2002. Nevertheless, the political changes he promoted represented a clear discontinuity with the policy choices of his old allies and their supporters. It was therefore a case of change within an existing elite rather than an elite shift.

The election of Jorge Viana represented the rise of a social group that was already organized and relatively powerful. We cannot underestimate Viana's leadership and political skills. Sooner or later this group would reap the state election. Eduardo Braga, on the other hand, had to build a whole new constituency in rural areas and, at the same time, please the old supporters from the state capital, particularly those whose interests revolve around the Free-Trade Zone.

Braga was defeated when he ran for the state office for the first time. He learned the hard way that intra-elite competition for votes in the Manaus area was fierce. Therefore, he had to reach out to the rural voters as a way to secure his election. Braga's electoral strategy paid off, and the implementation of his environmental policies secured the support from rural voters without antagonizing him with old urban elites. Accordingly, Viana also had a significant urban constituency, for he had served as mayor of the capital city before becoming governor. Such a broad support assured their re-election and the election of their allies as governors when they left office.

Apparently, forest policies have permanently entered the political agenda of those states, and investing in them brings payoffs to governors. If that proves to be true, it will be good news for forest conservation. No matter whether a candidate truly believes in sustainable development or whether he/she is an opportunistic rational actor, he/she will eventually pay attention to those issues.

Concerning innovation, even though Acre started earlier, Amazonas policies gained more visibility; this was so because the state focused on two simple main components: PAs and the Bolsa Verde. The PA program is particularly conspicuous due to the number and extension of the areas established after 2003. Amazonas is larger and richer than Acre, therefore it has more land and resources, which helps explain why the state could afford to create such a vast network of PAs.

Being a latecomer also helped Amazons develop their environmental programs faster. When Acre started discussing conservation and sustainable use of forests, deforestation control was almost exclusively a matter of command and control. By the mid-2000s, however, market incentives such as payments for environmental services and REDD+ became a reality. Governments in both states engaged in negotiations to develop those mechanisms as well as to reap the benefits from them. Amazonas was particularly successful in attracting private money to the Bolsa Verde program. Also, government officials in Amazonas may have learned from the Acre experience, but that is a question that remains open. Further research on bureaucratic and technical/scientific elites could shed some light on the mechanisms of policy innovation and diffusion.

## Notes

1  In 1965, the military government banned all existing political parties and created a two-party system. The *Aliança Renovadora Nacional* was the pro-government party, and the *Movimento Democrático Brasileiro* (MDB) was the only opposition party. *Aliança Renovadora Nacional* immediately became the majority party in both houses,

204 Fabiano Toni, Larissa C. L. Villarroel and Bruno Taitson Bueno

but the MDB grew steadily, particularly in local elections and started challenging the hegemony of the *Aliança Renovadora Nacional*. As government political strategists were aware of the ideological cleavages within MDB, in 1979 a new legislation allowing freedom of party association was passed, and the multi-party system came back to Brazilian politics. The strategy paid off, as MDB, which became PMDB, lost a significant share of its leaders and rank and file, who left to found new parties. Although some moderate liberals also left *Aliança Renovadora Nacional* (PDS, after the 1979 reform), the party kept most of its power.

2  Initially, IMAC could issue permits to clear up to 3 ha. The limit was then extended to 20 ha, in 2001, 60 ha in 2002 and, in 2003, the state gained control over all permits.

3  The PP-G7 was an international cooperation program that included Brazil, the G-7 countries and the Netherlands government. Its main goal was the conservation of Brazilian tropical rainforests. The program was created in 1992 and the first effective actions were launched in 1994. It had five thematic areas: (1) experimentation and demonstration projects; (2) conservation of PAs; (3) institutional strengthening; (4) scientific research; (5) lessons and dissemination. Between 1992 and 2012, the PP-G7 received US$430 million, through a fiduciary fund, managed by the World Bank.

4  In 1994 and 1998, PSDB's candidate—Fernando Henrique Cardos defeated PT's Lula in the presidential campaign. In 2002, when Viana was re-elected, Lula defeated PSDB's candidate, José Serra.

5  According to the Brazilian electoral law, mayors, governors, and the president can serve two consecutive terms and run again after another term out of office.

6  Rubens Alves, President of the NGO GTA (Amazon Working Group). Interview recorded on March 31, 2014.

7  Interview recorded on April 1, 2014.

8  Election for Mayor in capital cities and cities inside national security areas were re-established only in 1985.

9  The state government also created an agency to deal exclusively with PAs, the Center for Conservation Areas (CEUC), as part of the Sustainable Development Secretary (SDS).

10  Each one of the 26 states and the Federal District has three representatives in the Senate. The number of representatives in the Chamber of Deputies varies according to the population size, with a minimum of eight representatives.

# References

Abrucio, F. L. (1994) Os barões da federação [The barons of the federation]. *Lua Nova: Revista de Cultura e Política*, (33), 165.

Abrucio, F. L. and Samuels, D. (1997) A nova política dos governadores [The new politics of governors]. *Lua Nova: Revista de Cultura e Política*, 137, 40–41.

Arretche, M. (2013) Quando instituições federativas fortalecem o governo central? *Novos Estudos Cebrap*, 95, 39.

Bentes, G. M. (2006) Reserva de Desenvolvimento Sustentável: da realidade à legislação ambiental no estado do Amazonas. Master's thesis, Universidade Estadual do Amazonas.

Bezerra, M. J. (2006) *Invenções do Acre: de território a estado–um olhar social*. PhD, Tese de Doutorado, São Paulo.

Braga, E. (2012) O Amazonas e seus Desafios. *Amazônia*, 34, 38–39. Editora Círios, Belém.

CEPAL (2007) *Análise Ambiental e de Sustentabilidade do Estado do Amazonas*. CEPAL/SDS, Santiago, Chile.

FAS (2014) http://fas-amazonas.org (accessed 03/04/2014).

GCF (2010) Governor's Climate and Forests Task Force Home. Available at: http:// gcftaskforce.org/index.html (accessed June 2010).

Herculano, S. (1992) Desenvolvimento Sustentável: como passar do insuportável ao sofrível. *Tempo e Presença*, 14(261), 12–15.

Hoefler, S. (2003) Novas e velhas formas de patronagem na Amazônia central. *Revista Território*, 7(11), 49–62.

IBGE 2010 Censo Demográfico, available at: www.ibge.gov.br/home/estat%C3%ADstica/ popula%C3%A7%C3%A3o/censo2010/tabelas_pdf/amazonas.pdf (accessed 02/03/2014).

INPE (2014) Projeto Prodes: Monitoramento da Floresta Amazônica Brasileira por satélite. Available at: http://www.inpe.br (accessed 03/04/2014).

Lemos, A. L. F. and de Arimatea Silva, J. (2011) Desmatamento na Amazônia Legal: Evolução, Causas, Monitoramento e Possibilidades de Mitigação Através do Fundo Amazônia. *Floresta e Ambiente*, 18(1), 98–108.

Nickson, R. A. (1995) *Local Government in Latin America*. L. Rienner Publishers, Boulder, CO.

SEPLANDS (2004) Relatório Analítico das Políticas Públicas Estaduais para o Setor Extrativista da Borracha. Rio Branco, Acre: Secretaria de Estado de Planejamento e Desenvolvimento Econômico Sustentável (SEPLANDS), Governo do Estado do Acre.

Silva, J., Nobre, A., Joly, C., Nobre, C., Manzatto, C., Rech Filho, E. and Rodrigues, R. (2012) *Brazil Forest Code and Science: Contributions to the Dialogue*. The Brazilian Society for the Advancement of Science (SBPC), São Paulo, Brazil.

Stepan, A. (1999) Para uma nova análise comparativa do federalismo e da democracia: federações que restringem ou ampliam o poder do Demos. *Dados*, 42(2), 00. Available at: http://www.scielo.br/scielo.php?script=sci_arttext&pid=S0011-52581999000200001&lng=en&tlng=pt.10.1590/S0011-52581999000200001 (accessed 7/25/2014).

Toni, F. (2006) *Gestão florestal na Amazônia brasileira: avanços e obstáculos em um sistema federalista*. CIFOR, Bogor, Indonesia.

Viana, V. M. (2010) *Sustainable Development in Practice: Lessons Learned from Amazonas*. IIED, London.

Villarroel, L. C. L. and Toni, F. (2012) Política e Meio Ambienrte: A Inclusão das Unidades de Conservação na Agenda de Governo do Estado do Amazonas. *Raízes*, 32(1), 96–109.

# 12 Conclusion

## With or against elites? How to move towards more sustainable environmental governance in Latin America

*Benedicte Bull and Mariel Aguilar-Støen*

### Introduction

When Mosca (1939), Michels (1962) and Pareto ([1935] 1997) formulated their arguments about elites, they were convinced that elites would always be with us: we could only hope that elites circulated from time to time so as to ensure that new groups got represented and new talent was put to use. When the "pink tide" governments of Latin America came to power, it was with quite different expectations. The aim for many of them was to engender profound societal trans-formations away from the elitist democracies that many had opposed in the past, and towards more egalitarian societies. As shown in the chapters above, in many cases the visions for change also included new ways of relating to nature and of how to reach more sustainable forms of production.

However, as has been made quite clear, the picture is very mixed regarding the extent to which that has been achieved. The chapters in this book have discussed different ways in which elites have affected the changes that have occurred; we also discuss cases in which no change has been achieved. In this chapter we will summarize the main findings of the preceding chapters.

In Chapter 2 we discussed three processes that could lead to a shift in visions, practices and policies by the elites: an "elite shift" wherein old elites are replaced with new ones as a result of political disruptions or (often international) economic changes; an "elite reorientation" in which the elites adopt new ideas and ideologies; and an "elite settlement" in which different elite groups reach agreements that carve out new development policies and lay the ground for new institutions. In the discussions of change and continuity in the following, we will keep these three processes in mind. We will start by discussing the extent to which there have been elite shifts related to the entering of the "pink tide" governments to power in Latin America. We will then discuss whether we see tendencies towards "elite reorientation" and "elite settlements." We will argue more specifically that there have been two forms of elite shifts/reorientations that have had positive influence on environmental governance: the emergence of new elite groups with an environmental background (sometimes forming a new technocratic elite) and an elite reorientation towards greater sensitivity towards the views of subalterns. However, in spite of these positive trends, recent Latin American experiences illustrate many of the limitations that the combination of a capitalist economy, the imperative for new state elites to construct and strengthen states, and elitist histories and politics of place present.

## The "pink tide" and elite shifts

Many countries in Latin America have, as we argued in the introduction, experienced political disruptions of old elite dominance. However, as discussed in Chapter 2, a shift in government does not necessarily entail a shift in elites. To what extent have we seen a shift in elites, why and with what consequences? In the different chapters of this book we have seen the emergence of several new elites. One group has acquired their status due to the control of political and organizational resources (i.e. incipient new political elites). We have seen that in the case of Bolivia, where groups associated with the governing party MAS have also started to acquire significant economic resources, for example in the soy sector. These are people with a different profile and initially with far fewer economic resources than the traditional political elites in Bolivia. We have also seen that to some extent in El Salvador in the chapter by Bull, Cuéllar and Kandel. Although the old economic and political elite is still of major importance in El Salvador, due to the policies of the Funes government, a new elite is emerging from the cadres of the left-wing *Frente Farabundo Martí para la Liberación Nacional* (FMLN) party, but gaining additional resources due to investments in the Bolivarian Alliance for the Peoples of Our America (ALBA) companies related to the Venezuela-led regional ALBA initiative.

However, we have also seen new elites emerging for other reasons. In the cases of Argentina Ecuador and related to the regional Reduction of Emissions from Deforestation and Forest Degradation (REDD) process we saw new elites emerging as a result of their command over technology and knowledge or as a result of changing technology, such as in the case of genetically modified (GM) soy production in Argentina. However, new technology seldom produces new elites in and of itself: in all the cases analyzed there has been a combination of new technologies, political shifts and command over economic and knowledge resources that has resulted in the rise of new elite groups.

Of crucial importance for the shifts has been a change in the global political economic context. As has been emphasized in the chapter by Hogenboom, there has been a shift in what she calls the international elites, that to a significant extent is due to the increased importance of Chinese investors, lenders and trading partners, but also the rise of emerging economies and increased South–South integration in general. However, beyond a change in the composition of the international elites, this shift has allowed both states and new non-state elites to gain force. One example is the elites surrounding the ALBA companies, as discussed above . Had we included Nicaragua and Venezuela among our cases, we would probably have seen an even stronger tendency towards the emergence of a new elite that controls both key economic and political resources.

The emergence of such elites may challenge the pessimistic predictions by Block (1977; see Chapter 2). His argument was that the state cannot really be democratized within a capitalist economy in spite of the establishment of pluralist institutions. Consequently, a leftist party in power would always have to be concerned with "generating business confidence" since it depends on capitalists for investments and generating economic activity. Therefore, it has little policy space to pursue its agenda. This may, however, change if alternative sources of capital appear, as has happened in various countries in Latin America.

However, in many countries we still see a strong dominance of what we could label "old elites": groups that have controlled capital as well as a number of other resources for decades if not centuries, and that increasingly have become integrated with transnational capital (Bull *et al.*, 2014). They have not easily allowed new groups to compete for the same resources, and their different strength and strategies across the different countries explains much of the difference between the policies chosen by different centre-left regimes. The importance of the strategies of the "old elites" for understanding the policies of the centre-left governments, was illustrated clearly in the chapter by Bull, Cuéllar and Kandel on El Salvador. Here the old elites used any means available to retain their control of power, in spite of the fact that the new government did not present policies that would radically reduce their privileges. In the chapter by Aguilar-Støen on Guatemala, we saw entrenched elites adapting to upsurges in the global market for minerals, but without taking into consideration the interests of the local communities.

Thus, the general picture is quite mixed regarding whether we see an elite shift. The other question is whether there has been an elite reorientation. One issue that has appeared as important in that respect is new forms of knowledge and technology.

## Elite reorientation? The role of knowledge, technology and technocracies

Several chapters in this book highlight the important role played by knowledge, technology and technocracies in galvanizing shifts in the position or emergence of different elites in environmental governance.

For instance, shifting ideas about the regulation of genetically modified organisms and the position of the issue in the agenda of governments and other actors, as well as the importance of genetically modified crops for various countries' economies, have opened new political spaces to actors that control knowledge and technologies related to the issue. Chapter 6 by Andrade and Zenteno Hopp offers a clear example of how the dynamics between knowledge and policy making resulted, in part, in a new position of president Correa in relation to the regulation of genetically modified organisms (GMOs) in Ecuador. Chapter 5 by Zenteno Hopp, Hanche-Olsen and Sejenovich shows how controlling GM soy technology leads to reconfiguring the structure of land tenure in Argentina and to the increased role played by urban-based businessmen in the management of GM soy production. In Chapter 4, Zenteno Hopp and Høiby suggest that the expansion of GM soy, is justified by the assumed positive effects of the crop on the environment (higher productivity by unit of land and less use of chemical inputs) paradoxically ignoring that this agricultural expansion is happening at the expense of forest areas. There is little doubt that agricultural production is important for the economies of Ecuador, Bolivia and Argentina, and that in the case of the two latter countries, GM soy provides substantial revenues to the countries. It is within this context that actors controlling knowledge and technologies related to GM crops gain new spaces to influence governments' policies and positions. The effect is also prominent, when, as in the case of Ecuador, public servants are positive to GM crops. As a result, deeper and wider discussions of the effects of GM crops on the environment are left out of the national agenda, or subordinated to the pre-eminence of the economic gains of GM crops production.

While in the case of oil, gas and minerals extraction in South America, the role played by international elites (i.e., Chinese companies) is closely related to the funding these elites provide; in the case of countries with poorer techno-logical development, such as Guatemala, controlling technology is an important asset for the incursion and position of transnational elites in mineral extrac-tion. Consequently, these actors have considerably more leverage than others (i.e., social movements) to influence public policies related to environmental regulations.

However, as shown by Parker in Chapter 9, mining elites are not uniform in their views on environmental aspects of their activity. Their discourses on water and energy consumption differ, and some show a stronger inclination to take seriously the need for the mining industry to take its impact on the environment seriously.

In the case of the forestry sector, Chapter 10 demonstrates how access to and control of specialized knowledge is clearly involved in the emergence of a new science–policy elite that dominates policy-making arenas at national and inter-national levels. Furthermore, knowledge and knowledge production are central in determining how different groups are going to be included in national and international debates on how and who will benefit from global initiatives such as REDD.

The cases presented in this book illustrate how knowledge and technology are embedded in political processes in at least the following ways: first, because both technology and knowledge can be seen as assets that open new spaces for politi-cal participation, actors controlling these assets can gain positions within such spaces. Second, because there is no clear-cut separation between policy making and knowledge production processes, actors controlling knowledge production also have a privileged access to policy-making processes, reinforcing their posi-tions and contributing to shaping spaces for political participation. The results of these dynamics though, are logically strongly influenced by the context where they take place and determined by historical traits characterizing the paths taken in each context.

## Elite settlements? New elites and the state-building predicament

In the introduction we argued that many of the new, leftist governments in fact controlled limited resources resulting from weak state institutions and strong societal elites. In that situation they had the choice of attempting to strengthen the states, grooming new elites, allying with outside elites (economic elites, international elites, knowledge elites, etc.) or confronting competing elites. The chapters above show that they have indeed applied several of these strategies, but what has become particularly salient is an attempt to strengthen the states. While the reversal of the neoliberal development model with a focus on private sector development and a limited state was in the programs of most of the left-ist governments, the structural weaknesses of the state and its limited presence in many areas of the countries had been of much less concern. One explana-tion could be the personal experience by many of the leaders of the left-wing parties with the most oppressive aspects of the former authoritarian states. The list of current leaders that have been persecuted, imprisoned and even tortured during the dictatorships of the 1960s to 1980s is long, and includes Luiz Inácio Lula da Silva and Dilma Rousseff in Brazil, Evo Morales and his vice president Alvaro García Linera in Bolivia, Michelle Bachelet in Chile and José Mujica in Uruguay, to mention only some. For them, state strength might be seen as much more of a problem than state weakness. Nevertheless, state capacity (weak-ness/strength) is a multifaceted concept and a state might be perfectly capable of oppressing opposition while having weak capacity to implement policy in remote areas, as referred to in Chapter 2.

The need to build a strong state has become an imperative to the leftist gov-ernments for various reasons: only a strong state apparatus is able to distribute sufficient benefits to the most marginal of the population in accordance with the electoral promises of the leftist governments; a strong state apparatus is needed to implement development projects to ensure the national progress promised by the new leftist governments. In some cases, this has occurred in the context of an elite settlement, or an understanding with competing elites; elsewhere state strengthening has occurred as a strategy of weakening competing elites.

The latter dynamic is perhaps particularly clear in the case of Ecuador as discussed by Zenteno Hopp and Andrade, where Rafael Correa's government is seeking to set Ecuador off on a developmentalist path, predicated upon a stronger state that can drive technological and economic upgrading. This pro-cess has opened space for new influential groups, such as young technocrats in the ministry of Agriculture. It has also engendered significant poverty reduc-tion and improvement on a number of other social indicators (CEPAL, 2013). However, building a strong state has been dependent not only on technological progress but crucially in the short term on continued exploitation of natural resources. In the process, the ideas of a "good life" in harmony with nature and respect for a plurality of cultures as established in the new constitution have been repeatedly violated.

In the cases of Brazil and Chile there has been more of an "elite settlement" between economic elites and right-wing parties and elites of the left-wing parties. This has prevented major deviations in the environmental aspects of the devel-opment model from the former governments, but as explained by Toni, Villarroel and Taitson Bueno in Chapter 11, although this is true at the federal level, there is still space for more profound changes at the state levels, depending on the elites governing there.

This consideration points to the importance of space in understanding the dynamics of development and environmental governance to which we turn in the following.

## The politics of space and scalar tensions

Different chapters in this book highlight the centrality of space and scale dynamics in the shape and outcome of political processes and debates. At the broader sense, market developments and booming commodity prices have resulted in the decrease in importance of traditionally influential elites, including Western companies and international institutions such as the World Bank (WB), the InterAmerican Development Bank (IDB) and the International Monetary Fund (IMF), and in the rise of new international elites (i.e., Chinese companies and multilatinas). Booming market conditions have allowed South American countries to speed up debt payments to international institutions, and in this way South American countries have also, at least to some degree, been freed from the influence the US is able to exert, through these institutions and its own government agencies in South America's politics. Although in several countries the state, in a more centralizing fashion, is attempting to take control over the development of extractive sectors, multinational companies remain crucial for the development of such sectors. Thus, as a result, we are currently observing new relations and arrangements between on the one hand, national states and on the other hand, diverse international elites of various origins, including North American, European, Chinese and Latin American. Although it is too early to conclude on this respect, these new relationships would clearly have important implications for environmental governance in the region.

At the domestic level, we observe that the renewed effort of different governments to have a greater influence in controlling and managing natural resources often clash with the ideas, aspirations and visions of actors at local and regional levels, with varying outcomes. In some cases, such as the one exemplified by Brazil, local governments have been capable of crafting innovative and more ambitious environmental policies independently of the direction taken by the central government. On the other extreme we find Bolivia. In this case, in part because they control soy production and own large properties, local elites have been capable of influencing public policies at the national level in the direction they aspire to. The outcome in Argentina is rather different. Because of the way in which soy production is currently organized in the country, the urban–rural links have been reorganized. An urban based elite controls land and soy production, and consequently views land and natural resources in a different way than the traditional landed elite. The outcome is that within the current pattern in Argentina, natural resources and the sustainability of agricultural production take new and different meanings. Soy production in this way resembles other extractive activities (i.e., mining) rather than agricultural production, with clear environmental consequences.

In the two Central American cases on the other hand, we observe that historically based inequalities in access to power and decision-making processes continue to result in large obstacles to integrating lower scales into environmental planning, or to include the aspirations and desires of marginalized, often rural, actors in broader development plans. The role played by the state in the two Central American cases is substantially different although the responses from the economic elite are somehow comparable, resulting in rural areas continuing to be spaces devoted to profit maximization by a reduced elite, rather than places where sustainable development concerns take priority.

## Towards a more sustainable environmental governance

An overall summary of the situation would be that there has been a certain degree of elite shifts, but its significance for environmental governance varies. In general, it can be said that in the struggle to ensure economic growth and more equitable distribution of resources, governments of the "new left" have taken a rather pragmatic venue in their relation to different elites, which has not always resulted in taking greater consideration for the environmental consequences of such growth. This results, in most cases, in forms of environmental governance that have not brought the environmental concerns, visions, values and interests of marginalized or subaltern groups to the forefront.

Pointing, as we have done, to the role of elites has provided us with significant insight into why this is so, in spite of promising signals from several of the leftist regimes about a willingness to search for a more sustainable development model. Many of the findings were actually not very surprising: both class theory and elite theory have predicted the difficulties of leftist governments in transforming societies characterized by a high degree of concentration of resources and deep structural inequalities. While these theories never explicitly focused on the environment and natural resources, their conclusions also seem to be highly relevant for environmental governance and sustainable development.

Yet the picture is not entirely bleak. First, there is a strong difference between countries, and also, in large countries such as Brazil, between states in a country. Larger countries with stronger economies such as Brazil are transiting towards a path in which certain measures (such as those related to forest governance) are transformed by the dynamic interaction of new and old elites in a global context in which forests have taken a heightened significance in terms of global climate change. At the other extreme, smaller countries, with more vulnerable economies such as Guatemala do not seem to be transitioning towards a path that allows greater inclusion of the concerns and interests of marginalized groups in environmental governance. This is also related to the sectors we examined in these countries, and again to the links such sectors have with the global economy. Although not examined with the same depth in all cases, the case analyzed in Chapter 9 is extremely illustrative in terms of how important, how varied and how flexible the elites' views on the environment are, and at the same time how more conservative views (like those of the business elite) exert a greater influence on the overall output of different efforts to regulate the environment, because of the significance and variety of resources these elites control.

In other words, there seems to be some slight room for optimism. To the degree that new elites are capable of influencing the positions and views of old elites, there might be opportunities for reorienting the priorities of governing parties towards more inclusive and equitable environmental governance. How much new elites would be capable of influencing old elites in terms of environmental governance and sustainable development is, however, to some extent limited by ongoing power struggles in other arenas than the environmental one, as exemplified by many of the cases analyzed in this book.

# References

Block, F. (1977) The ruling class does not rule: Notes on the Marxist theory of the state. *Socialist Review*, 33, 6–27.

Bull, B., Castellacci, F. and Kasahara, Y. (2014) *Business Groups and Transnational Capitalism in Central America: Economic and Political Strategies*. Palgrave, London.

CEPAL (2013) *Panorama Social de América Latina*. Comisión Económica para América Latina y el Caribe, Santiago de Chile.

Michels, R. (1962) *Political Parties*. Free Press, New York.

Mosca, G. (1939) *The Ruling Class*. McGraw-Hill, New York.

Pareto, V. ([1935] 1997) The governing elite in present-day democracy, in E. Etzioni-Halevy (ed.), *Classes and Elites in Democracy and Democratization*. Garland Publishing, New York and London, 147–152.

# Index